THE LIFE OF JOHN MILTON

A. N. WILSON

The Life of John Milton

Oxford   New York

OXFORD UNIVERSITY PRESS

Oxford University Press, Walton Street, Oxford OX2 6DP

London Glasgow New York Toronto
Delhi Bombay Calcutta Madras Karachi
Kuala Lumpur Singapore Hong Kong Tokyo
Nairobi Dar es Salaam Cape Town
Melbourne Auckland

and associated companies in
Beirut Berlin Ibadan Mexico City Nicosia

Oxford is a trade mark of Oxford University Press

First published 1983
Reprinted with corrections 1983

British Library Cataloguing in Publication Data

Wilson, A. N.
The life of John Milton.
1. Milton John, 1608–1674—Biography
2. Poets, English—17th century—Biography
I. Title
821.4 PR381
ISBN 0-19-211776-9

Library of Congress Cataloging in Publication Data

Wilson, A. N., 1950
The life of John Milton.
Bibliography: p.
Includes index.
1. Milton, John, 1608–1674—Biography. 2. Poets,
English—Early modern, 1500–1700—Biography
I. Title
PR3581.W47 821'.4 82-6386
ISBN 0-19-211776-9 AACR2

Set by Rowland Phototypesetting Limited
Printed in Great Britain
at the University Press, Oxford
by Eric Buckley
Printer to the University

Ad patrem matremque

ACKNOWLEDGEMENTS

I AM very grateful for assistance from the Arts Council in the course of writing this book.

I am indebted to Mrs Duncan-Jones, who read the book in its entirety, and made many helpful suggestions and corrections. She is not responsible for the errors of taste or of fact which probably remain. Dame Veronica Wedgwood gave me useful information about Milton's blindness. Mrs Luna was a most patient and punctilious editor.

I would also like to thank Mr Timothy Tosswill, at whose feet I first learnt to love Milton's poetry. To me, as to so many others, his teaching remains a perpetual source of inspiration, for which I feel inexpressible gratitude.

London, July 1982

CONTENTS

	Prologue	I
1.	The Pigeon of Paul's	5
2.	The Lady of Christ's Coll:	17
3.	The Courtier	38
4.	'Lycidas'	54
5.	Continental	70
6.	Anti-Episcopal	94
7.	Mary Powell	109
8.	Miss Davis and the Liberties of England	124
9.	Barbican	149
10.	Propagandist	157
11.	Hard Season	173
12.	The Beginnings of *Paradise Lost*	186
13.	*Paradise Lost*	202
14.	Third Marriage	216
15.	*Samson Agonistes*	224
16.	*Paradise Regained*	240
17.	Death	253
	Notes and References	260
	Index	271

PROLOGUE

THERE is not much left of Milton's London. Bread Street, where he was born, and spent his boyhood, was destroyed in the Great Fire; and, having been rebuilt, it survived another 250 years only to be bombarded in the Second World War. Today it is a soulless, windy, straight thoroughfare; less a street than a gap between banks and office-blocks which are tall enough to disguise its proximity, at the one end to St Paul's Cathedral, and at the other, to the River Thames. To imagine what it was like in Milton's boyhood one must look at Vischer's engravings or read Stow's *Survey of London*.

In those days, Bread Street was a narrow row of predominantly wooden houses which ran down the very centre of a hugely over-crowded, fast-expanding Gothic town. In 1500 there had been a popula-tion of some 75,000 Londoners. In 1600 there were 220,000. By 1650 the population had swollen to 450,000. One has to think of a town like Bruges or Salisbury suddenly trying to accommodate the population of modern Birmingham or Brussels. Squashed about Bread Street on every side there were tenements and windmills, trees, theatres, brothels, bridges, and alleys; mansions and hovels. And every few yards, a church spire pointed its spindly cross to the sky. Month by month, more and more people flooded into the already overcrowded lanes and roads. For the most part, they were Englishmen from the provinces – like the Miltons themselves – who had come to the city to make their fortunes. Since the accession of James I, there were also more than a few Scots. There were European refugees, too, victims of religious wars, Protes-tants from France, the Low Countries, and Italy.

There were more people than the city could adequately feed or house; and there were strict rules against unauthorized or speculative building, so that the old houses burst at the seams. Food was in short supply. Drainage, and anything approximating to lavatories, were woefully inadequate. Stow, in his survey, describes St Katharine's-by-the-Tower as 'enclosed or pestered with small tenements and homely cottages, having inhabitants, English and strangers, more in number than some cities in England'.[1] There was never enough water. The place stank.

All around, the very skyline was changing, in that town where Milton grew up. Old men would have been able to remember when Hog Lane which stretched 'north toward St Mary Spital had once stood secluded in green fields where the citizens used to walk for recreation'.[2] There were no fields there in 1616, the year that Shakespeare died. Patches of green survived on the city's edges, which would be unimaginable in today's London. Clerkenwell was dotted with gardens and expanses of meadowland. Bunhill Fields, north-east of the Barbican, were still spacious and country-like. But encroachments were steadily being made on the green. Shadwell, Limehouse, and Wapping, outlying villages, had already been linked by continuous building by the time Milton was eight or nine. Even St Paul's Cathedral, a vast Noah's ark on the top of Ludgate Hill, one of the most splendid Gothic cathedrals in northern Europe, was changing its shape. Men feared 'its near approaching ruin, by the corroding quality of the coal smoke, especially in moist weather, whereunto it had been long subject'.[3] Inigo Jones had been commissioned to reface the exterior of the nave and the transepts with new stonework. The mysteriously dark interior (the numinous shadows increased by the thick layers of soot on the huge east window) was about to be radically altered. The pointed nave windows were to become rounded. The little church of St Faith's-under-St-Paul's, which clustered against the east of the Norman apse of the cathedral, was already being demolished, in preparation for the building of a new choir. Another church, St Gregory's, which nestled on the south side of the cathedral, was pulled down during Milton's school-days.

The last vestiges of Falstaff's London, bit by bit, were being crowded out or tidied away. But there were churches enough to spare. The Mermaid Tavern, at the top of Bread Street, where Shakespeare had been an *habitué*, and where the tribe of Ben still drank and roared and held their meetings of the Apollo Club, was surrounded by churches on every side. There were two in Bread Street alone: St Mildred's and All Hallows. Round the corner, there were St Augustine's and St Antholin's. And the churches teemed with people.

Preachers were now as popular as players had been in a previous generation. The bells of St Antholin's now clattered daily at five in the morning to summon the faithful to lectures: the latest thing. Ben Jonson and his cronies can only have staggered home a few hours before the din started up. Very tiresome it must have been for his namesake, William Johnson, the landlord of the Mermaid, to be woken so soon by the insistent chiming of the steeples, and by the crowds, flocking at dawn to hear the rector of St Antholin's, Charles Offspring, expounding the epistles of St Paul.[4]

Less of a cult figure than Offspring, but nearer the Mermaid, was the rector of All Hallows, Richard Stock. He had his following; he preached the new doctrines. He was a man who looked for the finishing of the Reformation in England, the purging of the last odours of popery which still clung to the Established Church and which the new King had done so disappointingly little to abolish. Stock wanted the new generation to be in no doubt of God's truth. He catechized the children of Bread Street every day for an hour before school: boys and girls on alternate mornings. His sermons were of an angry, woeful colouring. Above all, he was angered by his congregation when they showed ignorance of the Scriptures. For the first time in 1,600 years, Christians were expected to be literate. Their salvation apparently depended upon it. 'Your books are seldom in hand but when you go to church; they lie in your houses covered with dust.' Thus Stock ranted.[5]

By books, he did not mean what the tribe of Ben would have understood by the word. Stock was not thinking of *England's Helicon*, or Harington's Ariosto, or of *The Faerie Queene* or of the recent *History of the World* by Sir Walter Ralegh. Still less was he thinking of Terence, or Aristotle, or Ovid. He was thinking of one book only. A new version of the book had appeared in 1611, but it was merely a revision and collation of a century or more of translations. Some of Stock's congregation would possess copies. But most of them were letting dust settle not on newly printed 'Authorized Versions', but on the old Geneva Bibles that their parents had forgotten to read.

Yet now, more and more, the dust was being blown off the old book, and it was being read. The vintner and landlord of the Mermaid had seen some strange changes since his tenancy began there. He had watched Jack Donne, the drinking companion of Beaumont and Fletcher, turn parson. His sermons were probably of a different order from ranters like Stock. But his ordination pointed to the strange way things were going.

When the revellers had departed, one can imagine this William Johnson shutting his inn for the night, and walking down to the river, a short stroll before returning to bed. Most of the houses in Bread Street would be plunged into darkness, for men rose in those days at dawn. But, night after night, as he ambled down that fetid, narrow little street, the innkeeper who had served ale (in his day) to Shakespeare and Donne and Ben Jonson, would have seen a light burning in an upstairs window above the sign of the Spread Eagle. Every evening, defiant amid the surrounding blackness of London, the candles flickered at that window until midnight struck. It was not some learned divine, preparing a lecture for the morning; nor an advocate working late on a case; nor an alchemist dabbling in forbidden knowledge, though any passer-by might have guessed it to be one of these things.

It was a little boy, the eldest child of somewhat aged parents, a scrivener and his wife. There were three children now: John, Anne, and a baby, Christopher. The parents had lost their first infant, who was buried, unbaptized, in All Hallows in 1601, and it was perhaps this which made them cosset and pamper their eldest, John, who had been born on 9 December 1608. Private tutoring was arranged. The inhabitants of Bread Street must have been struck by the cherubic beauty of the boy, and by his expensive clothes as he flitted, a fey little creature, through the stinking alleys of the neighbourhood. Already, he led a studiously eccentric life. The maids who sat up late with him complained that it would do no good to his eyes. But still, night after night, a passer-by could see the candles flickering at his window.

In the very wet April of 1616,[6] the month they heard at the Mermaid that Shakespeare was dead, perhaps the innkeeper and his customers, stirred by such spectacles of mortality, followed the bells to church. The prescribed lectionary of Old Testament readings in the month of April would have filled their heads with stories from the Book of Judges, and from the first Book of Samuel. Walking back to the Mermaid at night, and looking with puzzlement at the lights burning late in the Milton household, the innkeeper might well have found himself thinking of singular Israelite infants, set apart for the Lord's service; of the child Samuel, dwelling with Eli in the Temple; and of Samson, who was 'a Nazarite unto God from the womb'.

CHAPTER I

THE PIGEON OF PAUL'S

Me tenet urbs reflua quam Thamesis alluit unda,
Meque nec invitum patria dulcis habet.

'Elegia prima ad Carolum Diodatum'

THEY were an Oxfordshire family, and papist. The scrivener was born in 1562, and brought up in Stanton St John, a village five miles north-east of Oxford. His father, Richard Milton, held to the old religion, and was a ranger or 'Keeper of the Forest of Shotover'.[1] Father and son parted company; because of religion, some believe. Probably the Keeper's son went to the University, and enjoyed the musical tradition of what had been called Cardinal College.

He was brought up in the University of Oxon: at Christchurch, and his father disinherited him because he kept not the Catholic religion (he found a Bible in English in his chamber), so thereupon he came to London, and became a Scrivener (brought up by a friend of his, was not an Apprentice) and got plentiful estate by it and left it off many years before he died. He was an ingenious man, delighted in music. Composed many songs now in print, especially that of Oriana.[2]

So Aubrey (an unreliable, but always interesting informant) records in his jottings. John Milton *père*, whatever the reasons were, joined the throngs who squeezed into London towards the end of the sixteenth century. He must have started in business at about the time Shakespeare began to look about for a patron. No one can doubt which was the more reliable means of making money. Something between, in modern terms, a stockbroker and a solicitor, John Milton was purchasing for himself and his children, if he were to have any, something infinitely more precious than capital.

By the age of forty he had made enough money to marry, and he chose a London girl called Sara Jeffrey, whose father was a merchant-tailor. Ties with Oxfordshire were probably not wholly cut. Indeed, as business

prospered, John Milton *père* seems to have acquired clients and credi-
tors in the region of his father's village, including the squire's family at
the neighbouring Forest Hill.

But there was not much question of going home. Old Richard Milton,
crustily paying out good money on fines rather than go to church, does
not appear to have seen much of his more prudent and conformist son in
these last years. When John and Sara were eventually blessed with
children of their own, they were all Londoners. The eldest and the
youngest came and went. Christopher Milton was to end his life as a
judge in Ipswich. But John Milton *fils* remained, except for very short
interludes, a Londoner throughout his life.

He was born into a London where the theatre audiences had not yet
seen *The Winter's Tale* or *The Tempest*; by the time he died, they were
queuing up to see Buckingham's *The Rehearsal* and the plays of Aphra
Behn. He was born into the Gothic, squalidly overcrowded capital that
Stow had surveyed. He grew up there, learnt his religion there, went to
school there. Every other day, like all the other boys in the street, he
presumably went to be catechized by Richard Stock; and, of the
hundreds he saw milling up and down Bread Street, he must have
known William Johnson the vintner, and perhaps even his client William
Shakespeare. Jonson, Donne, Fletcher, and Middleton must have
passed beneath his infant gaze, this London child. A Londoner he
stayed, throughout the political revolution of the 1640s; he saw the Civil
War, and the monarchy, out. Whitehall gave him his only job, in the
republican government of Cromwell. By the time the job was done, he
was still in London, but it was a London which he could not see. He
could only smell it, and hear it, and feel it teeming around him; and not
an inch of it was unknown to him. It gave him his shelter when, at
the Restoration, his life was endangered; and it was only at the last possible moment that he left it during the plague of 1665. He was on the environs of the City during the Great Fire. And his last decade of life,
blind and bewildering years, was spent hearing the new city grow up
around him.

The decision of the scrivener, in early life, to leave Stanton St John,
had therefore most momentous consequences for his son. Shakespeare
—'my Shakespeare' as the poet called that figure familiar to his
boyhood – could 'warble his native wood-notes wild'. Milton's native
notes were citified, not rural; bookish, not spontaneous. It was only by
flights of fancy that a Londoner in the early seventeenth century could
rise

Above the smoke and stir of this dim spot,
Which men call earth, and, with low-thoughted care
Confined, and pestered in this pinfold here,
Strive to keep up a frail, and feverish being . . .

(*Comus*, 5–8)

Fancy alone? No, for money also could do it. The scrivener strove to keep up a frail and feverish being so that he could be a musician, and so that his children could be independent. When he came to work his apprenticeship as a poet, as we shall see, the young John Milton actually did so in as old-fashioned a way as possible, by looking out for aristocratic patronage. But he did so in the confidence that it did not matter whether he received patronage or not. Milton, perhaps, is the most beautiful of capitalism's first-fruits. He belonged solidly to the prosperous, mercantile middle class by which the City of London was maintained, governed, and strengthened in the four decades after his birth; the commercial class whose prosperity and independence derived wholly from their wits. Every figure that the scrivener scratched in his ledger, every bill he signed, every document he wrote, and every venture he underwrote, the filling up of columns, the lending of moneys, the guaranteeing of mortgages purchased the years and years of independence which were necessary for the creation of *Paradise Lost*.

John Milton would have been a poet whether he was born in a barn or a castle; on board a Swedish ship or half-way up a French mountain. But he would not have been the poet he was, had he not been born into that London, crammed with trade, and merchants and clergymen, and schools.

Milton had a tutor before he went to school: a Scotsman called Thomas Young. It is usually assumed, because of Young's subsequent career, that he was engaged by the Miltons because of his fervent Protestant faith. The Scots, however, even in the seventeenth century, were an overeducated race. Young was a graduate of St Leonard's College in the University of St Andrews, of which he had become an MA in 1606. But so had dozens of others, and they had most of them learnt the painfully small value set by the world on those two letters, MA. They do not guarantee any person employment. When the English, for want of a monarch, proclaimed the Scottish sixth their first King James, that pedantic potentate came south followed by dozens and hundreds of Scottish university men, bringing their MAs with them, in hope of preferment. Some were lucky. Others had to make do with free-lance preaching jobs or 'lectureships' in churches which looked favourably on

their Presbyterian theology. Others got employment as tutors in private
houses, or as schoolmasters. And of such was Thomas Young. In all
probability he was engaged not because of his religious sensibilities but
because of his competence at languages. Thirteen years later, when he
looked back on his education and felt gratitude to his father for having
provided it with such care and intelligence, Milton thanked him specially for the gift of languages.[3] It is primarily this gift which Milton
celebrates in his poem to Thomas Young himself, 'Elegia quarta',
written in 1627. He fancifully compares this intelligent young Scotsman
to Phoenix, son of Amyntor, and to Chiron, son of the nymph Philyra
who were the tutors of Achilles.

> Qualis Amyntorides, qualis Philyreius heros
> Myrmidonum regi, talis et ille mihi.
>
> (27–8)

(To me he is as Amyntor's son and the heroic son of Philyra were to the king of
the Myrmidons.)

It was under his guidance, Milton continues rapturously, 'that I first
wandered through Parnassus, drank the Pierian spring and, through the
grace of Clio [muse of history] made my mouth happy with Castalian
wine'. This is his rapturous way of saying, presumably, that it was with
Young that he first slogged through Livy.

We do not know whether Young returned the compliment, and felt he
was teaching a new Achilles. But the Fourth Elegy makes it plain that,
for Milton, learning Latin was a great imaginative adventure, opening
up untold literary and linguistic riches. Before he had reached the age of
ten he was drunk with that Castalian wine; his head sang to the
complexities of Virgil; his mind ranged through Ovid's mythological
treasure-hoard. In our day, the knowledge of Latin has almost evapo-
rated from the minds of the educated classes. In a generation or two, it
will be as rare an accomplishment as Syriac. We think of it therefore as
something fusty, dry, difficult, the possession of ashen-faced pedants
and bespectacled women with brindled hair. For Milton, it was a burst of
Mediterranean sunshine into the grey little London street where he first
heard its varied music, a mingling of sensual and intellectual pleasure
which would never forsake him. Thomas Young, MA, was the instrument of this deep delight, and the ecstatic terms of 'Elegia quarta' are
scarcely hyperbole. Whether Milton *liked* him, still less whether he
shared his views of life, matters really as little as whether we share the
view of life of the head waiter in our favourite restaurant.

It was at this date that the first portrait of Milton was painted. His hair is cut short and parted well to the left. It has not yet deepened into the rich auburn which was to characterize it late into middle age. It is a perfectly oval face, with large serene eyes, a nose as yet unformed, and the ruby lips of a beautiful woman. Even at ten years old the corners of the mouth turn up a little, suggesting an amusement which is quizzical, but slightly haughty. Behind that high and oval brow rests a quiet and intellectual conviction of his indisputable superiority to the rest of the universe.

A stiff, lace Elizabethan collar juts in a semi-circle round his oval chin. He wears a neat little doublet, braided and buttoned with gold. Portraits of grown men and women reflect the personality of the painter and of the sitter. Portraits of children reflect the expectations of their parents. This is the portrait of a young gentleman. The sons of nobility, peering down to us from panels in Penshurst or Haddon or Hatfield or Knole do not have finer clothes or more supercilious expressions. This is not the face of a boy who is going to have to earn his living.

Yet the gentility of having a private tutor, rather than being sent to one of the City schools, did not last. Young went abroad when Milton was eleven – to minister to the English-speaking population of Hamburg: merchants mostly, with a sprinkling of voluntary exiles for whom the generality of Anglican clergy was insufficiently Calvinist.

John Milton, in consequence (or perhaps he was destined for it anyway?) was sent to school. London was rich in excellent grammar schools, founded in the previous century on Renaissance, humanist principles. He could have gone to Westminster, where the headmaster, Camden, had instructed Ben Jonson; he could have gone to the Merchant Taylors' school, where Spenser had been as a boy (as had Lodge, Lyly, and Kyd). But nearest to Bread Street, and of equally high reputation, was St Paul's.

Thither, early each morning, Milton would squelch his way through the pigeon-droppings and the scaffolding which littered St Paul's churchyard; for the tower and the great rose window were always thick with these birds. 'The scholars of Paul's, meeting with them of St Antony's, would call them Antony pigs, and they again would call the other pigeons of Paul's, because many pigeons were bred in Paul's Church, and Saint Antony was always figured with a pig following him.'[4]

The schoolroom had been built by Dean Colet (friend of Erasmus and Sir Thomas More) in 1519. It was, apparently, 'large and spacious, fronting the street on the east of St Paul's Cathedral'. Colet had dedicated the school to the boy Jesus. A picture of the Christ Child hung over the High Master's chair, and each day began with a prayer to the Divine Infant, in Latin: 'Sweet Jesus, my Lord, who, as a boy in the twelfth year of thine age didst dispute in the temple at Jerusalem among the doctors so that they all marvelled with amazement at thy superexcellent wisdom, I petition thee that in this thy school, of which thou art protector and defender, wherein I am taught daily in letters and wisdom, that I may chiefly come to know thee Jesus, who art thyself the true wisdom . . .'

The inducements to such knowledge were stringent. All boys everywhere were thrashed, until a few decades ago. But it tells us something about the severity of Milton's High Master, Alexander Gil, that in that somewhat brutalized age, he had a reputation as a flogger. Aubrey gleefully records his 'whipping fits'; and when his son, also called Alexander Gil, inherited the job, he was eventually to lose it because of his excessive use of corporal punishment. Milton never expressed an opinion on the subject. It is known that he used physical punishment himself when, as a grown-up, he undertook the education of boys. Gil the younger became a friend of his. But there were far more fascinating things to notice about his own High Master, the older Alexander, than his brutality with the birch.

He was one of the most brilliant spelling cranks of the age. 'Of all the reformed systems of spelling which were suggested in the sixteenth and seventeenth centuries none deserved to succeed more than that of Alexander Gil.'[5] As a pretty skilled phonetician, Gil was fully aware that the letters of the alphabet could not hope to reproduce all the sounds of current English speech, but, unlike previous reformers, he suggested only a modification and extension of the alphabet. Needless to say, no one ever adopted exactly the principles set out in his *Logonomia Anglica*, which was published in 1619, a year before Milton went to Gil's school. But the poet was certainly influenced in his spelling by his schoolmaster. Milton's later 'suttle', 'prisner', and 'buis'nesse' reflect some of the principles which gave rise to Gil's relentless 'sutl', 'prizner', and 'biznes'. Milton, like Gil, distinguished between the spellings 'me' and 'mee' depending on rhetorical stress. Milton, however, even when he did not copy Gil's forms exactly, shared his master's distaste for the 'cacography' which had overtaken the written language since the invention of printing.[6]

No one has been successful, since Gil's day, in reforming that cacography. We still spell like madmen. And the art of printing has declined to the point where it would be impossible to reproduce, at manageable expense, a passage of specimen spelling from *Logonomia Anglica*. Of more general interest, perhaps, than the theories enshrined in its pages, are the passages of literature he renders in his own characters. There is much English poetry here, especially Spenser. It would seem likely that Gil fostered and encouraged the love of poetry in his boys. In doing do, he showed himself fully a Protestant, and of his age.

Since Plato banished the poets from the *Republic*, men of God had been opposed to men of fancy. St Augustine, a Platonist long before he was a Christian, incorporated this mistrust of literature into the Catholic view of life and passed it on to the Church for the next thousand years. Never more vividly did it appear than in St Jerome's dream, when he was reproached with the words 'Ciceronianus es, non Christianus'. Chaucer, who ends both his great poems with apologies and retractions, would have understood that dream, Spenser, probably not. What Spenser's greatest disciple thought of the story, we know well. This 'Lenten dream' was 'a phantasm bred by the fever which had then seized him'.[7]

St Paul himself 'thought it no defilement to insert into Holy Scripture the sentences of three Greek poets and one of them a tragedian'.[8] But it was not until the generation of Spenser that Christians felt fully confident that there was no conflict between Christ and the Muses.

Reading *The Faerie Queene* was thus one of the most important features of Milton's childhood; 'our sage and serious Spenser', he called him, 'whom I dare be known to think a better teacher than Scotus or Aquinas'.[9] The sage seriousness is buried in the very midst of the great poem's fantastical narrative and richly elaborated rhetoric, like hard almonds lost in a sticky cake. To develop a taste for the language and the story is to develop the poet's patterns of thought. No sermon of Richard Stock's could ever teach a delight in virtue as vividly as Sir Guyon's sojourn in the Bower of Bliss, or Amoret's near escape from the House of Busyrane. Protestantism had no more powerful advocate than Spenser's Una making her way to the House of Holiness. Dryden later recalled that 'Milton hath acknowledged to me that Spenser was his original'.[10] Spenser's preoccupations – Platonic idealism, classical mythology, medieval legend, militant Protestantism dressed in the most Italianate poetic forms[11] – filled Milton's head while he was still a boy at St Paul's.

The Divine Weeks and Works of Guillaume de Saluste du Bartas would also have been known to him, a favourite of Elizabethan Protestants, and

popular in the translation of Josuah Sylvester. 'The world's a school',
Milton would have read,

> where (in a general story)
> God always reads dumb lectures of his glory:
> A pair of stairs, whereby our mounting soul
> Ascends by steps above the arched pole:
> A sumptuous hall, where God on every side
> His wealthy shop of wonders opens wide.[12]

A pleasing sentiment in that city of merchants.

Sylvester's translations were immensely popular in England, and
there were many editions.[13] *The Divine Weeks and Works* was a prolix
account in verse of the Creation narrative in the Book of Genesis,
followed by the Fall of Man, and the early stories of the Bible, such as
Noah's ark. Some of Sylvester's rendering lacks felicity:

> Lord, I acknowledge and confess before,
> This ocean hath no bottom, nor no shore;
> But (sacred pilot) thou canst safely steer
> My vent'rous pinnace to her wished peer,
> Where once arrive all dropping wet, I will
> Extol thy favours, and my vows fulfil.[14]

But on other occasions, as when he is contrasting Adam in his state of
innocence and us in our state of knowledge, sinful knowledge, Sylvester
is powerful and haunting:

> But our now-knowledge hath for tedious train,
> A drooping life, an over-racked brain,
> A face forlorn, a sad and sullen fashion
> A restless toil, and cares self-pining passion.
> Knowledge was then, even the soul's soul for light,
> The spirit's calm port; and lanthorn shining bright,
> To straight-stepped feet, clear knowledge; not confused:
> Not sour, but sweet: not gotten, but infused.[15]

Nor is it to be supposed that Du Bartas was regarded as a sort of churchy
substitute for real poetry. It was as much a triumphant example as *The
Faerie Queene* of the marriage of Christ and the Muses. Sir Philip Sidney
himself not only read Du Bartas but translated him.[16]

So Milton grew up with none of Chaucer's sense that poetry ('en-
ditynges of worldly vanitees')[17] was a sin to be revoked in order to save his
soul. On the contrary, his peculiar headmaster would have taught him to
love poetry above all other forms of literature.

The little pigeons of Paul's would undoubtedly have trooped down the high Gothic aisles of the cathedral, and listened to the anthems and the sermons. From that illustrious pulpit, once again, they would have heard reiterated the confident belief that there is no conflict between Christianity and the highest literary standards. 'And they mistake it much, that think, that the Holy Ghost hath rather chosen a low, barbarous, and homely style, than an eloquent, and powerful manner of expressing himself . . .' This is the voice of the Dean, John Donne, himself a poet. Sometimes he is terrifying in his odd conceits: 'If my soul could ask one of those worms which my dead body shall produce, Will you change with me? that worm would say, No; for you are like to live eternally in torment; for my part, I can live no longer, than the putrid moisture of your body will give me leave, and therefore I will not change; nay, would the Devil himself change with a damned soul? I cannot tell . . .' Sometimes his lightness commends God for giving us 'not only that which is merely necessary, but that which is convenient too; He does not only feed us, but *feed us with marrow, and with fatness*; he gives us our instruction in cheerful forms, not in a sour, and sullen, and angry, and unacceptable way, but cheerfully, in *Psalms* . . . Not in an *Oration*, not in *Prose*, but in *Psalms* . . .' Sometimes he speaks of God himself as if he were a poet: 'The Holy Ghost is an eloquent author, a vehement, and an abundant author . . .' Donne became Dean of St Paul's in 1621, when Milton was a boy at the school, and it would be very peculiar if the younger poet had never heard the older preach.

Cathedral life, for that sensitive and aesthetic boy, must have provided a wealth of delight to the eye, to the ear, to the brain. He lists cathedral worship as one of the deep pleasures of 'Il Penseroso':

> But let my due feet never fail,
> To walk the studious cloister's pale,
> And love the high embowed roof,
> With antique pillars' massy proof,
> And storied windows richly dight,
> Casting a dim religious light.
> There let the pealing organ blow,
> To the full-voiced choir below,
> In service high, and anthems clear,
> As may with sweetness, through mine ear,
> Dissolve me into ecstasies,
> And bring all heaven before mine eyes.
>
> (155–66)

Here, in St Paul's, Milton must often have witnessed, and taken part in, the seemly routines of mattins and evensong, and gazed, with a mixture of emotion, as canons and prebendaries hobbled into their stalls, bedecked 'not in robes of pure innocency, but of pure linen, with other deformed and fantastic dresses, in palls and mitres, gold, and gewgaws fetched from Aaron's old wardrobe'.[18] Perhaps as a boy he felt less strongly about ecclesiastical vestments than he did as a man. After all, he was at this date almost certainly destined for a career in the Church. As he heard the Dean preach or the Chaplain in Course read the lessson, he might well have imagined that he would be similarly occupied when he came to manhood. Whether gewgaws from old Aaron's wardrobe were frequently seen in the sanctuary of old St Paul's during the 1620s we may rather doubt, but almost certainly there were degrees of conservatism about the way the canons were dressed.[19] They wore, in winter, the same sort of grey hood or amice, made of squirrel fur, with which Skelton would have been familiar when he dresses his clerical aviary 'in their amice of grey'.[20] Perhaps the furry edges of these amices, glimpsed afar in the choir of the cathedral during his boyhood, suggested the mist of morning when he came to describe it in old age:

> Thus passed the night so foul till morning fair
> Came forth with pilgrim steps in amice grey . . .[21]

We cannot be sure. But the echoes of church-going which suggest a memory of this phase of Milton's existence do not immediately make us suppose that his hostility to the forms of the Established Church was formed during his boyhood. For, while assuming that he was one day to be an Anglican clergyman, he doubtless had other, and more interesting, things on his mind.

Lessons – the rehearsal of the old trivium of grammar, rhetoric, and logic – can have provided him with no difficulties. When he established a small academy himself, its syllabus of learning bore no conspicuous relation to the formal education he would have received at St Paul's. It would seem safe to assume that Milton was no exception to the rule that men of genius, whatever formal arrangements are made about their education, are largely self-taught; as little influenced by whatever academies they happen to attend as if they had never been to school or university.

Much more important than anything that happened in the classroom (except, perhaps, for the *personal* influence of Alexander Gil) was the great friendship Milton formed while a boy at St Paul's with Charles Diodati.

Diodati was the son of an English mother, but his father, who was a well-known London doctor, came from an exiled Italian family of Protestants. Dr Diodati had actually been born in Geneva, where his brother Giovanni was a famous theologian.

We do not know what it was that cemented the friendship of the two boys, but Charles Diodati's surviving letters to Milton – in Greek – are tribute to their shared erudition as well as to the depth of their feeling for one another.

> Multum crede iuvat terras aluisse remotas
> Pectus amans nostri tamque fidele caput,

Milton was to write to his friend in 'Elegia prima': 'Believe me, it is a great joy to know that lands afar have bred a heart that loves and a mind that is faithful to me'. Milton had many friends throughout his life, and was a passionately affectionate man. But his friendship with Diodati had the peculiar intensity which belongs to the almost romantic attachments of adolescence. When he looked back on the friendship after Diodati's untimely death, he missed the intimacy of a confidant ('Pectora cui credam?'), the talents of a fellow-musician, and the sharp, clever laughter of someone who shared his not always very kind sense of humour:

> Quis mihi blanditiasque tuas, quis tum mihi risus,
> Cecropiosque sales referet, cultosque lepores?[22]

'Who can bring back to me your caressing charms, your laughter, your flashes of Attic wit, your well-turned jokes?'

Perhaps it was under Diodati's influence that Milton learnt Italian and developed his distinctive felicity in that language. Together, doubtless, they encouraged each other to write verses. Milton, in the aristocratic tradition of sixteenth-century versifiers – like Wyatt, like Sidney, like the Countess of Pembroke – rendered psalms into metrical forms. It was probably at about the time that he was writing of

> The horned moon to shine by night,
> Amongst her spangled sisters bright,[23]

that Diodati managed to publish a Latin elegy to the memory of Camden, the recently deceased headmaster of Westminster.

Metrical psalms were ideally suited for musical settings, of course, and while the son laboured to turn the poems of King David into couplets of varying skill—

> Why fled the ocean? And why skipped the mountains?
> Why turned Jordan toward his crystal fountains?[24]

the father was responsible for many of the four-part settings of the tunes of *The Whole Book of Psalms*, published in 1621 by Thomas Ravenscroft.

Friendship, learning, laughter, and music colour the years of Milton's adolescence. One has no sense of it being fraught with anguish or rebellion. Holiday-times must have been spent much in the company of Charles Diodati. Evenings were spent reading late and perfecting his Latin, Greek, French, and Italian.

Perhaps the parents felt that the intensity of the friendship between the two boys called for a separation. Perhaps it was merely chance that Diodati was withdrawn rather early from St Paul's and sent to Trinity College, Oxford, where he matriculated at the age of thirteen in February 1623. Perhaps, too, this parental anxiety determined the place of Milton's own university education. On the other hand, even though his father was an Oxford man, his headmaster was not. In all likelihood it was Gil who suggested that Milton stayed on at St Paul's and went on to Cambridge. Unlike so many boys of this class and date, there seems to have been no question of Milton going to an Inn of Court. His future was settled. Cambridge; then a Fellowship; ordination, and preferment in the Established Church; a life in which he could serve as priest and teacher, while pursuing his own learning and becoming one who, like the Dean of St Paul's, used his skill as a versifier to the glory of his God.

Thus, while Diodati pursued his studies at Oxford, not five miles from the home of Milton's grandparents, Milton took his luggage up to the Bull Inn at Bishopsgate and waited for old Thomas Hobson, the carrier, to convey him to Cambridge. At eighty, the old man still insisted on making the weekly journey to London. Milton was obviously amused by him. As a somewhat exquisite, infinitely intelligent and very beautiful youth, Milton must have felt, as the carriage creaked northwards, that the University was rather lucky to be having him, and that life was full of wonderful possibilities. He was quite wrong. On 12 February 1625, at the age of sixteen, he was admitted to Christ's College and the time-wasting and depressing business of being an undergraduate had begun.

CHAPTER 2

THE LADY OF CHRIST'S COLL:

The crushing melancholy of the undergraduate condition.
Anthony Powell, *Books Do Furnish a Room*

MILTON did not settle down at Christ's easily. His first year at Cambridge could not be reckoned a success. Although he worked hard and, as his brother afterwards told Aubrey, 'performed all his exercises there with very good applause',[1] he was unappreciated, and therefore unhappy.

The college tutor, in a clever undergraduate's life, is important not as a teacher, but as an audience. If he fails to be appreciative, or thinks to cut his pupil down to size, life quickly becomes hellish. So it was with Milton and his tutor, William Chappell, who seems by all accounts to have been a disagreeable man.

University life in the seventeenth century was, of course, very much more limiting than in our own day. When Milton arrived at Christ's it must have been like signing on at a rather tough boarding-school. It was the third largest college in the university, about 265 men if one counted up the commoners, scholars, and fellows. It must have been crushingly dingy, settling down in such an institution in the middle of a tiny little market town when he had been used to the centre of London. And it can not have been pleasant to exchange the position of a rather pampered elder son in a small, well-run household for that of a lesser pensioner – not a very grand position socially – in something between a barracks and a monastery. Milton probably had to sleep in the attic room of a wooden building and to share his chamber with at least three other boys. Some of the undergraduates at this date even had to share a bed. It can hardly have been much fun for a youth who, from early years, was used to his own room and whose parents had allowed him to keep very grown-up nocturnal hours. 'When he was very young he studied very hard and sat up very late, commonly till 12 or one a clock at night, and his father ordered the maid to sit up for him.'[2] Here, the noise and silly, boyish chatter must have echoed in his ears from dawn till dark. And it is unlikely that, with his rather sophisticated and lofty manners, he was treated very kindly.

'He was so fair that they called him the Lady of Christ's Coll:'[3] It is easy to imagine the tone with which that nickname was invented. He had no close friends there, so far as is known. A few pigeons of Paul's were up at Christ's in Milton's time – Edward Collins and John Redrish were already there when he arrived, and Robert Pory, who had been in the same class at school, was matriculated on the same day. But there is no evidence that they were Milton's friends.

How did the Lady of Christ's Coll: spend his days? Presumably he managed to spend time in libraries, improving his Greek and Hebrew. Perhaps at this date, though more probably later, he began to imbibe Plato. He presumably attended lectures, which were compulsory. Perhaps he heard Andrew Downes, who had been Regius Professor of Greek since 1585 and whose wits had more or less gone. Perhaps he went to Joseph Mead's lectures on Homer in his own college. Perhaps they taught him a certain amount, but it is hard to imagine that he found any of the dons at Cambridge as distinctively, powerfully clever as Alexander Gil.

History does not record what made Milton fall out with his tutor. One does not envy William Chappell much, having so lofty and exquisite a pupil. His brother Christopher told Aubrey that he received 'some unkindness' from Chappell; Aubrey has added 'whipped him'[4] as a gloss to this vague assertion, from which follows Dr Johnson's mockery, 'I am ashamed to relate what I fear is true, that Milton was the last student in either university that suffered the public indignity of corporal correction'.[5]

It is most unlikely that, if Milton was whipped by Chappell, he was the last boy at Cambridge or Oxford to be punished in this way. There is no evidence, however, that the whipping was public, or even that it happened at all. Legend further goes on to state that Milton was almost certainly rusticated. And more credence has been given, even by the most sober biographers,[6] to the crude pamphleteer who said of Milton that 'being grown to an impostume in the breast of the University, he was at length vomited out thence into a suburb sink about London'[7] than to Milton's own very forceful denial of the charge. Twice in his pamphleteering utterances Milton denies having been sent down from Cambridge. One has either to conclude that he, or his enemies, were lying. Milton had many unamiable characteristics, particularly in his youth. He was arrogant, lofty, snobbish, and cruel. But it is hard to believe him to be a liar. And that leaves one with the rather dull conclusion that, although he obviously quarrelled with Chappell, he was not formally rusticated or 'sent down'. When the trouble died down, he transferred to another tutor, Nathaniel Tovey.

Milton was probably in Cambridge on 27 March 1625, when the town-crier announced at the market cross that James I was dead, and had been succeeded by Charles I. A thunderclap drowned the crier's voice. It is unlikely that Milton's quarrel broke out with Chappell as early as that; he was not even matriculated until April. But in that very month plague broke out in London and Milton's family probably took refuge in the country, since his married sister, Anne Phillips, was pregnant with her second child. By high summer the plague had reached Cambridge; it continued until autumn and was the reason for term starting late. I rather doubt whether Milton bothered to go back that Michaelmas. The family were back in London by Christmas; it was there that Anne gave birth to her baby, Anne, a child who was not destined to live long. Perhaps Milton returned to Cambridge, unwill-ingly enough, and missed the coronation of Charles I in Westminster Abbey in February; evidently, however, by springtime he was in London again, more beguiled by theatres than by lectures; by pretty girls than by undergraduates; and refreshed by the intelligent company of merchants, schoolmasters, musicians, and clergymen who made a pleasant change after the crushing boredom of the dons.

This moment is immortalized in one of his most delightful poems, the 'Elegia prima' which he wrote to Charles Diodati, who had recently taken his Oxford BA. 'I am still in the city which the Thames bathes with its tides', he writes:

> Me tenet urbs reflua quam Thamesis alluit unda,

'. . . I am glad to be here, and not exactly pining away after Cambridge, not missing my rooms, which not long ago I was forbidden'.

This only sounds like rustication if you are determined to believe the libellous pamphlet about Cambridge vomiting Milton out into a suburb sink.

> Nec dudum vetiti me laris angit amor

does not spell out why Milton is away from Cambridge; 'vetiti' no more implies rustication than we are to imagine by 'laris' an actual shrine of household gods in Christ's. Although 'vetiti' implies 'forbidden' it is plainly, in the context, ironical: 'I am being denied the wonderful privilege of sharing an attic room with four nose-picking little morons'. If he was indeed forbidden, it is just as likely that he is referring either to some tiresome dormitory prank, or to the earlier interdict on anyone returning to Cambridge because of the plague. It quite definitely does not mean, 'I have been sent down'.

He continues to meditate humorously on his exile from Cambridge: 'If this were the worst exile that Ovid had endured, he would have been a match for Homer and Virgil. If it could be called exile, to be living comfortably at home in his father's house, then he is revelling in his banishment.'

Once again, this has been understood much too literally by readers who believe the pamphleteering slander. The worst that has happened is that Milton has returned in a pique to London after a quarrel with his tutor. He writes humorously comparing himself to Ovid in exile, who was banished by the Emperor Augustus in AD 8 on pain of death. The very ludicrousness of the discrepancy between the two poets' positions should make clear the tone of Milton's joke.

What does the poem tell us, though, about Milton at this date, aged perhaps seventeen? Already, however playfully, he is starting to place himself in the company of the really great poets of the classical past. If one followed through the implications of his opening joke,

> O utinam vates nunquam graviora tulisset
>   Ille Tomitano flebilis exul agro,
> Non tunc Ionio quicquam cessisset Homero
>   Neve foret victo laus tibi prima Maro. . .

one could see that Milton was aiming for the highest stakes. To be as good as Ovid was not enough for him. He was going to be another Homer, another Virgil, as Ovid himself might have been, had he had the advantage of being born into a middle-class London home in the year 1608.

In mood, however, Milton is cockily Ovidian here, a young sensualist wandering through the streets of London, enjoying the plays and falling in love with a beautiful blonde girl.

> Nor always city-pent, or pent at home,
> I dwell; but when spring calls me forth to roam,
> Expatiate in our proud suburban shades
> Of branching elm, that never sun pervades.

Here many a virgin troop I may descry,
Like stars of mildest influence, gliding by.
Oh forms divine! Oh looks that might inspire
E'en Jove himself, grown old, with young desire![8]

Cowper's school-roomy translation cannot convey the boyish exuber-
ance of the Latin. It is a highly exhibitionistic poem; its learning and
competence are not worn lightly, nor does he want us to miss the fact
that, at seventeen, he is quite a ladies' man. How sad he is to be leaving
all these adorable creatures behind him! The girls of London are more
lovely than the Achaemenian damsels in turreted headgear, who live in
Susa and Nineveh; or the maidens of Greece and Troy and Rome.
There is an absurdity about these fantastical and pretentious compari-
sons. But in all probability they are a good deal less artificial than they
seem. Milton was actually meditating upon ancient and biblical history,
and on classical literature for most of his waking years. One completely
fails to understand him if this fact is not remembered. But this did not
make him into a prude or a killjoy, as he has so often been ludicrously
depicted; nor did it diminish his intense awareness of human beauty,
and his rich ability to convey the emotions of joy, and pleasure. His
happy vacation – and that is all it has been – in London is over. Now,
alas, he must return to Cambridge where, so far, he has been so
homesick and learnt so little:

Stat quoque iuncosas Cami remeare paludes,
Atque iterum raucae murmur adire Scholae.
Interea fidi parvum cape munus amici,
Paucaque in alternos verba coacta modos.

(Now I have got to go back to the reedy marshes of the Cam and the noisy uproar
of its University. Meanwhile accept this little tribute from a faithful friend – a
few words crammed into verse.)

His great love is still for Diodati. If he had been returning to Oxford with
him, Milton would doubtless have felt very differently about university
life.

As his second year in Cambridge began, with a new tutor, it is
conceivable that the academic syllabus began to offer Milton the chance
to read things he did not already know. One of the troubles with
Chappell, almost certainly, was that he had insisted on making Milton go
through the basic Aristotelian subjects – logic, ethics, physics and
metaphysics, and endless grammar – which any pigeon of Paul's would

have known by the time he was twelve.[9] The fact that tutorials and lectures were conducted in Latin – even on occasions in Greek – might have been difficult enough for some country-reared nobleman's son, or some child of a lesser personage. But it was absurd, for one who had been enjoying Greek and Latin poetry since Thomas Young taught him as a young child, to be bothering his head with constructions and irregular verbs. In his father's house he was used to intelligent grown-up conversation, from lawyers, theologians, and fellow-musicians. The state of the nation was being discussed, the state of Europe and the Church, the latest books, the rights and wrongs of everything in the universe. How dull it must have been to have to listen to some not very intelligent don, droning on about the rules of medieval disputation.

Some glimmerings of interest can always be found by lively minds, however, even in academic exercises. One of the tasks usually assigned to undergraduates in their second year was rendering Plato into Latin. First you had to go through it all with a lector, a hack little better than an usher, who made sure that you had mastered the Greek. This would happen in class, each pupil translating in turn.[10] Then the interesting task began of translating Plato into Latin, and probably Cicero into Greek.[11] Every undergraduate at Trinity at this date was required to possess copies of Plato, Aristotle, Demosthenes, Cicero, and the Greek Testament, or to suffer expulsion. Perhaps some similarly astringent rule applied at Christ's. Milton would certainly have owned them anyway.

Plato had been the ancient most revered by Milton's immediate literary antecedents, Sidney and Spenser, in the great age of Elizabethan Protestantism. They were fired by the idea, known largely through Neoplatonic writings, originating with the Italian humanists of the fifteenth and early sixteenth century, that Platonism, that most imaginatively attractive of all philosophical systems, was closely allied to Christianity. The long reign of Aristotle, perpetuated by medieval Catholicism, was over.[12] The soul, imprisoned in its clogging house of clay, could do more than systematize and categorize as the old schoolmen had done along Aristotelian lines. It could fly out of its cage and gaze into the heart of things. Music allowed it to do so; allegory, in painting and in poetry, taught generations of men and women to regard nature as a thin veil showing forth, and at the time concealing, heavenly things. Neoplatonism on this general level was responsible for the paintings of Botticelli and Bronzino, for the wardrobe of Queen Elizabeth and the fantasy world of *The Faerie Queene*.

For the theologians it meant a release not only from the Aristotelian restrictions of late-medieval Catholicism, but also from Calvinism, which strayed so happily into the enemy camp to attack them on their own ground. The passages in Plato's *Timaeus* describing the creation of the world were seen to be compatible with the doctrines of creation inherent in Genesis and in the Catholic creeds. Clement of Alexandria and Origen, those two Christian Platonists of the second century, became more popular than the later, Latin fathers of the Church. It was they who had first pointed out the resemblances between the *Timaeus* and the Pentateuch, and it was in Milton's undergraduate days that it again became common to hear Plato spoken of as 'that Attic Moses'.[13]

A younger man than Milton, Ralph Cudworth,[14] (who became Regius Professor of Hebrew in Cambridge at the age of twenty-eight in 1645) was to write that

Pythagoras drew his knowledge from the Hebrew fountains, is what all writers, sacred and profane, do testify and aver. That Plato took from him the principal part of that knowledge, touching God, the soul's immortality, and the conduct of life and good manners, has been doubted by no man. And that it went from him, into the schools of Aristotle, and so derived and diffused, almost into the whole world, is in like manner attested by all.[15]

The group of men, all very slightly younger than Milton, who came to be known as the Cambridge Platonists, were 'nursed upon the self-same hill' and were subject doubtless to the same influences. Gabriel Harvey, that endearing academic buffoon and friend of Spenser's, had written half a century earlier as though the University had been overrun by Platonists. But that craze had failed to affect the prevailing Aristotelianism of the syllabus, and produced no exciting new exponents of Christian philosophy such as, in the new generation, Cudworth, or Henry More, or Benjamin Whichcote who had asked, 'Give me religion that is grounded in reason . . . the religion that makes men courteous, affable and sociable, not sour, morose and dogged; that makes men ready to forgive, not implacable . . .'[16] Theirs are attractive voices in a century where religion so often seems menacing and maniacal. The development of these largely Low Church, largely Emmanuel men, is of course not immediately mirrored by Milton's. But it was similar; and there is reason to suppose that they had influence on him. Perhaps if he had stayed in Cambridge and become a don (as most biographers of Milton, being dons themselves, assume he was pining to do) he would have become a Cambridge Platonist himself.

What their emergence shows the student of Milton, however, quite apart from the many points where his poetry and thought seem to overlap with theirs,[17] is the much more general one that it was possible, in the opening decades of the seventeenth century, to revive the thought-patterns of the ancients without self-consciousness or absurdity. Few, if any, Anglican theologians of this date believed in apostolic succession as it was defined by Roman, later by Tractarian, thinkers. But most learned men of this date would have been fired by Cudworth's alternative, the wisdom of the ancients passing from Pythagoras to Plato and through the Schools of Aristotle, being diffused almost into the whole world. Milton, throughout his life, judged contemporary claptrap by the standards of the ancients. The mental habits engendered by translating Plato into Latin and Cicero into Greek are enough to explain a huge proportion of his later political attitudes.

Meanwhile, the budding poet and clergyman devoted the closing months of 1626 to writing poems about dead bishops. You did not have to feel personally the death of a public figure in order to write elegiac or commendatory poetry about him. Indeed, writing such verses was a perfectly legitimate way of drawing attention to one's talents. The beginning of the modern attitude of sincerity in these matters can be seen in the well-known incident when Wordsworth was at Cambridge, and the Master of St John's died. The coffin was carried into the college hall 'stuck over by copies of verses English or Latin' just as it would have been in Milton's day.

My uncle [wrote Wordsworth] seemed mortified when upon enquiring he learnt that none of these verses were from my pen, 'because', said he, 'it would have been a fair opportunity for you for distinguishing yourself'. I did not, however, regret that I had been silent on this occasion, as I felt no interest in the deceased person, with whom I had had no intercourse and whom I had never seen but during his walks in the College grounds.[18]

No such scruple deterred the young Milton when he heard of the death of the Bishop of Winchester.

The death of Lancelot Andrewes cannot really have been a personal grief to Milton; and when he came to examine that prelate's writings fifteen years later he had little time for his 'shallow reasonings'.[19] Nevertheless, it was not hypocrisy which made him exclaim, in 'Elegia tertia', that the death of this celibate High-Church Bishop of Winchester at the age of seventy-one was a calamity beside which the London plague of the previous year (which killed 35,000 people) and the Thirty Years War seemed but trifles. With the baroque playfulness of an Italianate tomb, encrusted with putti and goddesses, Milton's elegy for Lancelot Andrewes imagines the Bishop of Winchester appearing amid a cluster of vines, a white robe flowing down to his golden feet, before the angels clap their bejewelled wings and waft him heavenwards. The whole convention of elegy-writing, as the story of Wordsworth shows, has vanished from our consciences. If the present Bishop of Winchester dies in harness, he will get an obituary in *The Times*, a memorial service and, if the porter remembers, the flag at half-mast at New College, Oxford. That will be it. Anyone writing poems in which they imagined him being carried into the sky by a brigade of neo-classical figurines would be accused of bad taste, if not blatant satire. But this was not so in Milton's day. If you wished to be regarded as a poet, or even to be noticed in some other capacity, it was quite legitimate to be as fanciful as you liked about the deaths of public personages. And if you sought preferment in the Church (as Milton did) you would naturally want to be as ingenious as possible about the demise of prelates.

So, when the Bishop of Ely also died, a couple of weeks after Winchester, Milton was in luck. His cheeks were still wet, his eyes still swollen with weeping, he writes, from bewailing Andrewes, when he heard the news 'that you, the glory of humanity ("generis humani decus") who was as a king of holy men in the Isle of Eels, had succumbed to death and those iron-hearted fates, Clotho, Lachesis and Atropos'. What was his reaction? Of course, he spontaneously cursed the goddess who rules over the tomb and felt like Archilochus of Paros (eighth-century BC iambic poet) who cursed the low trickery of Lycambes.

What is the relevance of Archilochus? None, one suspects, except to give any but the most learned readers the uncomfortable feeling that they ought to have read him.

So much for dead clergymen. Live ones, it is tempting to suspect, played less part in Milton's consciousness at this date. Evidently, early in 1627 he received a letter from Thomas Young, still a chaplain to English exiles in Hamburg, complaining that his former charge never wrote to him. The result is 'Elegia quarta', a rather frivolous, not to say silly poem, which many commentators have misinterpreted. It is striking, not that Milton alludes to the persecution of the Low-Church party in this poem, but that he makes such slight allusion to it. The greater part of the poem is taken up with itself and its author. It begins with elegant nothings, begging Aeolus, God of the Wind, and Doris the Sea-

Goddess to blow the missive to Germany's golden shore; it continues with the tribute to Young for having taught him Latin, which we have already mentioned; and it alludes to the spring movement of troops at that stage of the Thirty Years War. Only late, in the passage beginning 'Patria dura parens' ('O native land, O hard-hearted parent') does it allude to Young's flock, exiled for reasons of conscience. And he adds a fanciful comparison between Young, sharing their exile in order to minister to them, and Elijah who fled from Ahab and Jezebel. A disparaging reference to the already unpopular French Queen of England, Henrietta Maria, is unmistakable here, but it is slight. It was inevitable, because of the subsequent developments of ecclesiastical controversy in England in which Milton played so conspicuous a role in the 1640s, that too much should have been made of 'Elegia quarta'. What it shows, by its own admission, is that Milton was giving less than a part of his mind to ecclesiastical controversy in 1627. When it came, it was perhaps already predictable which side Milton would be on. But it is quite mistaken to imagine that there were really sides to take in the early years of Charles I's reign. Milton could not have regarded Young's exile very seriously, any more than he really believed that his letter was going to be delivered by a goddess. In any case, it was only a matter of months before, on 26 March 1628, Young was instituted to the joint livings of St Peter and St Mary in Stowmarket.

More disturbing must have been the misfortunes of Milton's friend and correspondent Alexander Gil *fils*, who in the autumn of 1628 found himself in trouble with the law. The Duke of Buckingham, Chancellor of Milton's university, had been assassinated on 23 August by a man called John Felton. Buckingham, a generally detested favourite of Charles I's, was thought, probably quite rightly, to have been an unwholesome influence on his king. The Commons had pleaded for him to be removed and been immediately prorogued. So, it could scarcely have been a day of national mourning when the news of his death came, and joyful ballads, celebrating the murder, were soon on sale in the streets of London.

In the wine-cellar of Trinity College, Oxford, Alexander Gil the younger was drinking with friends and was rash enough to speak his mind about Buckingham and Charles. He was overt in his talk of Buckingham's homosexual proclivities and cheerfully imagined him in hell. As for the king, he was 'fitter to stand in a Cheapside shop with an apron before him and say "What lack ye" than to govern a kingdom'.[20]

Was Charles Diodati among Gil's bibulous audience? Unfortunately,

one of William Laud's godsons was. Gil found himself hauled in front of
the Star Chamber. He was deprived of his holy orders and his degrees,
fined £2,000 and sentenced to the pillory and to lose both his ears. His
father interceded for him, and doubtless pulled strings: his ears were
spared, but the prison sentence was not remitted.

These things must have given Milton pause: not, as I say, made him
wonder which side he was on, because as yet there were no sides; no one
in England could have dreamed, in 1628, what was going to happen. Nor
should we judge Gil's sentence by modern standards. But it cannot have
done much to attract Milton, then aged twenty, to the figure of Bishop
Laud, at that date much in the ascendant, nor to Laud's vision of the
Church.

What sort of a Church was it, this Church of England in which Milton
was destined to serve as a priest?

It was a Church which was still evolving. While claiming a continuity
with its Catholic past, it was, as a national, Protestant Church, only some
seventy years old when Milton grew to manhood.[21] It contained, as it has
always contained since, Christians of almost every conceivable shade of
opinion. They ranged from Godfrey Goodman, who was Bishop of
Gloucester from 1625 to 1643, to parsons like Milton's London neighbour Charles Offspring. Goodman, who never actually joined the
Roman Church,[22] used to say a Latin mass and recite the Roman
breviary. Offspring was a Calvinist who made St Antholin's famous for
its Geneva-style lectures.[23] Both men belonged to the Church of
England, as did multitudes of other Christian people whose theological
opinions had little in common with either. All were agreed, of course, on
the fundamental truths of Christianity – the Resurrection, the hope of
everlasting life for the redeemed, and the divinity of Christ on which all
this hung. Few, except Sir Thomas Browne, were bold enough to think
that diversity of opinion was desirable in a Church. If some Christians,
for instance the Calvinists, were right, inevitably others, such as Ar-
minians, who disputed such doctrines as supralapsarianism and insisted
on human free will, must inevitably have been wrong. You cannot both
insist that, before the fall of man, and even before the creation of the
world, God has decreed salvation to one human soul, damnation to
another, while at the same time believing the human race to be free to
choose their own salvation. You cannot both believe that Christ died
exclusively for the 144,000 whose garments have been washed in the
blood of the Lamb, *and* believe that Christ died for the salvation of all.
The modern Christian uncertainty about the truth in these matters did

not obtain in the seventeenth century. They believed Christianity to be true, and it was therefore important that they got it right. Nothing less than the risk of hell depended upon it.

Nevertheless, even if the Reformation was slow in coming, and even if the National Church seemed to be stuck in some unsatisfactory half-way house, neither fully reformed like the Churches of Geneva or Holland, nor fully Catholic like the Church of Rome, there were many who felt that it would be disastrous if the Church split itself up into sects as soon as any body of Christians discovered themselves to be in exclusive and full possession of theological truth.

He is a good Christian that can ride out, or board out, or hull out a storm, that by industry, as long as he can, and by patience, when he can do no more, over-lives a storm and does not forsake his ship for it, that is not scandalized with that State, nor that Church, of which he is a member, for those abuses that are in it. The Ark is peace, peace is good dispositions to one another, good interpretations of one another; for, if our impatience put us from our peace, and so out of the Ark, all without the Ark is sea: the bottomless and boundless See of Rome, will hope to swallow us, if we dis-unite ourselves, in uncharitable mis-interpretations of one another.[24]

So urged the Christian punster who was Dean of Paul's. The greatest tact, as Donne saw, was necessary to steer the National Church through its crisis years, the greatest charity, and above all the most delicate political sense. It required a man, or men, who could be firm in essentials, when the essential things had become manifest, and tolerant in inessentials. But Providence instead chose to raise up Charles I and William Laud.

Charles I was the first monarch in history to be brought up as a member of the Church of England. He was a pious man, and unflinchingly loyal to his vision of Anglicanism, which found an echo in the opinions of the red-faced, diminutive, bad-tempered little figure of Laud who, having been President of St John's College, Oxford since 1611 rapidly collected preferments (Dean of Gloucester, 1616; Bishop of St David's, 1621, of Bath and Wells, 1626, of London, 1628, and finally Archbishop of Canterbury, 1633). It is not the place, in a life of Milton, to discuss whether Laud's view of the Church was right or wrong. If one believes it to be right, one lumps him together with more attractive figures such as George Herbert, Lancelot Andrewes or Jeremy Taylor; one considers the beauty of the middle way, the elegance of Laudian communion-tables pushed back against the east wall of churches like altars; the loveliness of the Anglican liturgy, and the wisdom of its church in keeping 'the mean between the two extremes, of too much stiffness in refusing, and of too much easiness in admitting any variation from it'.[25] One thinks of the beautification of churches at this date, Inigo Jones adding his Italianate windows and porticoes to cathedrals, and college chapels, incense being gingerly burned ('In Peter House there was on the altar a pot which they usually called the incense pot'),[26] copes worn, and everything seemly, while a clear distance was kept, in practice and in attitudes, from Romish abuses. If, on the other hand, one believes Laud to have been wrong in his view of the Church, one tends to emphasize his activities in the High Commission Court, and the Star Chamber. Alexander Gil was very far from being the only person threatened with losing his ears for quite trivial offences. It was one thing to have restored the beauty of holiness in our sanctuaries; but did every parish want it? One old lady in Norwich, seeing her new Arminian parson standing at the holy table in scarlet mass-vestments asked why the mayor was officiating in church.[27] Every parish in England was asked to conform to the Laudian way of doing things, once Laud became Primate. Such things as the position of the holy table, the liturgical garments of the parson, the contents of his homilies, the ornaments in his church were made subject to the scrutiny of Laud's petty-minded Visitors. Nothing could have been more calculated to whip up offence all over the country. In the seventeenth century, far more than in our own day, people were very little aware of what the government was up to in London, whether they had a good King or a bad King. But they were all aware of what was happening in church, and there is no better way of infuriating people (as even modern controversies about the liturgy show) than needlessly tinkering with church services just when the congregations have got used to them. It was Laud, with his bossy desire to impose his will on every parish in England who, throughout the 1630s, was unconsciously rallying support for the Roundheads as yet unshorn.

So much for the Church in general. Milton must have been wondering, throughout his Cambridge career, what sort of position he could appropriately occupy in it: a chaplain, perhaps, at some great house, or even at Court? Perhaps, with his great musical ability, he dreamed of becoming precentor of some cathedral or abbey. It is conceivable that his father imagined some such pleasant combination of musical and scholarly life at Christ Church, Oxford, his old college. Certainly, while the younger John Milton was still at Christ's, the older kept up his Oxfordshire contacts. On 11 June 1627 he lent £300 to one Robert Powell, the young squire of Forest Hill just outside Oxford. The loan, at 8 per cent, would bring in £24 annually and it was to be paid, not to the scrivener, but to his undergraduate son. It is not known how this little contract came to be undertaken, who introduced Powell to the Miltons, or whether the families, as near Oxfordshire neighbours, had known each other for generations. But it was to have momentous consequences in the life of the poet. The scrivener, in beginning to tie up his business arrangements with a view to an early retirement in such a way as to guarantee his son a little genteel security, had unwittingly prepared the way for Milton to meet his future wife. He was also purchasing for his son the luxury of being able to discard, when the prospect began to seem utterly distasteful, the necessity of taking orders in the peculiar hybrid institution which has just been described.

Was he really called by God to the sacred ministry? What an august question for a young man to ask himself! Without his private income it is unlikely that any such self-doubt could have occurred to the clever product of a London grammar school. As Laud's career showed, with his vulgar Berkshire accent that his enemies so snobbishly mocked, there was no better way of rising in the world than ordination, if you were compelled to live on your wits rather than on your birth. Milton was of a higher social class than Laud, of course; he was what we would think of as on the upper edges of the middle class. But it is unlikely that he would have been very happy as a scrivener, like his father.

If he was not to become the Precentor of Christ Church, some other career equally appropriate would have been found in the Church; how eloquent he would have been as the Master of the Temple, what a distinctive successor to Donne as Dean of St Paul's.

Yet, in an egotist's choice of career, much depends on looking about at others in the same line and asking if it is possible to imagine oneself in their company. The Pharisee's prayer: 'I thank thee that I am not as other men are!' has been the ruin of many a career; and it is a prayer which must have been hovering in Milton's soul ever since he became articulate.

So, looking about him at Christ's, who did he see? On the one hand, there was a handful of good, serious, and intelligent people destined for a career in the Church, some of the younger MAs already perhaps in deacon's or priest's orders. George Ecoppe, Robert Chestlin, or Milton's old schoolmate Robert Pory were all High Church, all destined for careers as parsons, all, as it happens, turfed out of their London livings by Presbyterians in the 1640s. Slightly younger than Milton was Edward King, who had been admitted to Christ's on 9 June 1626. He was a clever young man who had written a little Latin poetry; perhaps talked to Milton about it. It was possible to imagine him as a decent-enough parson.

But the same, alas, could not be said for the generality. How embarrassingly stupid they were! Lamentably ignorant in class and lecture-hall, loud and coarse in their sports. Milton recalled the excruciating amateur dramatics they put on, their attempts to get their mouths around Latin plays, above all the ludicrously undignified behaviour of the young clergy and the college chaplains. As 'Elegia prima' shows, Milton was very fond of the drama when it was well done. Throughout his life it was his ambition to be a great dramatist. But the displays of these idiotic young ordinands and clergymen left a lasting impression on his mind, and fourteen years later he could recall those ghastly evenings

when in the colleges so many of the young divines, and those in next aptitude to divinity, have been seen so oft upon the stage writhing and unboning their clergy limbs to all the antic and dishonest gestures of Trinculos, buffoons, and bawds – prostituting the shame of that ministry which either they had, or were nigh having, to the eyes of courtiers and court-ladies, with their grooms and mademoiselles. There while they acted, and overacted, among other young scholars I was a spectator. They thought themselves gallant men, and I thought them fools; they made sport, and I laughed; they mispronounced, and I misliked; and to make up the atticism, they were out, and I hissed.[28]

'This merriment of parsons is mighty offensive',[29] as Milton's most merciless biographer, in a different context, observed. This little vignette of Milton's young, laughing face, should not be forgotten. He is often spoken about as humourless, dour, and sombre, where it would be more appropriate to think of him as shrill, fantastical, and malicious. Some take it as axiomatic that laughter, like love, must always be shared to be wholesome. The satirist is very often one who has enjoyed the wicked pleasures of solitary laughter. Milton, like Pope, was one such. 'They made sport, and I laughed . . .'

We know what he looked like, from the face in the National Portrait Gallery in London. The oval face of the childhood portrait has lengthened into one of intelligent, sharp beauty. The long hair is auburn now. It fringes the rosy colour and soft complexion of his strong cheek-bones; it forms a careless parting at the top of his high, white brow. The nose is now sharp and aquiline; the lips, cherry-red and sensual and barely suppressing a scornful smile, and the dark eyes stare like a faintly disapproving bird and make any but the most self-confident observer feel a little foolish. The perfect, oval chin is vainly framed with a wide, stiff, expensively-laundered ruff.

This is the dazzling face which burst into laughter at the unfortunate antics of those contorted clergy-limbs, during a performance of some bad play like Thomas Vincent's *Paria* or Edmund Stubbe's *Fraus Honesta*. In some lives there are epiphanies, when a man or a woman suddenly knows the direction in which they are to go, or not to go. At some such pantomime, I believe, Milton's fate was decided. Whatever else he was to be, and whatever else the Lord required of him, he could not seriously entertain the notion of being ordained in the Church of England along with those idiotic characters with unpleasant accents and ill-fitting theatrical costumes.

It was before the dawn of Christmas 1629 – the first Christmas after his twenty-first birthday, that Milton woke early and began to compose his Nativity ode. The writing of that poem sealed his fate, for it shows that, in Milton's person, the tension between Christ and the Muses had been perfectly resolved. His natural medium, henceforth, in speaking of the things of God, will be verse. Describing the writing of the ode to Diodati, Milton implies that it came to him fast, and that it took little perfecting. The Spenserian convention of thinking of Christ as the great Pan has here suggested a whole mythologized description of the Incarnation. At its centre is the placid pastoral which confirms, what Milton so many years later declared to Dryden, that Spenser was his master:

> The shepherds on the lawn,
> Or ere the point of dawn,
>   Sat simply chatting in a rustic row;
> Full little thought they then
> That the mighty Pan
>   Was kindly come to live with them below . . .
>
> (85–90)

But, of course, the poem is infinitely more than a Nativity painting. Compressed into its inexhaustibly rich few lines is a whole vision of Christianity. It draws on innumerable traditions, historical, theological, iconographical: the peace of Augustus, the mysterious fourth eclogue of Virgil, the angelic appearances in the Gospels, and the liturgical convention that it is on Christmas Day that the Church sings, 'Let God arise, and let his enemies be scattered'. All these conventions are richly drawn upon, the inheritance of Milton's Christian upbringing. And much of his reading, not only of his English masters, of Spenser, of Shakespeare, of Sylvester's Du Bartas, but also of Virgil, Horace, Homer and Ovid is found here.

> Say heavenly Muse, shall not thy sacred vein
> Afford a present to the infant God?
> Hast thou no verse, no hymn, or solemn strain,
> To welcome him to this his new abode . . .?
>
> (15–18)

Milton, in asking this question, is testing his entire future. Has he anything to say which all his great masters have not said before?

Let others expound the greatness of the ode. The biographer must note it as a turning-point in Milton's life. For, after this, he knew that he was a great poet. He had *thought* a poem. Hitherto, he had made up Latin verses; he had thought in prose. But now his whole conception of his religion is transformed into poetic terms. Sadly, the subjects which Virgil and Homer and Ovid wrote about withdraw into the shades:

> The lonely mountains o'er,
> And the resounding shore,
>   A voice of weeping heard, and loud lament;
> From haunted spring, and dale
> Edged with poplar pale,
>   The parting genius is with sighing sent,
> With flower-inwoven tresses torn
> The nymphs in twilight shade of tangled thickets mourn.
>
> (181–8)

The world had waited with peaceful anticipation for the great Pan; the angels sang his coming. But the old gods, the very stuff of ancient poetry (it was why Plato had banished poets from his *Republic*), are sent packing:

> Our babe to show his Godhead true,
> Can in his swaddling bands control the damned crew.
>
> (227)

This particular way of writing – that of externalizing or mythologizing theological truth – is something to which Milton, in fact, never aspired after he had finished the ode. But a beginning had been made. He was now much more than a postulant. He was one of the great English poets.

His excitement bursts out happily in those companion-pieces

'L'Allegro' and 'Il Penseroso', which he wrote in the next couple of
years. Both poems depict *pleasures*. We are not meant to choose between
them. The rustic good-cheer, the Shakespearian fancy of 'L'Allegro' is
balanced by the pleasures in 'Il Penseroso' of reading and solitude. If we
take the pleasures expounded as being ones which Milton felt keenly, we
should judge that at the age of twenty-one he loved the summer
landscape of the journey to Cambridge; he loved good food, the beauty
of women; he loved reading, theatre-going and philosophical speculation; and, for all the absurdities of the clergy, he loved going to church.

Again, as of the Nativity ode, the critics have said so much that the
biographer need record no more than that Milton was widening his
English range all the time, writing poems which were at once profoundly
original, and dense with echoes of the past.

But of the handful of poems he wrote in the two years 1629–31, the
biographer must point to ones of lesser literary importance for the light
they throw on Milton's interests at this date. And first, one must mention
his Italian sonnets:

> Donna leggiadra il cui bel nome honora
> L'herbosa val di Rheno . . .
>
> ('Sonnet II')

'My lady fair, whose lovely name honours the grassy Reno valley . . .'
Milton by this date was fairly fluent in Italian. Perhaps it was the
language of friendship between him and Diodati. He was steeped in
Petrarch, Dante, Ariosto, and Tasso, and in this delightful, if mannered
sonnet, he tries his skill as an Italian poet. For those without a crossword
mentality, it should be explained that the name which honours the grassy
valley of the Reno is Emilia. Milton, it appears, was in love with a girl
called Emily, or Emilia, a foreign beauty, 'pellegrina bellezza'. Even if
she knew of it, we need not suppose that the love affair ever came to
anything. In a series of poems he pours out his youthful adoration for the
young lady. He positively has to burst into the beautiful language of
Italian, he says, to describe her charms, even though his fellow-
countrymen will not understand what he is saying. Actually, he rather
likes (and will always rather like) the idea of people finding him slightly
above their heads. His dear friend Diodati understands and that is as
important as anything. With great excitement, in his 'Sonnet IV', he
confides to his friend the thrill of being in love: 'Diodati, e te'l dirò con
maraviglia . . .'

The first object of his affections had dark eyes and lashes and crisp dark hair. It is these two features, her eyes and her hair, which he celebrates in his fifth sonnet. These poems are, perhaps, conventional enough. But there is no reason to suppose that they do not represent a quite genuine experience. Milton always felt feminine beauty keenly. (He was always particularly attracted to nice hair.) And it would seem from later experience that he fell in love quite easily. And one is faced with the first biographical puzzle: why did he wait thirteen years after falling in love with Emilia before he got married? It is not a puzzle which will ever be answered. Something in him held back. He was, throughout his early manhood, always in a state of preparation, of unfulfilment. He was emotionally timorous, even though he felt things so keenly. In the same way, shuddering under the power of his poetic calling, he did not pour forth, like Keats or Shelley, torrents of youthful verse. He was waiting. His lines on Shakespeare show what he was waiting *for*. The poem was not printed in the Shakespeare Second Folio until 1632, but the lines were probably written in 1630. Strikingly, Milton speaks of the bard in the most personal terms possible:

> What needs my Shakespeare for his honoured bones
> The labour of an age in piled stones . . .

His Shakespeare; the Shakespeare he has absorbed and read and reread and made his own. The figure (who can resist the thought?) familiar to him from his early childhood in Bread Street. That fame lives in verse more than in marble or the gilded monuments of princes is a conventional enough thought. But one can have no doubt, in the light of Milton's subsequent utterance on the subject, that it really was a desire for fame which made him 'Scorn delights and live laborious days'. Emilia had to be forgotten. Perhaps she was easy enough to forget, only a passing phase. Perhaps when he next came back to London she had found a lover or a husband. We shall never know. It seems unromantic in a poet to put his own career before affairs of the heart but, in the case of Milton, there is a sort of admirable sturdiness which makes up for the absence of romance. And there is humour, too. Milton joined with the many other Cambridge men in lamenting the passing of Thomas Hobson, the University carrier, who died on 1 January 1631. Milton pays tribute to Hobson's sensationally bad driving:

> Death was half glad when he had got him down;
> For he had any time this ten years full,
> Dodged with him, betwixt Cambridge and the Bull.

But the playfulness of the ending is affectionate, delicate, gentle. He imagines Death 'in the kind office of a chamberlain' to the old man,

> Showed him his room where he must lodge that night,
> Pulled off his boots, and took away the light:
> If any ask for him, it shall be said,
> Hobson has supped, and 's newly gone to bed.

His other elegy of this date is of an altogether different tone. 'An Epitaph on the Marchioness of Winchester' points the direction in which Milton felt his life to be going. It is a harmless, conventional thing. As a papist with strong Protestant sympathies the marchioness is celebrated as a saint. But the death of a lady is very different from the death of an absurd old carrier. Everyone valued rank and title and hierarchy in the past much more than it is acceptable to do so now. Yet even by the standards of that most obsequious age, Milton was a crashing snob. Nearly all the women he really admired in later life – Lady Margaret Ley, Lady Ranelagh – were above the common rank. Death, for the Marchioness of Winchester, is seen as a wonderful opportunity to rise even higher in some celestial Debrett. She who was 'A viscount's daughter, an earl's heir' could hope to be 'No marchioness, but now a queen'. As we shall see, Milton deliberately chose, even though he had the support of his father and the means to live without the support of aristocrats, to seek out the patronage of the Countess of Derby.

The *Penseroso* student; the lover; the wit – he had ever, we are told, a most satirical wit – and the social climber. These are all elements of the young Milton. But he was dissatisfied with his performance as a poet. This diffidence, that in his emotional life held him back from involvement with Emilia, seemed poor when compared with his more prolific coevals:

> How soon hath time the subtle thief of youth,
> Stol'n on his wing my three and twentieth year!
> ('Sonnet VII')

He associates his lack of poetic output with a general quality of late developing: 'my late spring no bud or blossom sheweth'. Physically, he had been a slow developer. His nickname, as the Lady of Christ's Coll:, rankled. Perhaps a bashfulness about his still boyish appearance had thwarted his ardours for Emilia. He will not be rushed. He knows that he will do great things, that he will write great poems, read all the books in the world, learn all the languages:

All is, if I have grace to use it so,
As ever in my great task-master's eye.

The mighty Pan is not a loving God; or, if he is a loving God, Milton
does not feel towards him the sentiments of tenderness which might
have come from the pen of, say, Crashaw. Certain passages of Scripture
mean more to individual men than to others. For Milton, undoubtedly,
the story of the Fall, and the story of Samson are the obvious ones to
mention. But also, throughout his life, he meditated on the parable of
the talents. The task-master's eye was not to be forgotten as Milton's
undergraduate career came to a successful conclusion, and he went
home (a different home) to live with his mother and father.

CHAPTER 3

THE COURTIER

Milton was a Courtier when he wrote the Masque at
Ludlow Castle, and still more a Courtier when he
composed the Arcades.

Charles Lamb, *The Last Essays of Elia*

ONCE he had decided that he was not going to be ordained Milton's
Cambridge career ceased to be of the slightest importance. He was
granted the degree of Master of Arts *cum laude* on 3 July 1632, but no
ceremony can ever have meant less to him. His centre of interest had
already shifted. He was no longer writing poems about deceased
prelates; and he had not yet turned his satirical attention to the question
of whether prelates were or were not a desirable thing. He was looking
rather, as Shakespeare, Donne, and Jonson had looked, for an aristocratic patron. With a curiously appropriate piece of luck, he found a
patroness who had also been Spenser's.

For the first time in Milton's life the interest shifts to the country. We
are not in a university town, nor back in Bread Street. Harefield is the
last little patch, to this day, of rural Middlesex. Its parish church of flint
and brick is still surrounded by fields. It is hard to believe, walking
through the churchyard, that Piccadilly Circus is less than half an hour
away by motor-car.

Pushing open the church door one finds an interior which demonstrates the pleasingly chaotic mixture of styles which can be found in
village churches: real Gothic of the fourteenth century patched up with
Tractarian Gothic of the nineteenth; a stately Georgian pulpit, with a
reading desk beneath for the parish clerk; eighteenth-century-looking
Ten Commandments, spindly lower-case gilt Roman lettering against a
black background; a somewhat baroque late seventeenth-century rere-
dos with (apparently) Flemish communion rails to match. It is a splendid
hotchpotch. But the prize of the church is its assembly of monuments;

and the most splendid of these is a brightly coloured four-poster pressed up against the chancel wall.

It is the work of Maximilian Colt,[1] who used to design royal barges and the props for pageants and masques at the court of Charles I. Standing before it, one gets a glimpse into the splendour of life in the 1630s. At the top, almost out of sight unless one stands well back, heraldic birds with coronets on their hook-beaked heads spread their wings and perch on yet other coronets at each corner of the vast domed tester. Elaborately carved bright scarlet damask cascades down the black marble columns, tied back like drapery around a bed. And there beneath, with her golden hair streaming about her, and her coronet on her head, her hands together in prayer, her girdle loose about her dress, lies the person for whom this glorious monument was erected. She first came to Harefield in 1601. The following year she entertained Queen Elizabeth there. And even now, she looks as if she has merely 'supp'd and . . . newly gone to bed', before the next elaborate social ritual is enacted.

She had come to Harefield to be the third wife of Sir Thomas Egerton, but she was always known as the Countess of Derby by virtue of her fifteen years of marriage to Ferdinando Stanley, the fifth Earl of Derby. She is the great link between the author of *Paradise Lost* and the author of *The Faerie Queene*. Not only did she patronize Spenser; not only were she and her sisters celebrated in his poems (his 'Tears of the Muses' is dedicated to her), but they were probably remote cousins. Her father was Sir John Spencer of Althorp (an ancestor, incidentally, of the present Princess of Wales).

The three women kneeling devoutly at the foot of her tomb are her daughters by the Earl of Derby: Lady Frances married John Egerton, later Earl of Bridgewater; they had three children. Lady Elizabeth married the Earl of Huntingdon. Lady Anne married Lord Chandos, by whom she had four children and then, on being widowed, Lord Audley, who subsequently became the Earl of Castlehaven. The three demure statues at the bottom of the tomb, all stiffly kneeling in the same direction and labelled with the appropriate quarterings, all look much alike. They give no clue that one of them was involved in one of the most sordid sexual scandals in history.

Alas, the scandal cannot go unmentioned. But first, how did Milton come to meet them all, as he must have done; what is the connection between Harefield and Bread Street?

The simple answer is music, and in particular, the music of Henry Lawes. He was a Wiltshire man of about twenty when, in 1615, he settled in London and met Milton's father. The scrivener, who was himself an accomplished player, knew most of the musicians of the day, and would have watched, with wistful pleasure, the swift success of his young friend. Lawes quickly got to know most of the poets and patrons of the day. He became the music teacher to the children of the Earl of Bridgewater (stepson and son-in-law of the Countess of Derby) and, in 1630, a gentleman of the King's Chapel, and a member of the King's Music. Years later, in 1646, Milton was to address Lawes in a flattering sonnet which suggests, with exaggerated devotion, that all Lawes's musical predecessors in England habitually failed to set words harmoniously to music without misjoining strong musical accents and unaccented syllables.[2] If this is somewhat unfair to Dowland and Campion, it shows the strength of Milton's feeling for Lawes; and the reasons, apart from those of obvious affection and friendship, are given in the sestet of the sonnet:

> Thou honour'st verse, and verse must send her wing
> To honour thee, the priest of Phoebus' choir
> That tun'st their happiest lines in hymn, or story.
> Dante shall give Fame leave to set thee higher
> Than his Casella, whom he wooed to sing,
> Met in the milder shades of Purgatory.
>   ('Sonnet XIII')

It is one of his most apparently relaxed, but technically stylish, sonnets and the allusion to the *Purgatorio* is clear. The Italian musician named, whom Dante addresses in the *Purgatorio* as 'Casella mia', had set the great Florentine's canzoni to music; just so, Lawes was to be glorified for having set Milton's verse to music. The egotism is blatant and uncomplicated, Lawes is to be flattered, to consider himself highly fortunate, for having been associated with the greatest poet of the age.

It cannot have seemed like that to Lawes himself when, as a young man rising in the world, he decided to do a good turn to the undergraduate son of his friend the scrivener. The Countess of Derby had commissioned a musical entertainment at Harefield. Could the young Milton (twelve years Lawes's junior) manage some verses for the occasion? Something in Ben Jonson's manner? Jonson had written things for the family often; there was that entertainment of his performed for the Countess's father at Althorp nearly thirty years before: 'The Satyr'.

> This is she,
> This is she,
> In whose world of grace
> Every season, person, place,
> That receive her, happy be . . .³

Milton went away and came up with

> Look nymphs, and shepherds look,
> What sudden blaze of majesty
> Is that which we from hence descry
> Too divine to be mistook:
>   This this is she
> To whom our vows and wishes bend,
> Here our solemn search hath end.

The songs of 'Arcades' have almost the mark of pastiche, so much are they 'in the average manner of Elizabethan and Jacobean pastoral'.⁴ But, on the day of its performance, 'presented to the Countess Dowager of Derby at Harefield by some noble persons of her family', it must have been a pretty thing.

One of the most delightful achievements of modern scholarship has been to reconstruct for us what masques were like. They must have been something between a pageant and a light opera, performed, like 'Arcades', by amateurs, usually under the direction of professional or semi-professional poets and musicians and perhaps theatrical men. The greatest poet of the masque-form is, of course, Ben Jonson; in so far as masques are dramatized occasional poetry, usually neo-classical manifestations of private preoccupations for small audiences of intimates at great houses, inns of court and the like, they are the most quintessential product of his genius. But above all the masque is a musical entertainment, accompanied by mime and dance and pageant. The words, in a sense, are subservient to all this. Harry Lawes's part in the 'Arcades' is much more important than Milton's.

Still, we may imagine the words being appreciated, and the combined genius of Milton and Lawes, and the rather elaborate scenery and props – the Countess Dowager being charmed as she watched her great-nieces and nephews or her grandchildren cavorting on the lawns of Harefield. Harefield, which was transformed for the sake of one summer evening into the woods of Arcadia, whose presiding Genius speaks a flattering oration 'to the great mistress of yon princely shrine' and then goes on to make playful allusion to the myth of Necessity towards the close of Plato's *Republic* – the Fates, the spheres, and the sirens. It is a meditation on the nature of music which Milton was to rework in a much better poem when 'Arcades' was finished:

> But else in deep of night when drowsiness
> Hath locked up mortal sense, then listen I
> To the celestial sirens' harmony,
> That sit upon the nine enfolded spheres,
> And sing to those that hold the vital shears,
> And turn the adamantine spindle round,
> On which the fate of gods and men is wound.
> Such sweet compulsion doth in music lie,
> To lull the daughters of Necessity,
> And keep unsteady Nature to her law,
> And the low world in measured motion draw
> After the heavenly tune, which none can hear
> Of human mould with gross unpurged ear . . .

The notion that only purged ears can hear the music of the heavenly places seems to have been grafted on to Plato's myth by Milton himself.[5] Purgation might perhaps have seemed all too needful to that family in the eyes of the old lady as she watched them scamper towards her out of the trees in their pastoral costumes.

> O'er the smooth enamelled green
> Where no print of step hath been,
> Follow me as I sing,
> And touch the warbled string.
> Under the shady roof
> Of branching elm star-proof.
> Follow me,
> I will bring you where she sits
> Clad in splendour as befits
> Her deity.
> Such a rural queen
> All Arcadia hath not seen.

She who had entertained Queen Elizabeth, and befriended most of the great wits of the previous age was now troubled by the most disturbing possible scandal. Among the children who scampered were those of her daughter, Lady Anne, married to the Earl of Castlehaven, who was executed in August 1631. Milton, however, was probably apprised by Lawes of the fact that all was not well with the Earl of Castlehaven's family, long before he was brought before his peers, in April 1631, and tried for the most abominable crimes.

Both Lady Anne and the Earl had been married before. Her daughter Elizabeth, at little more than twelve years old, was married to his son James. In the trial which followed, the Earl's wife and son were both constrained to give evidence against him.

If half of what was alleged against Lord Castlehaven is true, then counsel for the prosecution scarcely exaggerated when he said that 'although Suetonius hath curiously set out the lives of some of the emperors who had absolute power and might make them fearless of all manner of punishments and besides were heathens and knew not God: yet none of them came near this Lord's crimes'.

Castlehaven was a Roman Catholic and a homosexual. He had the classic homosexual delight in having love-affairs with men of the lowest class, on whom he then bestowed great favours. One of these was a servant called Antil whom he married to one of his daughters. Antil, as well as being adopted as the peer's son-in-law, was invited, with other servants in the household, to commit indecencies with the Countess, the Earl usually a cheerful onlooker, sometimes a participant in the proceedings. Castlehaven's exact behaviour with these servants led to an absurd piece of legal wrangling during the trial, the attorney in his charge submitting to the judgement of their lordships 'whether it were to be accounted buggery . . . without penetration'.[6]

Trials of this nature play a peculiar role in modern life, as they did in the seventeenth century: great cleansing rituals in which we can heap our feelings of sexual guilt on to some convenient scapegoat whose excesses outnumber the average, in frequency, or imaginative range. Of Castlehaven's wickedness, as the prosecuting counsel said in his opening speech, 'The one is a crime in our nation of that variety that we seldom have known the like, and the other we scarce ever heard of before. And they are both of that pestilent and pestiferous nature that if they be not punished they will draw from heaven God's heavy judgement upon this kingdom . . .' Yet, as always on these occasions, there is an element of glee about the trial, and the way it was reported. Transcripts survive in abundance.[7] The trial was everywhere talked about and the Earl's execution, when it came, well attended. Here was something almost everyone could cluck about; something worse, more exotic, more vile than the ordinary private citizen could dream up for themselves. The salacious legal questionings (could it be accounted buggery without penetration?); the cruelly extracted evidence of the

Countess and the servants make appalling reading because, as with the trial of Wilde, one feels that the desire to have such matters publicly aired is primitive, savage, and therefore compulsively necessary for the societies which enact such vile rituals.

Castlehaven was the perfect instrument of such a ritual because his crimes were so terrible. Plainly mad with perverted lust, he was also a Roman Catholic, which made it even easier to create the feeling that the monster in the midst must be throttled and done away with. By far the most scabrous detail in the trial, apart from his keeping a prostitute in the house[8] – 'one Blandina . . . who bestowed an ill disease there and therefore he sent her away';[9] and his sodomy, and his enforced rapes of his Countess by his servants, was his treatment of Lady Anne's daughter Elizabeth (the child of her previous marriage), who in 1628, at the age of about twelve, had been married to the Earl's son James, the eldest of six children by *his* previous marriage.

The evidence, truly horrifying, was given by Skipwith, another of Castlehaven's servants-cum-boyfriends. He told the court, with a wealth of circumstantial detail too vile to have been invented, that the Earl had forced him to rape Elizabeth when she was only twelve years old. Every standard is violated by his account. It is above all horrifying, of course, that the young Elizabeth has been lured into marrying Lord Audley for purely dynastic reasons, and before the age when she might reasonably be expected to consummate the marriage, only to find herself at the mercy of her father-in-law's cruel fantasies. Further evidence suggested that she was used as a whore by the entire household at Fonthill. Lord Audley, incidentally, who succeeded to the earldom when his father was eventually beheaded (on Saturday 14 May 1631 on Tower Hill at about nine in the morning) was the pillar of respectability, and had a very creditable military career.

It has been necessary to dwell upon this distressing episode because without doing so, the next major development in Milton's literary career is incomprehensible. Everybody had followed the Castlehaven trial avidly, in the way that people always do follow public scandals. But for Milton, who was now directly involved with the family, it was of more than voyeuristic interest. The old Countess of Derby would not have young Elizabeth into her house, but the three other children, Elizabeth's sisters, were taken into her care at Harefield. And, while being unable to have her defiled granddaughter and daughter in her house, she did make petition on their behalf to the King. On 6 August she sent a petition to Secretary Dorchester that 'unless the King's mercy may be obtained for the dowager Lady Castlehaven and her daughter, they are left most miserable: the mother, by secret conveyance of the late Earl, and by wasting the estate she had from Ld. Chandos her former husband; the writer's grandchild by being left by her husband without comfort or any estate at all. Intreats him to move his Majesty to extend his favour to them . . .'[10]

Was 'Arcades' written before or after this terrible calamity in the family of a distinguished old Elizabethan lady? At least one critic has wished it could have been *after*. 'The fulness of compliment, the assurance that she was unshakeably a "rural queen" most fit to rule over the realms of pastoral, would take on a beauty, if they were intended as consolation and support, that as merely formal tribute they necessarily lack'.[11] But we do not know.

Certainly, the Castlehaven scandal was not easily forgotten. William Prynne, an extreme Protestant barrister of Lincoln's Inn, published in the following year a book called *Histriomastix*. It was a work primarily directed to attacking stage-plays, but in the course of it he suggested that having male actors who played the parts of women inevitably encouraged the sin of Sodom which the Scriptures condemned and 'Councils, heathen states and in our English statutes (which have made it capital, as a late example of a memorable act of justice on an English peer can witness) do more than testify . . .'[12]

Prynne's book, although on its title-page principally concerned to show 'That popular stage-plays (the very pomps of the Devil which we renounce in baptism, if we believe the Fathers) are sinful, heathenish, lewd, ungodly spectacles, and most pernicious corruptions, condemned in all ages as intolerable mischiefs to churches, to republics, to the manners, minds and souls of men', is equally fierce in its condemnation of just about everything else. He hates men with long hair ('our effeminate hairy men monsters')[13] and he 'would our overgrown lock-wearers and frizzle-pared men-women would well consider' what Scripture says on the matter of coiffure in 'I Cor. 1: 14. Ezek 44: 20. Lev. 19: 27 and 21: 5. Dan. 4: 33. Rev. 9: 7, 8. 1 Tim 2: 9. 1 Pet. 3: 3. Isa. 3: 24.'.[14] English gentlewomen do even worse 'as if they all intended to turn men outright and wear the breeches, or to become Popish nuns . . . are now grown so far past shame, past modesty, grace and nature, as to clip their hair like men with locks and foretops, and to make this whorish cut, the very guise and fashion of the times, to the eternal infamy of their sex, their nation and the great scandal of religion'.[15]

Prynne never makes his religious position more clear than when he

says that 'the Apostles and the Christians in the Primitive Church . . .
were for the most part weepers, not laughers'[16] and that 'Christ Jesus our
pattern, our example, whose steps we all must follow, if ever we expect
salvation from him: was always mourning, never laughing; (I am sure not
at a stage-play, which he and his condemn, as worthy tears, not
smiles)'.[17]

Did Milton share the view of this clever, somewhat fanatical lawyer?
Evidently not. Whether he went in for frizzling or nourishing it, we are
not told, but he wore his own hair long. The embarrassing experience of
seeing Latin plays badly acted by apprentice clergymen at Cambridge
did not seem to have changed his taste for the drama. He could still be
lured to the theatre

> If Jonson's learned sock be on,
> Or sweetest Shakespeare, fancy's child,
> Warble his native wood-notes wild,
> And ever against eating cares
> Lap me in soft Lydian airs . . .
> ('L'Allegro', 132–6)

and, if he were asked to write another masque, he would do so.

The chance came when the Countess of Derby's family achieved
fame of a rather happier kind. On 26 June 1631, her stepson and
son-in-law, the Earl of Bridgewater, was made President of the Council
of Wales; and, a little later, on 8 July, Lord Lieutenant of Wales and the
Counties on the Welsh border.

Lord Bridgewater was going to celebrate his arrival in the Marches on
Michaelmas Night. When Henry Lawes heard of this, he almost
certainly got in touch with Milton at once. They had three months to
draw up an entertainment together. It was to happen at Ludlow Castle.
This would inevitably mean that it could not be an affair with vastly
elaborate scenery, of the sort provided by Inigo Jones for Ben Jonson's
Court masques. Lavish costumes there could be, and of course, singing.
Dance, on the other hand, would have to be more limited than in a
London masque. This was a major drawback, for in many definitions of
the nature of the genre, it has been said that the masque *is* dance.[18]
Lawes evidently thought that the masquers of Ludlow could not be
trusted to have any very elaborate measures. Why not, instead, place the
burden of the entertainment on his young pupils the Earl's children,
whom Lawes knew well, and whom he could drill mercilessly into
learning lines, movements, and measures?

Surely flattered to be asked, Milton went away and thought about his commission. In his mind, there were many things mingled. He had to envisage something suitable for a young girl of about fifteen, and her two younger brothers. In such a family, nubile young adolescent girls might provoke memories too recent and too horrible to be uttered, and yet too strong to be passed by. *Histriomastix* had been possessed of a carping, angry tone, and spiritual stinginess. Surely God's world, and God's plenty, were to be enjoyed, and particularly when one is young. 'What lesson is that unto you, but that in the april of your age, you should be like April?'[19] But that was the counsel of the wicked aunt in the *Arcadia*, not the virtuous Pamela. The knowledge of God teaches us true moderation; not lean and sallow abstinence, but a right sense that, as vessels of the Holy Ghost, we keep a sense of proportion about our physical appetites. Plato had taught the same doctrine in the *Phaedo*. The soul only became flesh by a sort of corruption; and the soul of the corrupted person can never really become detached from the flesh. Corruption! Corruption! The Earl of Bridgewater's brother-in-law certainly knew of that; even to know of him and his story was to be polluted. Lust had such power to contaminate life that by looks and gesture and talk, we can be corrupted by it.

Milton, who remained the supreme egotist, could not fail to feel the relevance of these thoughts to his own position. He had had flirtations, and innocently thought himself in love with pretty girls. There had been Emilia. But his virginity remained undefiled. His soul was unclotted by the contagion of sex. It could fly up to God, like the soul of any good Platonist, by contemplation and high thinking; it could rise above the flesh, above the 'smoke and stir of this dim spot which men call earth'. Yet this was not the thought of a weeper, but of a laugher. The fruits of such detachment were harmony and gaiety. How could he convey these thoughts in a masque?

Dance, Lawes had said, was to be limited. Perhaps it was as well. What was it the old vicar of St Thomas's, Oxford, said in his extraordinary book *The Anatomy of Melancholy*? 'Young lasses are never better pleased than whenas upon a holiday, after evensong, they may meet their sweethearts, and dance about a maypole, or in a town-green under a shady elm . . . Yea many times this love will make old men and women, that have more toes than teeth, dance, "John come kiss me now", mask and mum; for Comus and Hymen love masks and all such merriments above measure . . .'[20]

Comus. The Greek word for revelry. 'Voluptuous Comus, god of cheer'²¹ Jonson had called him in a masque Milton had certainly read in manuscript, *Pleasure Reconciled to Virtue*.²² It was an entertainment in which Prince Charles (later Charles I) had taken a part: his first masquing role. Comus entered the stage (all designed by Inigo Jones) in a low chariot like a Bath chair, with an arbour of vine over his head; he was naked, with a huge belly. Three naked followers pushed the thing along.²³ After the dance and the anti-masque these figures were scattered and there is a speech in favour of virtue:

> She, she it is, in darkness shines.
>   'Tis she it still herself refines,
>   By her own light, to every eye,
> More seen, more known, when vice stands by.
>   And though a stranger here on earth,
>   In heaven she hath her right of birth.
>   There, there is Virtue's seat.
>   Strive to keep her your own,
>   'Tis only she, can make you great,
>   Though place, here, make you known.²⁴

Jonson's great original was, then, the starting point for Milton; Lawes's specifications (perhaps the absence of a great number of professional actors) determined the shape of the thing. With these potent ideas brewing, and these suggested restraints, Milton went away and wrote his masque. With these unpromising beginnings, one of the most lovely poems in our language blossomed out. Milton was never more Shakespearian than when he wrote the 'masque presented at Ludlow Castle'. Yet although the suggestion of the masque is Jonsonian, the language Shakespearian, there is no other poet who could have written it. It is the lightest and the most joyous of all Milton's poems, suggesting everywhere harmony and musicality, reaching out, as it were to the music which accompanies it, imitating its cadences and providing dance where dancers were none.

Lawes, when he first read it, was, however, evidently anxious. Was it really imaginable that Lady Alice Egerton, who was to play the lady, could speak lines like these:

> Hast thou betrayed my credulous innocence
> With vizored falsehood and base forgery,
> And wouldst thou seek again to trap me here
> With liquorish baits fit to ensnare a brute?
>   (696–9)

What member of the family, watching Lady Alice have this encounter with her tempter, could fail to remember her cousin Elizabeth, who, so recently, really had been ensnared in the most brutish fashion by her stepfather and his band of monstrous revellers? Who, remembering the disgusting way in which Lady Elizabeth Audley lost her virtue at the age of twelve, could fail to think of that disturbing fact when Comus lures the lady on with his sneering speech:

> List Lady be not coy, and be not cozened
> With that same vaunted name virginity,
> Beauty is Nature's coin, must not be hoarded,
> But must be current, and the good thereof
> Consists in mutual and partaken bliss . . .
>
> (736–40)

That was another passage which Lawes quietly omitted from the players' copy. He made one or two other cuts, perhaps on musical grounds, but there was no possibility of cutting the parts of the masque which were going to remind the audience of the Castlehaven scandal. The whole performance, delicately, beautifully, but firmly, was concerned with the preservation of a young person's chastity.

The masque, as a form, is designed to celebrate, in a ritualized way, the virtues appropriately embodied in a particular aristocratic or royal family. It was 'a celebration and a demonstration of those qualities by which the aristocrat justified his power'.[25] So, Milton's little masque, or pastoral drama, depicts the children of the Earl of Bridgewater as lost in a dark wood on their way to Ludlow, and separated from one another, the Lady and her two brothers. On the other hand they are befriended by the unseen Attendant Spirit, played by Harry Lawes, whose position as their tutor and mentor is ritualized as he sings of the Earl as

> A noble peer of mickle trust, and power
> Has in his charge, with tempered awe to guide
> An old, and haughty nation proud in arms:
> Where his fair offspring nursed in princely lore,
> Are coming to attend their father's state,
> And new-entrusted sceptre . . .
>
> (31–6)

On the other hand, the Lady is beset and threatened by Comus, with his magic, his charming-rod, his lustful designs, his playful and most attractive dalliance:

> The sounds, and seas with all their finny drove
> Now to the moon in wavering morris move,

And on the tawny sands and shelves,
Trip the pert fairies and the dapper elves;
By dimpled brook, and fountain-brim,
The wood-nymphs, decked with daisies trim,
Their merry wakes and pastimes keep:
What hath night to do with sleep?
Night hath better sweets to prove,
Venus now wakes, and wakens Love.

(115–24)

The gaiety, and above all the supreme tastefulness of this is what lends the verse such charm. Lovers of Milton have always regarded his *Masque* as his prettiest work; wholly his own, and yet in diction and structure and feeling owing so much to *his* Shakespeare who 'warbled his native wood-notes wild'. More recent scholarship has emphasized the appropriateness of a masque on the theme of chastity in the light, or rather the shade, of the Castlehaven scandal. And yet, perhaps the most striking feature of the *Masque* is not the grace with which he emphasizes the beauty of chastity – any hack, writing for this family after Lord Castlehaven's execution could have thought of that. Is it not rather more remarkable that without any offensiveness, Milton has enabled Comus to retain the amusing, gay, and almost innocent debauchery that he has in Jonson's masque? It requires far more delicacy and tact to give Comus good lines, in this particular set of circumstances, than it does to provide good lines for the Attendant Spirit or the Lady or the two brothers.

It is hard not to believe that Milton himself took the part of Comus on that Michaelmas Night in Ludlow Castle. With a good singing voice, a delicate ear, and graceful movements, how unlike he would be to the Cambridge bumpkins unboning their clergy limbs! Here he was with people of the world, with whom he was always more happy than with a narrow academic or literary circle; but not with worldlings, for the Earl's family was pious, serious, and learned. Lady Alice's two older sisters were noted for their Protestant piety. Lady Frances Egerton had a Huguenot governess as a child and learned to be 'a Calvinist in point of doctrine and a Presbyterian as to discipline'. Later in her life she was to lament wasting 'part of many Lord's days in masques and other court pastimes . . . this she would often mention with bitterness, and honourably mention and prefer before herself one of her noble sisters, who in her youth had a just sense of that error, and courage enough to resist the temptations to it'.[26]

But the brilliant thing about Milton's *Masque*, from this point of view, is that it would not offend the most serious sensibility. There was no needless or silly extravagance about the designs for the scenery; no needless nudity as there had been in *Pleasure Reconciled to Virtue*, and much of the high spiritual joy of a Platonic dialogue set to music as the brothers discover what it is that can protect their sister lost in the woods.

> How charming is divine philosophy!
> Not harsh, and crabbed as dull fools suppose,
> But musical as is Apollo's lute,
> And a perpetual feast of nectared sweets,
> Where no crude surfeit reigns.
>
> (475–9)

The *Masque* is Milton's first and most glorious expression of his belief, from which he never wavered, that virtue and the good are their own protection. Masques have been likened to 'cleansing rituals'; and there must indeed have been a moving and cleansing sense of joy as Lady Alice Egerton's young voice loftily reproached her tempter:

> Thou hast nor ear, nor soul to apprehend
> The sublime notion, and high mystery
> That must be uttered to unfold the sage
> And serious doctrine of virginity . . .
>
> (783–6)

There is an attitude to virtue itself betrayed here which is deeply Miltonic; more Stoic than strictly Christian; discernible in everything he wrote from the *Areopagitica* to *Paradise Regained*. Vice is associated with stupidity. The virtuous rise above the vicious through will-power and achieve a measure of Platonic deification. There is nothing here of the Atonement, or the Redemption, or the sense that though we are all sinners, some of us, or all of us, have been washed in the blood of the Lamb. It is true that at the end the Lady's virtue is of course not enough to save her; she needs the intervention of the Attendant Spirit before, unblemished, she and her brothers are led by Lawes to her enthroned parents with the final song:

> Mortals that would follow me,
> Love Virtue, she alone is free,
> She can teach ye how to climb
> Higher than the sphery chime;
> Or if Virtue feeble were,
> Heaven itself would stoop to her.
>
> (1018–23)

In this of course is implied the notion that God will help us to be good. But it completely evades the mainstream of Protestant theological preoccupation: the idea of grace. Those, like Richard Stock or Lady Frances Egerton, who believed themselves to be saved, achieved their salvation not through their own virtue but through the merits of Christ. Their righteousnesses were as filthy rags. Not so Milton's, who was proud of his and regarded them as lifting him above the vulgar rabble. The *Masque* reveals him to have had much in common with the Platonism of men like Henry More, Ralph Cudworth, or John Smith; not much with the extreme Calvinists or Presbyterians. He was fascinated by Christianity, and was always a devout Christian; but he never really had the slightest feeling for the sort of Christianity which takes the Epistle to the Romans as its inspiration. By Luther's standards, or Calvin's, or Zwingli's, or Cranmer's, Milton was probably not a Christian at all. In his Arminianism, at this phase of his life, he had much more in common with Laudians than with the more Genevan faction in the Church, however much he might have despised their lifestyle. Spiritually, he was more at home with the emergent Cambridge Platonists. But then, as for the rest of his life, he was too much his own man to be classifiable in terms of party. Doubtless he still loved church for musical reasons. But he had already developed an almost Shavian habit of mind which automatically produced a feeling of contempt for almost every opinion which it was possible for the human mind to entertain; combined with very strong, but effervescent and ever-changing opinions of his own. But one opinion he did not change, and that was the opinion expressed in the last lines of the *Masque*.

So, the scene changed in the hall, '*presenting Ludlow Town and the President's Castle; then come in Country Dancers, after them the Attendant Spirit, with the two Brothers and the Lady*', and the evening came to an end.

It remains the most delightful entertainment. In the early years of the eighteenth century it was popular as a little opera. Thomas Arne wrote music for it in 1738, and in 1750 there was a revival, with a prologue by Dr Johnson, in the presence of Milton's granddaughter. Asthma-ridden and ill at the age of sixty-one, she needed the money raised by this performance. It was during this period that the *Masque* came to be known as *Comus*. Thus a masque written to entertain the Egertons in 1634 provided a pension for a member of Milton's family in the reign of George II; and a single bridge, as it were, divides the patroness of Spenser and the hero of Boswell.

As Milton turned away from Ludlow, however, in the autumn of 1634, he must have wondered profoundly what direction his life was going to take. If, at twenty-three, his late spring no bud or blossom had shown, what did it show at twenty-five? A considerable body of poetry in four languages. But a man could not live by writing poetry, not merely because poetry makes no money, but because poetry cannot possibly take up the whole of a man's day. Study, learning, the 'curious search into knowledge' was, as his nephew said after his death, 'the grand affair perpetually of his life'. Where there was a good library, Milton would always be happy. But was this enough? Poetry, in the previous generation, had all been produced by men who were either full-time courtiers following the pattern of Sir Philip Sidney, or otherwise men of action or business.[27] Sir John Davies was a lawyer; Campion a physician; Spenser an administrator in Ireland; Shakespeare an actor-manager. Sandys had translated Ovid as he sailed across the Atlantic to take up his post as Treasurer in Virginia; Middleton completed his Welsh translation of the Psalms in the West Indies; Donne wrote poems on the Islands voyage, and then . . . Milton knew too well what then. Donne had taken orders. Milton could not do the same. He could not bring himself to unbone his clergy limbs with the buffoons of his old university. He had not become a fellow of Christ's; I do not believe that he had hoped for it. Then what? It must have been hard not to hope that his connection with the Bridgewater world would not bring patronage and preferment of some kind, some position at court, some honorific sinecure in the civil service. But no such offer came. Could it be that, far from regarding the *Masque* as a great cleansing ritual, the Earl thought it in rather bad taste? It is not unlikely. So, with nothing much to look forward to, Milton returned to live with his parents.

CHAPTER 4

'LYCIDAS'

Era già l'ora che volge il disio
ai naviganti, e intenerisce il core
lo dì ch'han detto ai dolci amici addio

Dante, *Purgatorio*, VIII. 1–3

MILTON'S father had given up the house and business in Bread Street in September 1631. His seventies were devoted to a peripatetic and rather restless retirement, never living for long in the same place. First the family moved to Hammersmith, in those days a tiny village on the edge of the rural suburb of Fulham. Then they moved further away, some seventeen miles out of London, to the dull little village of Horton in Buckinghamshire. What charm it must have had then has since been destroyed by ribbon development before and after Hitler's war; and by the unending drone of nearby Heathrow.

Milton later summarized his life during these years – from 1632–7 – in these terms:

On my father's estate where he had determined to pass the remainder of his days, I enjoyed an interval of uninterrupted leisure, which I devoted entirely to the study of Greek and Latin authors; though I occasionally visited the metropolis either for the sake of purchasing books, or of learning something new in mathematics or in music, in which I, at that time, found a source of pleasure and amusement. In this manner I spent five years till my mother's death.[1]

The memory distorts. Milton's five years were not, as this passage implies, all spent in the same place. He would have had the disturbance of his parents moving house. Nor does he reveal that his involvement in music took the form, as we have seen in the last chapter, of collaborating with one of the foremost musicians of the age in two musical entertainments for a great house. Horton is not all that far from Harefield. It is possible that Milton maintained his ties with the Countess of Derby until her death in 1637.

But memory did not distort that these were years of quietness, reflection, and study. Looking back from a time when his days had been greatly taken up with political involvement, the five years before his mother's death must have seemed idyllically peaceful. At the time, his mentors were worried by it. Why was he not doing something? He had not yet confessed to his old tutor Thomas Young, for instance, with whom he still kept up a quiet friendship, that he had abandoned the idea of taking orders. It was almost certainly to Young that he wrote the 'Letter to a Friend' which survives in a manuscript in Trinity College, Cambridge. The friend, whoever he was, had seen Milton on the previous day, and asked him why he delayed.

You are often to me, and were yesterday especially, as a good man to admonish that the hours of the night pass on (for so I call my life as yet obscure and unserviceable to mankind) and that the day with me is at hand wherein Christ commands all to labour while there is light.[2]

The letter seems almost eerily pregnant with the pattern and poetry of Milton's later years. As a passionate capitalist, he has a quite morbid horror of not *using* his talents, of not yielding returns on the capital invested in him by the great task-master of 'Sonnet VII'. And yet, at the same time, he cowers from the brink of experience and is diffident about what to do next. With endearing and characteristic self-absorption, he proceeds: 'I therefore think myself bound though unasked, to give you account, as oft as occasion is, of this my tardy moving'. As in 'Sonnet VII', he has a sense that life is proceeding more slowly for him than for others; that he is a late starter; just as, presumably, the nickname he had at Christ's implied a retarded physical development. Yet, he assures his friend, his endless, self-absorbed programme of reading and study is not without purpose:

If you think, as you said, that too much love of learning is in fault, and that I have given up myself to dream away my years in the arms of studious retirement like Endymion with the moon, as the tale of Latmus goes, yet consider that if it were no more but the mere love of learning, whether it proceed from a principle bad, good, or natural, it could not have held out thus long against so strong opposition on the other side of every kind.

Clearly, Milton had been under pressure, from his College, perhaps, from his friends, and from his people, to take some kind of employment; ideally, to be ordained and seek preferment in the Church. Surely he echoes his father's words, or any father's words, when he says that, far from scholarship being the promptings of a mere 'natural proneness', 'there is against it a much more potent inclination inbred, which about this time of a man's life solicits most the desire of house and family of his own to which nothing is esteemed more helpful than the early entering into credible employment, and nothing more hindering than this affected solitariness . . .'

The most remarkable portion of the 'Letter' then follows. All this, Milton concedes, would be true. If he were intended for orders, there would be no excuse; he should realize that the night was far passed and the day at hand; if he were thinking of marrying and buying a house of his own, it would, equally, be more prudent to seek out some lucrative living or patronage. But he was not doing these things.

To judge from the entries in his commonplace-book of this date, marriage was obviously much on his mind. The jottings dating from the Horton period are full of patristic references to the lawfulness of marriage, but the desirability of the virgin state. Cyprian's *De disciplina et habitu virginum*, Gregory of Nyssa's *De virginitate* appear to have been perused by Milton at this date, even though, as he noted, Gregory of Nyssa was himself married, and the papists only forbid the clergy to marry for 'shrewd reasons',[3] rather than high, Platonic ones. As has often been pointed out, the theme of chastity in the *Masque at Ludlow Castle* is shot through with a preoccupation with 'the serious doctrine of virginity': an odd concern to foist on the Earl of Bridgewater, who was to be the father of fifteen children.

Milton had put the idea of marriage out of his mind. Having fallen out of love with Emilia, he had translated, in his first and beautiful essay into blank verse, the fifth ode of Horace ('Quis multa gracilis te puer in rosa') and captured perfectly the tone of his original:

> What slender youth bedewed with liquid odours
> Courts thee on roses in some pleasant cave,
> Pyrrha for whom bind'st thou
> In wreaths thy golden hair,
> Plain in thy neatness; O how oft shall he
> On faith and changed gods complain: and seas
> Rough with black winds and storms
> Unwonted shall admire . . .

Horace gazes back at a self released from love, its storms and gales. And Milton likewise has found a quiet haven:

> Me in my vowed
> Picture the sacred wall declares t'have hung

> My dank and dropping weeds
> To the stern god of sea.

The self of the Italian sonnets, or of 'Elegia prima', has given way to the *Penseroso*, the scholar, the magician, almost the mystic:

> Or let my lamp at midnight hour,
> Be seen in some high lonely tower,
> Where I may oft outwatch the Bear,
> With thrice great Hermes, or unsphere
> The spirit of Plato to unfold
> What worlds, or what vast regions hold
> The immortal mind that hath forsook
> Her mansion in this fleshly nook:
> And of those demons that are found
> In fire, air, flood, or under ground,
> Whose power hath a true consent
> With planet, or with element.
>
> ('Il Penseroso', 85–96)

While at Cambridge one of his academic exercises had been on the music of the spheres, 'De Sphaerarum Concentu', the Platonic myth (expounded in the *Timaeus* and towards the close of the *Republic*) that the sun, the moon, the five planets, and the heaven of the fixed stars were each tenanted by a siren, who, singing in monotone their proper note, together formed a scale or octave. Milton adds to the myth this proviso:

The reason why we are quite unable to hear this harmony is the foolhardy theft of Prometheus which, among so many ills brought to mankind, robbed us of this faculty of hearing. Nor shall we be allowed to enjoy the faculty again, so long as we are overwhelmed by sin and grow brutish with beastly desires. But if our hearts should grow to a snowy purity, then our ears would be filled with the most sweet music of the revolving stars . . .[4]

There is plenty of this preoccupation in the *Masque*. Some have believed that Milton was deliberately chaste 'like the great ascetics of primitive magic in order to acquire supernatural powers'.[5] The 'Letter to a Friend' at least makes it clear that for the time being he had deferred the ambition to marry, if he had ever had it. He had deferred it, and this is the really remarkable thing, in favour of a higher vocation: the desire to achieve fame. He sees love as the greatest threat to 'this affected solitariness' and

though this were another yet to this another act if not of pure, yet of refined nature no less available to dissuade prolonged obscurity, a desire of honour and repute, and immortal fame seated in the breast of every true scholar which all make haste to by the readiest ways of publishing and divulging conceived merits, as well as those that shall, as those that never shall obtain it, nature therefore would presently work the more prevalent way if there were nothing but the inferior bent of herself to restrain her.

In this convoluted sentence, Milton leaves no doubt that he hopes, and is confident, that he is one of those who shall 'obtain immortal fame'. He is pursuing not 'the empty and fantastic chase of shadows and notions' but a better way, informed by a 'due and timely obedience to that command in the gospel set out by the terrible seizing of him that hid the talent'.

Milton scarcely knows what this awful vocation is to be; and so he bides his time. But he feels it, powerfully, certainly, strongly. The task-master is being served even now, as, in his loneliness and solitariness, the young man unspheres the spirit of Plato.

How so? The scrivener, now able to devote long days to his music, was evidently impatient with the idea. Other poets have not felt called to do nothing else. But this young poet appears to do nothing but sit all day, perusing the pages of Matthew Paris's Latin chronicles, the proceedings of the Council of Trent, the *Paedagogus* of Clement of Alexandria. This is parson's work, not poet's. Why won't the lad hurry up and get himself a decent living? Perhaps the Countess of Derby could fix something up? Harry Lawes had found him two poetic commissions for her family. He had executed them stylishly, though one can doubt the tact of a masque about chastity at this particular juncture in the family history, and was a hall full of Welsh gentry and the Mayor of Ludlow really supposed to catch all those references in the masque to the Hermetic books and the 'budge doctors of the Stoic fur'? Some such impatience, if the old man felt it, would have been understandable. Some such feeling was obviously expressed. And the result was . . . yet another poem: a Latin one: 'To my Father'.

'Ad Patrem' is an affectionate rebuke. It is also a hymn of filial gratitude. He invokes the Pierian fountains to flow through his heart, so that his Muse, forgetting his trifling, thin, reedy *tenues* songs, might fly up on brave wings and pay homage to his father. Whether you approve or not, dearest father, this little thing, this poem is being dreamed up, and really, there is no more fitting way of repaying your gifts to me . . .

So he cheekily begins, and he implores his father not to despise the gift of divine poetry:

Nec tu vatis opus divinum despice carmen . . .

There follows a predictable catalogue of how the gods love poetry, of how the sybils of Apollo reveal their secrets in verse; of how, in the golden age, it was usual to have a bard at royal feasts, his brows crowned with a garland of oak-leaves as he sang of heroes and of gods.

Although, Milton goes on, although you pretend to hate the delicate, *teneras* muses, you don't really. You have not forced me into some money-making profession; you have not made me become a lawyer (unlike, he could have added, his brother Christopher, who was admitted to the Inner Temple on 22 September 1632);[6] you do not make me take an interest in the absurdities of politicians. Instead, you have allowed me the peace and quiet of the countryside, to walk as the cheerful companion of Phoebus amid the leisurely delights of the Aonian spring.

He continues to say that the kindnesses which his father have lavished upon him are numberless; but not least among them is having taught him languages: Latin, Greek, French and Italian, as well as Hebrew.

The poem ends with a hymn of scorn to those who have chosen money-making careers, like his father. Go on then, pile up your riches, those of you who hanker after the royal heirlooms of Austria or the Peruvian realm:

> I nunc, confer opes quisquis malesanus avitas
> Austriaci gazas, Peruanaque regna praeoptas.

But he, the poet, is different. Already he has a slight place among the ranks of the learned; one day he will be crowned with ivy and laurel. He will no longer mix with the unskilled mob, his steps will shun the gaze of common folk . . .

> Iamque nec obscurus populo miscebor inerti,
> Vitabuntque oculos vestigia nostra profanos.

The poem ends with a pretty compliment to his father, suggesting that, just as his own juvenilia will achieve immortality, so will his father's name be perpetuated for endless ages.

Milton was never in any doubts about his own genius. The persona of 'Ad Patrem' is unattractive, absurd, and posturing, when the poem is read in isolation. It is unattractive, because no one likes a boast; and it seems absurd for a young man of twenty-five to be telling his father that his only claim to immortality will be having been the parent of a poet of genius. Moreover, since the leisurely lifestyle which Milton enjoyed was based entirely on money raised by his father's career in the City, he is hardly in a position to sneer at those who devote their lives to making money.

Yet, we must remember always, when dealing with Milton's egotism, that he had something to be egotistical about. There is almost a humility about his acceptance of the great gift that has been given him. He looks at what he has already written – 'L'Allegro', 'Il Penseroso', *A Masque*, 'At a Solemn Music', 'On the Morning of Christ's Nativity'. To have written such things must have been akin to having received a divine visitation. Milton had read the whole of English poetry, most of Latin, Greek, French, and Italian poetry. He knew that what had poured from his brain was among the most sublime poetry in the literature of the world. With patience and gratitude he accepts the gift, and presents it, baldly, to his father. There is no mention in 'Ad Patrem' of a career in the Church. Milton had by this stage abandoned any such notion. His father had evidently asked him what he intended to do with himself. 'Ad Patrem' is not actually a boast. It is, on the contrary, a plea for patience. Almost embarrassed by his great gift, Milton is aware that he is capable of greater, much greater things. But, in an almost god-like way, he senses that his hour is not yet come. He feels that the great poem which he will one day write must be prepared for, by learning, by scholarship, by solitude, by withdrawal, by prayer. For never, at any stage after this point in Milton's life, does he have any doubt that he is a man with a divine vocation.

Quietly then, at Horton, he nursed his gift. He saw friends occasionally. He saw the Diodatis in London. He kept up, doubtless, with friends at Cambridge. His nephew tells us that he had contracted a 'particular friendship and intimacy' with a younger undergraduate at Christ's, Edward King, who evidently did not share Milton's disillusionment with the Church and was destined for a career as a clergyman. King, as we have already mentioned, had written Latin verses which he had evidently shown to Milton.

But, for the most part, his life in Buckinghamshire was quiet. Presumably he occasionally went over to Oxford, where he had been incorporated as an MA in 1635,[7] to consult books in the Bodleian Library. Presumably he saw Lawes from time to time, and hoped, who knows, for some place in the household of the Earl of Bridgewater. At the beginning of 1637 he presented the Earl with a printed copy of the *Masque*,[8] with a number of manuscript corrections. Some even believe that he presented a copy of the book to King Charles I. It is not impossible.[9] There was no hope of any more patronage from the old

Countess of Derby. She died on 23 January 1637 and was buried in splendour at Harefield.

It was to be a year of deaths.

Milton's parents were both ill throughout the spring of that year. Even in his retirement the scrivener had debtors, or litigants who came his way in the course of business. He had two or three cases on the go in the Court of Chancery, and these, combined with the increasing decrepitude of his wife, were wearing. On April Fool's Day Christopher Milton made an affidavit that his father was too ill to attend the court in London to answer a litigant's bill.[10] But it was really Sara Milton, and not John the elder, who was ailing. Three days later, on 3 April, she died.

The poet, who had written elegies on the deaths of Lancelot Andrewes and the Marchioness of Winchester, was not moved to verse by the death of his mother. We are not to conclude from this that he did not grieve for her. Poetry for Milton, as for nearly all the pre-Romantic poets, was a public occupation. Milton is remarkable for the extent to which, compared with other Renaissance poets, he reveals himself in his poetry. But some moments were too private for him to versify and this was one. They buried her in Horton, even though she had not lived there for more than a couple of her sixty-five years; and there she remains, an exile from London, to this day.

Meanwhile the Last Will and Testament of John Cotton Esquire went on being disputed in the Court of Chancery and Milton versus Cotton continued to make lawyers some money. It was perhaps refreshing to have an excuse to be in London, away from the scenes of Sara Milton's last illness. The case provided the distraction needed for John Milton *père* to get over the first few months of his grief; and Milton *fils* appears to have accompanied his father, now changed as all men who have lost their mothers are changed.

If Diodati was in London in the earlier part of the summer, we know that he was not there in September. 'I was told, quite wrongly', Milton wrote to his friend, 'that you were in London, and I rushed to your cell with whoops of delight, but it was all, as the Greeks have it, the vision of a shadow!' Doubtless, he felt particularly anxious for companionship of his own age. Chilling news had come in August of the death of Edward King, who was drowned in the Irish sea on 10 August when his ship, not far from the English coast, struck a rock. King evidently died rather heroically, making little effort to save himself, and commending himself to God; he was on his knees in prayer as the boat went down.

So in this great year of deaths (Ben Jonson had died earlier in the

summer), Milton was brought uncomfortably to the fact that even his
own age-group was not immortal. It is always disturbing for a young
person when a contemporary dies. For Milton, who had such a sense of
his own destiny, waiting to be fulfilled after a sufficient gestation of his
genius, it was a rude blow. King had been a year younger than himself.
He was evidently prized and loved by Cambridge. When it was known
that Oxford was going to bring out a commemorative volume for Ben
Jonson, *Jonsonus Virbius*, Cambridge followed suit with a rival book.
Milton was asked to contribute.

Enough has already been said in this book about elegies to make it
plain that this memorial volume would not be the place for deeply
personal expressions of grief. Most of the contributions to the volume,
therefore, strain after ingenuity rather than trying to recapture what
each individual contributor felt about Edward King when he was alive.
So, when one of the contributors in Latin, a man called Coke, contrived
to say that he was sad to think of dumb fishes swallowing into their
entrails King's tongue, which had dripped with the sweetness of Latin
and Greek honey, we should not condemn him for ill judgement until we
have acclimatized ourselves to the spirit of the whole volume. There are
nineteen Latin poems and three Greek ones in the first half of the book,
entitled 'Justa Edouardo King'; there follow thirteen English poems,
'Obsequies to the memory of Mr Edward King'.

Even making allowances for the different conventions which in those
days obtained, it is hard not to think some of the English contributions a
little silly. Sampson Briggs, a Fellow of King's, felt that King had been
so full of qualities that

> Such general disturbance did proclaim,
> 'Twas no slight hurt to Nature but a maim:
> Nor did it seem one private man to die,
> But a well ordered University.

Another Fellow of King's College, Isaac Olivier, asked

> Why did not some officious dolphin hie
> To be his ship and pilot through the fry
> Of wondering Nymphs?

Why could not King have swum the Irish sea as Achelous ran untainted
through salt Doris to meet Arethusa? Or, Olivier goes on to suggest,

> Or else (like Peter) trod the waves: but he
> Then stood most upright when he bent his knee . . .

This is typical of what might be called the metaphysical 'wit' of the English contributions. Milton's poem goes back to the much older tradition of pastoral lament, perfected in English by Spenser but, of course, owing its origins to Virgil and Theocritus.

Far more ink has been wasted on 'Lycidas' than tears were spent for Edward King. For some readers it will always remain the peak of Milton's career;[11] not because they dislike *Paradise Lost*, but because they regard 'Lycidas' as the most beautiful thing in English. By choosing the pastoral mode, Milton declared himself, albeit unready, as the new Spenser. The laurels are not ready for picking, and the poet must wrench them from their branch, 'Shatter your leaves before the mellowing year.' This untimely putting of himself forward is purely ritualistic. Milton has written poetry before; enough, by the standards of modern poets aged twenty-nine, to fill a couple of volumes. But here he speaks of himself being forced to write before he is ready because it is fitting in the case of one who died so young.

> For Lycidas is dead, dead ere his prime . . .

The death of King, as much as in the other contributions to the 1638 volume, has been ritualized; so have Milton's reactions to it. The effect is to universalize the experience, of course. But, paradoxically, it also allows Milton to be far more particular, far more autobiographical, far more self-concerned than a poem merely about 'Edward King' could ever have been. In 'Lycidas' we see the first great evidence of Milton using art as a great vehicle of self-transformation. He is here the uncouth swain, 'warbling his Doric lay'; after the experience of controversy in the pamphlets, in which, of necessity, he adopted a range of different personae, he will be sufficiently rehearsed to transform himself into Samson and into Christ.

So King becomes Lycidas. Why Lycidas? In Theocritus, he was the 'best of pipers'. Further appropriate associations are caused by the memory of Spenser's 'May Eclogue' in *The Shepheardes Calendar*, in which Piers, the Protestant pastor, is called Lycidas. So Lycidas is a poet-priest. Of King the actual Fellow of Christ's, Milton makes little. He makes Lycidas as much as possible like himself:

> he knew
> Himself to sing, and build the lofty rhyme.

Moreover, although he will never forget how farcical it all was, he recalls with nostalgic affection the days when he and King, the uncouth swain and Lycidas, were at college together.

> Together both, ere the high lawns appeared
> Under the opening eye-lids of the morn,
> We drove a-field, and both together heard
> What time the grey-fly winds her sultry horn,
> Battening our flocks with the fresh dews of night,
> Oft till the star that rose, at evening, bright,
> Toward heaven's descent had sloped his westering wheel.
> Meanwhile the rural ditties were not mute,
> Tempered to the oaten flute;
> Rough satyrs danced, and fauns with cloven heel,
> From the glad sound would not be absent long,
> And old Damaetas loved to hear our song.
>
> (25–36)

This suggests a certain distancing of the two young friends from the rural clowning of the others.

> Meanwhile *the* [not *our*] rural ditties were not mute . . .

While they, the shepherds, contributed songs which pleased their clownish mentor, Damaetas (presumably one of the dons), the other undergraduates are viewed as rough satyrs and fauns with cloven heels. Attempts have been made to identify these characters, as one might in a *roman-à-clef*. It is fairly obvious that any such identification is impossible, because the mode Milton has chosen to write in makes anonymous and universal, and suggestive, things which, if made particular, would lose their edge. A line like

> And Doctor Chappell loved to hear our song

would have been absurd. Not only do we know it was untrue, in Chappell's case (even though he is a favourite among those who like to identify Damaetas);[12] it destroys the point of the line. As it stands, the line allows us to believe that Damaetas might very well not have loved their song, which, with the egotism of youth, the uncouth swain believes to have been so charming. But, at the same time, because Damaetas is traditionally a clown, his loving the song does not suggest very discriminating taste. So the line is held in perpetual irony which, mercifully, can never be unravelled.

After the beautiful and conventional passage of lament – 'But O the heavy change', in which Milton imagines 'universal nature' lamenting for Lycidas, and this having no more effect than it had when the muse sobbed for Orpheus as his dismembered body floated down the Hebrus, Milton reaches the central question posed by this death. If a poet's life can be so brutally and pointlessly cut short, what is the point of living a life of austere scholarship and contemplation such as he has been doing in Horton? Why not sow wild oats? The question, on Milton's lips, answers itself. The reward the task-master will give to him is fame.

> Alas! what boots it with uncessant care
> To tend the homely slighted shepherd's trade,
> And strictly meditate the thankless muse,
> Were it not better done as others use,
> To sport with Amaryllis in the shade,
> Or with the tangles of Neaera's hair?
> Fame is the spur that the clear spirit doth raise
> (That last infirmity of noble mind)
> To scorn delights, and live laborious days;
> But the fair guerdon when we hope to find,
> And think to burst out into sudden blaze,
> Comes the blind Fury with th'abhorred shears,
> And slits the thin-spun life. But not the praise,
> Phoebus replied, and touched my trembling ears;
> Fame is no plant that grows on mortal soil,
> Nor in the glistering foil
> Set off to the world, nor in broad rumour lies,
> But lives and spreads aloft by those pure eyes,
> And perfect witness of all-judging Jove;
> As he pronounces lastly on each deed,
> Of so much fame in heaven expect thy meed.
>
> (64–84)

The relevance of all this to the circumstances of King's life is hazy. King was not, like Milton, trying to win everlasting fame as a poet.

There follows the passage of the poem to which Milton's enemies have taken most exception: the emblematic procession of the winds, then of Camus or Cambridge, and then of St Peter, all commenting on the demise of Lycidas.

First, the 'waves and felon winds', questioned by Neptune about the reason for Lycidas's death. As has already been mentioned, King's boat went down in a storm on the Irish sea when it struck against rocks. King died piously and heroically: having tried to rescue fellow-passengers, he sank to his knees in prayer and, as Olivier put it, he

> Then stood most upright when he bent his knee . . .

Milton is not, however, writing a poem just about the death of E. King on 10 August 1637. He is writing about the meaningless cutting-short of life, the terrible arbitrariness of death, which we all carry about with us in our mortal bodies which, since the curse of Adam brought death into the world, have no more hope of life than a badly-built ship could hope to cross the seas. So, when the winds and waves are questioned, they say that Lycidas, unlike King, died mysteriously on a perfectly fine day:

> The air was calm, and on the level brine,
> Sleek Panope with all her sisters played.
> It was that fatal and perfidious bark
> Built in the eclipse, and rigged with curses dark,
> That sunk so low that sacred head of thine.
>
> (98–102)

This generalizing, this making of Lycidas's death more emblematic than King's, sits, to some tastes, oddly beside the next phase of the poem, in which St Peter appears, the first bishop, shaking his mitred locks and complaining about the low calibre of men coming forward for ordination in the Church of England. It seems, to these tastes, either absurd or profane; and Dr Johnson's censure of this passage (indeed of the whole poem) is too well known to be worth quoting.

Once again, however, it shows how Milton's personal preoccupations creep and intrude and climb into this poem and give it its peculiar and somewhat grotesque energy, transforming themselves into the poem's idioms while changing its flavour. There is a witty and delightful progression, not without Spenserian precedent, from the notion of shepherds as poets, a Theocritan, Virgilian notion to the Christian vision of Christ as the Good Shepherd and bishops as shepherds and pastors of their flocks; the clergy, as the bishops' representatives, as shepherds in their turn. The language of Christendom itself suggests the passage. Only Milton, however, could have put these words into the mouth of St Peter:

> How well could I have spared for thee, young swain,
> Enow of such as for their bellies' sake,
> Creep and intrude, and climb into the fold?
> Of other care they little reckoning make,
> Than how to scramble at the shearer's feast,
> And shove away the worthy bidden guest;
> Blind mouths! that scarce themselves know how to hold
> A sheep-hook, or have learned aught else the least
> That to the faithful herdman's art belongs!
>
> (113–21)

It has puzzled some readers so much that Milton gives these lines to St Peter that they have tried to make 'the pilot of the Galilean lake' into Christ. But St Peter it is, with the emblematic pair of keys with which he is always represented, and a mitre on his head. Though Christ is spoken of as 'the Shepherd and Bishop of your souls' in I Peter 2:25, he is not iconographically thought of as having 'mitred locks', a phrase which perfectly summons up a baroque statue of the Prince of the Apostles. How can it be, the puzzlers go on to ask, that Milton, the arch-anti-episcopalian, could be producing this statuesque figure of St Peter arrayed in the 'gewgaws out of old Aaron's wardrobe'?

There are two very clear answers which must be given. The first is that while having a sublime egotism, Milton's self-transformations into art always sublimate what is heterodox and odd in favour of what is conventional. By the time he wrote *Paradise Lost*, for instance, he had believed all manner of Christian heresies; but although scholars have looked for, and therefore found, evidence of them in the great epic, it is fundamentally true that he wrote it *as if from* the position of orthodoxy. He did so, not out of hypocrisy, but for the same reason that, if you were writing a poem about Father Christmas, you would not make him into a green-coated Frenchman with a black waxed moustache. Milton saw, and realized poetically, the full mythological solidity of Christian theology and cosmology. For the same reason, whatever his opinions about bishops, there is nothing more appropriate, iconographically, than having the first bishop lamenting the death of King, who was an episcopalian, with a life of priesthood in front of him. So, whatever Milton thought personally about bishops in 1637 would not have changed his picture of St Peter having mitred locks.

And that leads to the second, very necessary biographical point to make. Milton changed his mind with very great frequency in matters of religion. In the years in which his religious opinions are chronicled it would seem that he managed to be an Independent, a Presbyterian, a mortalist, an Arian, a semi-Quaker, an advocate of divorce, a celebrant of Christian marriage, a polygamist: not all at once, and not all in that order, but that is only a sample of the opinions he entertained between, say, 1640 and 1660.

At no stage in those years did he ever belong to a Nonconformist sect. Had the seventeenth century been tolerant of such deviants, and bureaucratic enough to inquire which denomination Milton belonged to, he would have had to say, throughout the most heretical phases of his late middle age, that he was C. of E. That was the Church that he was born, reared, died, and was buried in. There is no evidence, apart from 'Lycidas', for the state of Milton's religious opinions in this particular year. Many of his friends, as is well known, belonged to the Low-Church party. Some had been persecuted by the Laudian authorities for this preference. Milton was probably in sympathy with them; and everything he knew at first hand of the rising generation of clergy filled him with contempt.

> The hungry sheep look up, and are not fed,
> But swoll'n with wind, and the rank mist they draw,
> Rot inwardly, and foul contagion spread:
> Besides what the grim wolf with privy paw
> Daily devours apace, and nothing said . . .
>
> (125–8)

Despondent as it is, this sentiment is very Anglican. If Milton had been deeply anti-episcopalian at this period, or allowed his poem to be, it would have lacked the Anglican irony which it in fact possesses. To the fury of Roman Catholics and extreme Protestants alike, the Church of England under Laud claimed full continuity with the Church before the Reformation. Although quite manifestly a break had occurred, the mass had been replaced by an ambiguous communion service, the religious orders had been suppressed, and links with Continental Catholicism had been severed, the Anglicans had retained, in a somewhat mutilated ordinal, the threefold order of bishops, priests, and deacons. Hooker, it is true, had seen bishops as no more than the *bonum esse* of a church; not the *esse*. But Laud's High-Church notions went beyond this, and the new generation of Anglicans, of which Milton was one, had become accustomed to the apparent insolence of this National, Protestant Church's claim to retain its ancient historic links with the apostles: a claim which dismayed papists by its blatant untruth, and Protestants by its disloyalty to the first principles of the Reformation.

Milton, however, whatever his own views at the time of writing the poem, delights in adopting this point of view for the literary purpose of making St Peter, on whom all papalist claims rest, sadly shake his mitred locks at the prospect of Roman Catholic infiltrators making headway in England because of the idleness or stupidity of the Anglicans. The 'grim wolf with privy paw' is a clear reference to the Jesuits who, rather like Communists in the days of McCarthy in America, not only were thought to be everywhere by panicky witch-hunters, but actually were everywhere. I personally find it hard to believe that Milton was simply trying

on the episcopalian idea for size. 'Lycidas' makes it plain that, in 1638, he
was still hoping, though he had abandoned any intention of taking
orders in it, that the National Church would reform itself from within.
'Lycidas' is not the first voice of the pamphleteer who wrote *Of
Reformation*: it is the final *cri de cœur* of the man who had written the elegy
on the death of Lancelot Andrewes. Even as he concluded the poem,
with its matchless floral passage, its confidence that Lycidas will be
raised up 'Through the dear might of him that walked the waves' while,
in a playful neo-classical fancy, he becomes the 'genius of the shore',
Milton was already thinking of the next stage of his own life. He was now
in his thirtieth year. His mother was dead. His sister, Anne Phillips, had
remarried and was now called Mrs Agar. His papist brother Christopher, starting his career at the Bar, was already married, at the age of
twenty-five, to Thomasine Webber. So the elder John Milton was not to
be without companionship in his widowerhood.

What should the younger John do? If he had been a scholar in the old
Renaissance tradition, like More or Tyndale or Erasmus or Colet; had
he been an Englishman of the High Renaissance like Sir Philip Sidney,
there would have been no doubt what he should do: he would have gone
abroad, met all the greatest scholars of the age, seen Paris, Florence,
Pisa, and Rome; seen their great libraries, paintings, and architecture.
Why not do so now? It was a suggestion of the Provost of Eton which
prompted him to it. His elegy ends with confidence. His ecclesiastical
career has been banished; submerged, as it were, with Lycidas beneath
the waves. But he is only twenty-nine, and he puts on a garment of hope.
Blue is hope's colour; Speranza in *The Faerie Queene* had worn it:

> And now the sun had stretched out all the hills,
> And now was dropped into the western bay;
> At last he rose, and twitched his mantle blue:
> Tomorrow to fresh woods, and pastures new.

CHAPTER 5

CONTINENTAL

> There, unseen,
> In manly beauty Milton stood before him,
> Gazing with reverent awe – Milton, his guest,
> Just then come forth, all life and enterprise;
> *He* in his old age and extremity,
> Blind, at noon-day exploring with his staff;
> His eyes upturned as to the golden sun,
> His eye-balls idly rolling. Little then,
> Did Galileo think whom he received;
> That in his hand he held the hand of one
> Who could requite him – who would spread his name
> O'er lands and seas – great as himself, nay, greater;
> Milton as little that in him he saw,
> As in a glass, what he himself should be,'
> Destined so soon to fall on evil days
> And evil tongues – so soon, alas, to live
> In darkness, and with dangers compassed round,
> And solitude.
>
> Samuel Rogers, 'Italy'

ETON is no distance from Horton. Milton must often have visited the College – perhaps to enjoy anthems, sung by the boys in the chapel, perhaps to consult the library. The distinguished old Provost, Sir Henry Wotton, became a friend of the young scholar-poet, and a letter, now preserved in the British Museum,[1] makes it clear that Milton had discussed with him the possibility of travelling abroad.

Wotton, at this date aged seventy, was no schoolmaster, though he had been the Provost of Eton for the previous fifteen years, and had even taken deacon's orders in 1627. He was a famous diplomat, traveller, and poet, and had been knighted after a distinguished career in government service under the Earl of Essex in 1595. After that he had been ambassador to the Court of Venice, as well as making diplomatic visits to Augsburg, Paris, the Hague, and Vienna. So he was a useful man to know if you were embarking on a Continental tour.

Milton had sent him a copy of *Comus* (printed the previous year) and the old man had been delighted by it. ('Wherein I should much commend the tragical part if the lyrical did not ravish me with a certain Doric delicacy in your songs and odes, whereunto I must plainly confess to have seen nothing parallel in our language . . .') Clearly, Wotton had seen and admired it (*Comus*, of course, was published anonymously) before Milton sent him a copy and he thanks the young poet 'for intimating unto me (how modestly soever) the true artificer . . .'

The letter continues, 'Now, Sir, concerning your travels, wherein I may challenge a little more privilege of discourse with you; I suppose you will not blanch Paris in your way [clearly in conversation, Milton had made pretty plain his hostility to the French and their influence, through the Queen Henrietta Maria, on English life and customs] . . . therefore I have been bold to trouble you with a few lines to Mr M.B. whom you shall easily find attending the young Lord S. as his governor [this is one Michael Branthwait, a tutor to the son of Lord Scudamore, who was Charles I's ambassador in Paris] . . . and you may surely receive from him good directions for the shaping of your farther journey into Italy'.

Nevertheless, the old man cannot resist offering a further two paragraphs of slightly Polonius-like advice. As it happens, though, it was good advice; and the letter is given poignancy by the fact that they were never to meet again. Wotton died before Milton's return home:

I should think that your best line will be through the whole length of France to Marseilles, and thence by sea to Genoa, whence the passage into Tuscany is as diurnal as a Gravesend barge: I hasten as you do to Florence, or Siena, the rather to tell you a short story from the interest you have given me in your safety.

At Siena I was tabled in the house of one Alberto Scipioni, an old Roman courtier in dangerous times, having been Steward to the Duca di Pagliano, who with all his family were strangled, save this only man that escaped by much foresight of the tempest: with him I had often much chat of those affairs: into which he took pleasure to look back from his native harbour; and at my departure toward Rome (which had been the centre of his experience) I had won confidence enough to beg his advice, how I might carry myself securely there, without offence to others, or of my own conscience. 'Signior Arrigo mio', says he, 'I pensieri stretti e il viso sciolto² will go safely over the whole world': of which Delphian Oracle (for so I have found it) your judgement doth need no commentary; and therefore (sir) I will commit you, with it, to the best of all securities, God's dear love, remaining

Your friend as much at command as any of longer date,
Henry Wotton.

Thus prepared, he had only to procure a passport. Henry Lawes got one for him from the Warden of the Cinque Ports. Some time in May a trim, slight, well-dressed figure, accompanied by a servant, he boarded the ship for France. How much one would give for the journal or recollections of this unnamed Jeeves.

Milton's Continental travels only took up a little over fifteen months of his life. But they are proportionately much more important than that. Civil war and the propaganda it generates make nations inward-looking and provincial. Even the greatest minds stoop to silliness in times of national emergency. Milton was not above the absurdity of believing that God reveals himself 'to his servants and, as his manner is, first to his Englishmen'.[3] His fifteen months abroad strengthened, rather than diminished, his puckish chauvinism. But it also shows him in a larger, grander light. Sir Henry Wotton was most unusual in discerning that there was 'nothing parallel in our language' to the *Masque*. Milton was not appreciated as a poet on any wide scale in England, until he was nearly dead. On the Continent, he was lionized. There is an appropriateness about this because, intellectually, this polyglot young man was living a life of deliberate isolation from the English literary scene. Spenser and Shakespeare: of course they were important to him. So, too, was Ben Jonson. But he did not write like the 'tribe of Ben'; and the metaphysical school of writing made almost no impression on his poetry at all. Plato, Theocritus, Virgil, Dante, Tasso, Du Bartas . . . these had been 'his' authors since boyhood, and he had known them in their own tongues. The Diodatis had been his dearest friends in London. Wotton, a much-travelled cosmopolitan figure, was a recent and revered acquaintance. Milton consciously chose, or felt called, to enrich his native tongue with a great epic; he could equally have written it in Latin, Greek, Italian, or French. When Dryden spoke of Milton in the company of Homer and Virgil, he sketched a perspective which was Milton's own:

> Three poets, in three distant ages born,
> Greece, Italy and England did adorn . . .

The vast divide between the classical Mediterranean world of Virgil and the narrow confines of seventeenth-century England was bridged by the wealth of Milton's reading:

> The force of Nature could no farther go:
> To make a third she joined the former two.

This is why he had found Cambridge so stifling, its provincialism, its stupid, ill-read undergraduates, its dons 'never heard-of half a mile from home'. As he 'twitched his mantle blue' and set forth for the Continent, he was of course setting out on an adventure. Dangers, of the Websterian kind promised by Sir Henry Wotton, perhaps lay ahead: 'dukes who with all their family were strangled'. But, in another sense, as he disembarked, he must have had a heady sense of homecoming.

With the wisdom of hindsight, it is possible to see that Milton travelled abroad only four years before the outbreak of the Civil War in England. Historians used to speak of Charles I 'pushing his country to the brink' of civil war, as though there was an inevitability about it. Events which ordinarily would have seemed quite commonplace have therefore assumed an importance they probably lacked at the time. William Prynne, the author of *Histriomastix*, a work which attacked masques and playacting, and had some caustic things to say about the lifestyle at the court of Queen Henrietta Maria, had been tried the previous June, fined £5,000, and had his ears cut off. Tried with him were Henry Burton, a London parson who had described all bishops as 'upstart mushrumps' and had objected to wearing a surplice; and a parishioner of Burton's, John Bastwicke, another anti-episcopalian. Of course, by modern standards, the sentences imposed on these three men were barbaric enough. 'Their sin was against Laud and his surplices at Allhallowtide, not against any other man or thing', as Carlyle puts it in an emotive passage,[4] where the sufferings of this trio in the pillory are associated mysteriously with Jenny Geddes throwing the stool at the 'pretended-Bishop' of Edinburgh on 23 July 1637, and Hampden refusing to pay the Ship Money in November. In all probability these are still regarded as 'causes of the Civil War' by historians. Certainly, the rule of 'thorough' practised by Charles I and his ministers Laud and Strafford was very unpopular. Certainly, their policy in Scotland, and their attempt to raise tax without parliamentary authority gave rise to general concern, and certainly Parliament had not been assembled since 1628. Milton later referred to 'the sad breaking of that Parliament' in a sonnet to Lady Margaret Ley.

But few would have dreamed, in the spring of 1638, what lay ahead. There was a constitutional crisis brewing, as Charles I and everyone else knew; a crisis which would come to a head as soon as he was obliged to summon Parliament to raise money for the Irish and Scottish insurrections. But all this was comparatively mild compared with what was going on abroad.

Milton himself was struck, when in Italy, that the Florentines regarded him as being born in 'such a place of philosophic freedom as they
supposed England was';[5] and they supposed correctly, because England,
even during the so-called 'eleven years' tyranny' of Charles I was a good
deal gentler than many Continental countries.

Moreover, far from feeling that he had escaped a country almost torn
apart by near civil war, Milton must have been struck immediately, on
setting foot in France, by the very prickly and war-like atmosphere
which prevailed, compared with the comparative calm of home. The
French provinces were in a perpetual state of rebellion against Louis
XIII during the 1630s, and in the Paris of Cardinal Richelieu one would
have heard much about the progress of the war: for Europe had been at
war—the so-called Thirty Years War—since 1618.

Thanks largely to the diplomatic expertise of Richelieu, Paris was
actually enjoying a period of relative peacefulness in May 1638 when, in
all probability, Milton arrived there. For one thing the Queen, Anne of
Austria, was pregnant, for the first time in a twenty-two year marriage.
Louis XIII, as a result of the prayers of the Virgin Mary and the
Pandar-like activities of his cardinal, had been brought to bed with his
consort, during a heavy shower of rain four days after the Feast of the
Immaculate Conception in the previous December. The French people
could at last look forward to a Dauphin.

They could also look forward to a lull in the war. There was a new
Emperor (Ferdinand III), and that spring the Duke of Pomerania,
Bogislav XIV, died. Richelieu used these facts as an excuse for en-
gineering a respite in the war, urging the Emperor to accept the Swedish
occupation of Pomerania. In mid-March the treaty was signed.[6] The
Swedish ambassador, confusingly, was a Dutchman, Huigh de Groot,
or, as he was known to his wide readership throughout Europe, Hugo
Grotius.

Grotius was the greatest living authority on international law; he was
also a poet, a dramatist, a theologian – a man of parts in the great
humanist tradition. Born in Delft, he arrived in France as a very young
man; Henry IV called him 'the miracle of Holland'. Before he was
twenty he had edited the literary remains of Aratus di Soli, and
Martianus Capella's encyclopaedia *(De nuptiis Mercurii et Philologiae)*.
He had also written an epic, and two Latin plays, the first of which,
Adamus Exul, was widely regarded as a work of genius. Having, at the age
of twenty-two, written an authoritative work called *De jure Belli et Pacis*,
he tried to return to his native Holland, which was torn by religious and

political conflict. From a political point of view he backed the wrong horse, and declared himself as an Erastian, anti-Calvinist thinker who believed in a state-controlled Church rather like that of England. So, he stayed in France. Louis XIII offered him a pension if he would become a papist, but he refused, and eventually his diplomatic experience, his staunch Protestantism, and his knowledge of the French court made him an obvious choice, by Axel Oxenstierna, as Swedish ambassador. It was largely through Grotius's influence that Richelieu saw the advantages (to the horror of the Pope) of allying himself to Sweden during the Thirty Years War; and it was largely through his zeal (in spite of some restlessness on the part of Oxenstierna) that the alliance held.

Milton did not have long in Paris. But when his host, the British ambassador Lord Scudamore, asked him who he would like to meet, Milton had no hesitation in asking to be introduced to Grotius.[7] It is symptomatic of how Milton envisaged his Continental tour taking shape. It was something much more than sight-seeing, or holiday-making. He wanted to meet the great men of the age, and he was starting with one of the most eminent, the darling of princes and an all-purpose humanist genius.

Grotius was devoting his (as it happened) declining years in France to schemes of ecumenism similar to ideas which had fired Sir Philip Sidney's generation forty or fifty years before. Sidney, Hubert Languet, and such distinguished Huguenots as Du Plessis-Mornay had dreamed of forming a Pan-Protestant League uniting all the reformed churches of Europe,[8] and this was an idea dear to Grotius's heart. In his will (of 1645), he prayed 'to unite the Christians in one church under a holy reformation'. From this he excluded Calvinists and was hoping for a formation of national Churches with a more wishy-washy tradition, such as those of England, Denmark, and Sweden. Nor was it entirely impossible, given the extreme Gallicanism of the French hierarchy of bishops, that the French Church could not have been included. Milton doubtless heard of these ecumenical pipe-dreams from the lips of the great man himself. And of course, no biographer of the poet has ever been able to resist wondering whether they discussed that early play of Grotius's, *Adamus Exul*. Like most interesting questions, it is unanswerable, but it is quite likely that his meeting with Grotius planted the seeds of *Adam Unparadised* in the poet's brain. Perhaps the ecumenical idea struck both men, at the time, as more interesting. An all-Protestant league; it must have been an appealing idea to the cosmopolitan young poet, though he probably had cause to reflect that with their incense-pots and their mass-vestments, and their holy tables, adorned with frontals and candles, like altars, the new Laudian clergy seemed more like papists every year. Really, explaining the Church of England to foreigners, even to foreigners as astute as Grotius, was very difficult; and there was not much time to do it in. It is hard to imagine that Milton tried to speak of his national Church in tones of great loyalty.

He was, in any case, in Paris only a matter of days. Sir Henry Wotton had suggested his route. He should sail from Marseilles. Guided by an instinct to contradict, Milton at once set out for Nice, where he boarded, still accompanied by that unnamed manservant, the packet for Genoa.

In chronological terms Milton's year abroad occupies only a tiny fraction of his life, but by his own confession it was a year of personal crisis, a turning-point. Italy was to hasten the direction in which his mind was moving. If not a political equivalent of the road to Damascus, it accentuated radical and republican tendencies which had hitherto been merely latent; it sharpened and redefined his Protestantism. It was, moreover, the year in which he learnt the chilling news that he had lost his best friend with the death of Charles Diodati.

It is very easy to anticipate later developments in the life of a great man; to find, because one has been looking for them, hints of the mature man in his youthfulness. Modern biographers have not been slow to look for early whiffs of sectarian radicalism, even in the childhood of Milton; and it is assumed that, by the time he has rude things to say, in 1637–8, about 'our corrupted clergy then in their height', he was probably in league with what has been called 'the radical underground'.[9] Because Milton was to become, by turns, an anti-episcopal pamphleteer, a short-lived enthusiast for Presbyterianism, a sympathizer with the Independents, a defender of regicide, the Latin Secretary to Cromwell and a Wanted Man at the time of the Restoration, it has been assumed that all these manifestations were inherent in the pigeon of Paul's and the Lady of Christ's. So, we have a story of the boy Milton imbibing the extreme Calvinism of Richard Stock; it is strange, if he did so, that he never once in any of his writings showed sympathy for the fundamental tenets of Calvinism. We further have a picture of Milton, the young radical friend of Thomas Young, following the fortunes of religious exiles in Hamburg; the friend, too, of Alexander Gil the younger, who lost his ears and his liberty for toasting the murderer of Buckingham.

There is nothing specifically wrong in the idea of Milton, in his youth, mixing with people who were later on the side of Parliament when war broke out. But it is a distorted view if it sees nothing in the first thirty years of this life except clues for the later radicalism. Milton was to join forces with the side that killed King Charles I. So, for instance, was Algernon Sidney; so, had he been alive, if such guesses are worth anything, would Sir Philip Sidney. But we do not, for that reason, suppose *Arcadia* to be infiltrated from 'the radical underground'. Until he went to Italy Milton was training himself, in a rather old-fashioned way, to be a great poet, in much the same way that Sidney had done: by a conscious programme of reading, and by a cultivation of learned and aristocratic friends and patrons. His own testimony, in *De Doctrina Christiana*, is that, up to this point, he had not so much as opened pamphlets or books emanating from 'the radical underground'. He had not read them, he informs us, until the 1640s at the earliest.[10]

I am not suggesting, of course, that he had strong royalist sympathies. But his own testimony suggests that, until he went to Italy, his *political* sympathies had not become fully engaged. One sees this happening among dissidents in our own day, from behind the Iron Curtain, or from Africa, whose rebellious sentiments are crystallized by sojourns abroad. It is easy to assume that Milton was burning with indignation against the government of Charles I from the moment, say, that Gil's ears were sliced from his head. It requires greater imagination to see, an imagination so great that we cannot attain to it, that the pillory and the Star Chamber, hated as they might have been, were an accepted fact of existence in seventeenth-century England. Milton would no more have questioned their use than he would have questioned the lawfulness of the death penalty for cattle-thieving. The fact that friends had suffered in this way would not *necessarily* produce the anger and revulsion which it would in us.

Nevertheless, Italy changed Milton's view of his own country. When he first went there he had been intending to go further, and to explore Greece and the rest of the Mediterranean. Yet, as he tells us in the *Defensio Secunda*, 'when I was preparing to pass over into Sicily and Greece, the melancholy intelligence which I had received of the civil commotions in England made me alter my purpose; for I thought it base to be travelling for amusement abroad, while my fellow-citizens were fighting for liberty at home . . .'

Milton's biographers have been unwilling to accept this rather strange testimony at face value. It has been conjectured that he actually heard of Diodati's death while he was in Naples in, perhaps, November 1638, and it was this, rather than the stirrings of a political conscience, which made him feel unequal to a visit to the Areopagus.[11] But, even if there was evidence that Milton lied in the *Defensio Secunda* and his reasons for turning back were ones of dejection over his dead friend, one still has to explain why he did not come straight home. He spent nearly eight months abroad after he heard the news of the Bishops' War. Satirists can delight in this fact. And some of the apologies for Milton's 'delay' seem worse than the accusations. 'It was not as if war had actually broken out or Parliament again been summoned, but only that events were shaping themselves to a point where a man of his convictions might be of use. He might feel that he would rather be journeying toward than away from the scene of duty and yet see no urgent reason for cutting his time short.'[12]

The notion that Milton was at least facing north rather than south after he heard the news of civil broils at home does not excuse him if we understand, as generations of biographers have done since Dr Johnson, the sentences in *Defensio Secunda* to mean that Milton felt he ought to hurry home to advance the war effort. It sounds all too like W. H. Auden's mother assuring friends that 'Wystan is doing wonderful work for the Allies' as he steamed towards New York in 1939, safe from Luftwaffe and call-up papers alike.

But this is to misunderstand what Milton is saying. He does not claim that he hastened home. He claims that the news from England altered his purpose in being abroad. 'I thought it base to be travelling for amusement abroad . . .' He had set out as a budding poet, and such he still was. But his experience of Italy changed the *feel* of his journey. He was no longer purely a Renaissance man in quest of the great paintings, the famous thinkers, the most illustrious works of architecture with which to furnish his future memories. This played its part, still, in his journey, of course; but it was not the object of his journey. In spite of himself, he found that Italy forced political positions on to him. After 1638, he had to take sides.

This was for a variety of reasons. First, he began to see England through Italian eyes. On the one hand, there were those who saw it as the very nurse and seat of liberty. What a contrast with the reality Milton knew at home! And yet, compared with Italy, how abundantly true! His sense that there was a work about to be finished by God in his native country was confirmed by his talks, not with English radicals, but with Italians. Secondly, as well as seeing England through Italian eyes, he met his fellow-countrymen abroad. There is nothing more calculated to quicken one's sense of alienation from some elements in one's own culture than the polarizing effect of meeting fellow-exiles abroad. Am I really like that? Further, meeting these exiles, Milton was able to see the picture of England which some of them passed on to the Italians. He came face to face with the hard-line papist infiltrators, the Jesuit spies, the inquisitorial Gestapo. Some of them were anxious to shut him up, for he was free with his opinions. He was more than once in danger of his life. But finally Italy, and later Geneva, were important because they gave Milton the chance to see societies very different from his own, in which the polarities latent in the English scene were overt and extreme: here were not merely a few archbishop's commissioners sent to the parish to check that the holy table was correctly positioned, but a whole secret police. Where did the distinction lie? Here was the very nest of popery, and yet, at the same time, was it not 'the home of humane studies and of all civilised teachings'? There was matter for reflection there. Here, republicanism flourished without anarchy, an aristocratic republicanism, based at the same time on the wealth of cities. In Pisa, Florence, and Venice, the parallels and contrasts between these autonomous city-states and his own native London must have struck him again and again.

He went on being taken with the ravishing beauty of it all; and he was a great social success. Not until Byron went to Italy was another English poet to be so lionized. But – and this is the point he was making in the *Defensio Secunda* – the nature of his journey was different from what he · had expected. He had thought it was going to be purely, in our terms, cultural. It turned out to be a political education. He went there as a young man who had written some of the finest poetry in our language, but who, having decided not to become a clergyman, had no idea what to do with himself. He discovered, while he was there, a new vocation. That it came to him as a divine revelation is hard for the sceptical modern historian to accept.

> Promise was that I
> Should Israel from Philistian yoke deliver . . .

That promise was vouchsafed to Milton from on high while he was in Italy. It interrupted, delayed, and changed his poetic endeavours for the next quarter of a century, so that, though he went on speaking of himself as a poet, he wrote only a tiny handful of poems. It was Italy which was responsible for this. It was there that Samson, as it were, came to understand who the Philistines were; and what the yoke was which he had the power to unloose from his fellow-countrymen's shoulders. As far as lovers of his poetry are concerned, twenty-three or four years are on the point of being given to the locusts. As far as students of Milton's ideas are concerned, he is just on the point of getting interesting. In the Italian cities Milton began the process of his own re-education, and began to collect his ammunition against the Philistines. The papist bias of the Yale edition of Milton's works seems nowhere more marked than when it quotes, in an amusing but superfluous footnote, the reflections of Father Faber, the Victorian convert to Catholicism: 'I spent a delicious evening at Fiesole yesterday, and not being, as I had feared, tormented by a single thought of that execrable rebel and heretic Milton ... Milton (accursed be his blasphemous memory) spent great part of his life in writing down my Lord's divinity, my sole trust, my sole love; and that thought poisons Comus.'[13]

There is a strange aptness about that soft-hearted and obese versifier's thoughts in Fiesole. For it was in Tuscany that the thoughts which poison *Comus* began to dawn in Milton's mind. All that, however, lay ahead, as he disembarked at Genoa.

Genoa was the first Italian sight to meet his eyes. 'Never was any artificial scene more beautiful to the eye of the beholder', thought John Evelyn six years later.[14] Milton probably paused to explore briefly the palaces and churches over which Evelyn rhapsodized, before going on, as Evelyn did, to Leghorn and to Pisa. Splendid as these cities are, were, and full of varied delights as they must have been to Milton, he remembered them in after-years as little more than stopping-places for the first grand end of his journey: Florence, which, as he wrote later, 'I have always cherished more than others for its elegance of speech and manners'.[15]

It was, of course, historically, the city which had nourished Dante and Petrarch, and from which they were exiled. These forgers of the *dolce stil nuovo* were Milton's great examples. It was in Italy that the concept of great poetry in a vernacular tongue had been born. Ariosto had perpetuated the idea at the end of the fifteenth century, Tasso in the sixteenth, Spenser's great masters. It was in Florence that Milton felt the call most acutely to write his great work in English. 'For which cause, and not only for that I knew it would be hard to arrive at the second rank among the Latins, I applied myself to that resolution which Ariosto followed against the persuasions of Bembo, to fix all the industry and art I could unite to the adorning of my native tongue.'[16]

But, in the course of his discovery of these Italian authors, Milton had been fired with a love of their writing and an intimacy with their manner which were outstanding. Dr Johnson, himself a prodigious linguist, observed that one of the sources of Milton's peculiar diction was 'his familiarity with the Tuscan poets: the disposition of his words is, I think, frequently Italian; perhaps sometimes combined with other tongues'.[17]

Milton, then, was arriving at a city which had formed part of his dreams since boyhood, and whose accents were almost as familiar to him as English. His dearest friend, Charles Diodati, was of Tuscan descent. His people came from Lucca. So, when Milton arrived in Florence, it was almost as if he was coming to a second home.

What did he see, who did he meet as he arrived in the late summer haze of 1638? A city of medieval sturdiness was in the process of being made baroque. The church of Ognissanti, for instance, had a new façade that year. Santa Trinita already had its baroque façade by Buontalenti, which 'presented to the view that half-theatrical, half-pastoral idealisation of holiness that is at the heart of the baroque inspiration'.[18] From earlier manifestations of Renaissance excellence Milton could see Michelangelo's Bibliotheca Laurenziana, and his magnificent brooding statues in the burial-vault of the Medici mausoleum, the Cappella dei Principi; he would have seen the Donatellos at Or San Michele and Ghiberti's bronze doors at the baptistry. Solidly built *palazzi* and cooling squares would have met him at every street corner; compared with London, how spacious, seemly, and grand.

More wonderful than any of these things to Milton was the society which this splendid city provided. Here were groups of young men formed into sessions worthy of the title (worthy in that precise Platonic mind) of *academic*. There had never been anything like this in Cambridge. He was overwhelmed by their intelligence, and by the affection and warmth with which they received him. 'There I quickly contracted intimacy with many truly noble and learned men. I also assiduously attended their private academies *[privatas academias]*, an institution which is most highly to be praised there, not only for preserving the arts but also for cementing friendships. Time shall never efface the memory, forever grateful and pleasing to me, of you, Jacopo Gaddi, Carlo Dati, Frescobaldi, Coltellini, Bonmatthei, Chimentelli, Francini, and numerous others.'[19]

The form these meetings took, of the two Platonic academic societies, the Svogliati and the Apatisti, was that one member would bring along a poem, a dissertation on literature, philosophy, or theology, and the other members would discuss them. Sometimes there would be saints' lives read; sometimes attempts at character-writing on the model of Theophrastus.[20] The young men who took part in these discussions were delighted by Milton. They were flattered by his almost native fluency in their own language, and in his prodigious facility in Greek, Latin, Spanish, and French, as well as Hebrew. They were delighted by him as a man. All his life Milton had the power of attracting strong affection from friends of both sexes. It is a fact which, from time to time, needs to be reiterated. Throughout his middle life the strongest documentary evidence of his opinions and the workings of his mind comes from the pamphlets which he wrote after his return from Italy. They show him as a harsh, combative figure, often grotesquely funny, but at the same time bullying, arrogant, self-centred, and tortuous. Yet a man's public self, the self he reveals to his readers, is very often a distortion of what he is like in private conversation. The testimony of Milton's friends suggests a different man from the author of the more scabrous assaults on his pamphleteering adversaries.

So it was, then, that Milton, who had failed to find much intellectual companionship at Cambridge, and who despised the unboning of Protestant clergy-limbs, found himself happily a member of a Roman Catholic literary set. Dati, Gaddi, and the rest were brilliant polymaths after Milton's own heart, pursuing researches into every branch of learning – from law to Syriac, from medicine to epic poetry, from philosophy to astronomy. 'Whatever anyone desired to know of him, he would teach them',[21] was said of Coltellini, one of this group. He was the official censor at the Uffizi. Two other members of the group, Chimentelli and Bonmatthei whom Milton mentions with especial warmth, were Catholic priests. Milton never wavered in his hatred of popery, and he made no secret of this fact to his Italian friends. They remained his friends. That speaks more eloquently than the venom of his tub-thumping anti-Catholic views in the pamphlets. There was certainly freedom in the company of the Apatisti for Milton to speak his mind, and he was not howled down for doing so. He read them his Latin and Italian work and it went down well:

In the private academies of Italy, whither I was favoured to resort, perceiving that some trifles which I had in memory, composed at under twenty or thereabout (for the manner is that every one must give some proof of his wit and reading) there met with some acceptance above what was looked for, and other things which I had shifted in scarsity of books and conveniences to patch up amongst them were received with written encomiums, which the Italian is not forward to bestow on men of this side of the Alps.[22]

Astonishing as it now seems, Milton's genius went almost entirely unrecognized in his own country until a few years before his death. Lawes had arranged for him to write the masques for the Bridgewater family, but no record survives of their having thought *Comus* remarkable. Nobody singled out 'Lycidas' for special praise when the 1638 volume of tributes to Edward King was published. Apart from Sir Henry Wotton's letter, there is almost no hint that Milton's English contemporaries thought highly of him as a poet.

All artists need praise. That is why they seek patrons; the need for praise equalling the desire for financial reward. The Italians' enthusiasm for Milton was to suggest to him, for the rest of his life, the possibility of a universal audience. Shakespeare, 'not our poet, but the world's', as Landor said, wrote almost entirely for London theatre audiences; Milton wrote decidedly for posterity, and the enthusiasm of the Italians partly suggests why. The minutes of the Accademia degli Svogliati in Florence record that on 16 September 1638 the members gathered in some numbers to hear compositions read. There can be no doubt that there was a specially large turn-out because the Florentines wanted to hear 'e particolarmz il Giovanni Miltone Inglese lesse una poesia Latina di versi esametri molto erudita'.[23]

There is a lot of evidence surviving about Milton's short stay in Florence: glowing letters between himself and Bonmatthei. Another Florentine, Antonio Malatesta, dedicated a volume of poetry to the great English poet, John Milton, 'al grande poeta inghilese Giovanni Milton Londra . . .'[24]

In addition, Milton attended concerts, saw galleries, churches, paintings, sculptures; and went to the theatre. There is no reason to doubt Voltaire's story that while he was in Florence, Milton saw Andreini's *Adamo*:

Milton, as he was travelling through Italy in his youth, saw at Florence a comedy called *Adamo*, writ by one Andreino a player, and dedicated to Mary de Medicis Queen of France. The subject of the play was the Fall of Man; the actors, God, the devils, the angels, Adam, Eve, the Serpent, Death, and the seven mortal Sins. That topic so improper for a drama, but so suitable to the absurd genius of the Italian stage (as it was at that time) was handled in a manner entirely conformable to the extravagance of the design. The scene opens with a chorus of angels, and a cherubim thus speaks for the rest. 'Let the rainbow be the fiddlestick of the fiddle of the heavens, let the planets be the notes of our music,

let time beat carefully the measure, and the wind make the sharps etc.' Thus the
play begins, and every scene rises above the last in profusion of impertinence.

Milton pierced through the absurdity of that performance to the hidden
majesty of the subject, which being altogether unfit for the stage, yet might be
(for the genius of Milton and for his only) the foundation of an epic poem.[25]

So, with the praises of his new-found admirers ringing in his ears and
the sublime absurdities of Andreini's play in his mind, Milton took leave
of his Florentine friends for a while and headed south, via Siena, to
Rome.

'Triumphalist' is something that popes try to avoid being these days.
Not so in 1638. Urban VIII was an unashamedly triumphalist pope, a
distinguished international politician, forever meddling in the Thirty
Years War, a patron of the arts, and above all, like the best popes, fond of
his family. When he was elected, as Cardinal Maffeo Barberini, to the
throne of St Peter in 1623, there were very few cardinals. By the time
Milton reached Rome there were seventy-four of them, and a very high
proportion called Barberini. Urban VIII was the pope who first granted
the title of Eminence to his cardinals; it gives the flavour of his
pontificate. Where brothers, cousins, and nephews could not be advanced to clerical eminence, he handed out jobs of secular importance.
Carlo Barberini, his elder brother, and Don Taddeo, his nephew, held
high secular office in Rome.

What did Milton think of the splendours of the Vatican, its superb
collections of manuscripts, paintings, and sculptures, and in the very
midst of it, the most magnificent temple in the world?

> Built like a temple, where pilasters round
> Were set, and Doric pillars overlaid
> With golden architrave; nor did there want
> Cornice or frieze, with bossy sculptures graven,
> The roof was fretted gold. Not Babilon,
> Nor great Alcairo such magnificence
> Equalled in all their glories, to enshrine
> Belus or Serapis their gods, or seat
> Their kings, when Egypt with Assyria strove
> In wealth and luxury.
>   (PL I. 713–22)

The ambivalence of *Paradise Lost* itself, the fact of Satan's abundant
attractiveness, is surely a general reflection on Milton's attitudes to life.
For, while he is magnificent, he is yet the Devil. Everything about Rome
must have impressed Milton: as great potentates and princes and

scholars, the men he met there charmed and impressed him. But nor was he the first or the last man to wonder what all this magnificence, this sounding brass and clashing of cymbals, had to do with the Christian religion, with self-purification, with the prayer of humility?

Milton evidently made no secret of expressing these thoughts, but, as we have seen, he did so politely, and it did not stop him receiving invitations. On 30 October he and his manservant were entertained at the English College, the seminary for exiled papist priests. His fellow guests were the brother of Lord Falkland, a Lancashireman called Dr Holding, and Sir Nicholas Fortescue. The traveller's book at the English College implies that the dinner was a success.

Not all the people he met in Rome were to Milton's taste. The Italians charmed him. His fellow-countrymen much less so. One of the young men he bumped into that October was called Thomas Gawen, a Fellow of New College, Oxford. It seems that Milton and he spent some time together, but Gawen was a bad lot. Perhaps it was meeting him that began to throw the political crises at home into a lurid light for Milton. Here was one of those sinister figures he had written about in Lycidas when he described what

> the grim wolf with privy paw
> Daily devours apace and nothing said.

When he went back to England Gawen became a chaplain to the Bishop of Winchester, but in 1641 he was abroad again. In Paris he was met by an old Oxford friend who found 'His discourse changed and some tincture therein of the Romish dye'. Gawen was indeed a papist, but not one with the courage of his convictions. He would not go near the court of Henrietta Maria in Paris for fear that he would be thought of as a fellow-traveller by English papists and thus damage his chances of preferment in the Church of England, should things eventually go the Laudian way. So he bided his time, chopping and changing. He did eventually get small preferment in the Church of England, he was Rector of Bishopstoke in Hampshire, but when it was discovered that he was a Catholic he fled the country and ended his days in a rather sordid way with an Italian mistress and a number of illegitimate children in Rome.[26]

All this, of course, lay ahead when Milton knew Gawen in his twenties. But it must have given Milton pause. Here was a time-serving, cynical man, who honestly thought that it was in his interests to be a papist in England. For Milton, this must have confirmed his uneasy sense that whatever the protestations of the King, he was leading England, with the help of his French papist consort and his quasi-inquisitorial Archbishop of Canterbury, in the direction of Catholic absolutism. Meeting Gawen must have been not unlike meeting crypto-Communists in the 1930s, and having a chilling sense that it might not take much for Stalinism to take root in England.

As December advanced and Rome became wintry, Milton went down to Naples, accompanied still by his manservant, and with some eremite friar as their guide – 'per Eremitam quendam'. The unnamed hermit did not live so detached from the world that he was unable to introduce Milton to a figure of extraordinary literary eminence. This was a man who had been the friend of two of Italy's greatest poets, Tasso and Marini. Tasso had dedicated to him his treatise on friendship: he was Giovanni Battista Manso, Marquis of Villa and Lord of Bisaccio and Panca. What would Spenser have given to have met this man!

Manso was not merely Tasso's friend, he was his protector, from persecutions real and imagined. Milton's reputation had evidently travelled ahead of him. He had been fêted and lionized in Florence and Rome. Now, Manso, the grand old patron of great poets, took an interest in 'il grande poeta', Giovanni Miltone the *erudito*.

By him I was treated in the most friendly fashion as long as I stayed there. Indeed he took me himself through the whole city and the court of the Viceroy, and more than once he came to my hotel to see me. When I left, he seriously excused himself, because, though he had been most desirous of showing me much greater attention, he had not been able to do so in that city, because I had not been willing to be more guarded in religion . . .[27]

Milton was no time-server, no Gawen of New College. He was perfectly polite to the Italians about their religion, not mentioning it unless they were first to raise the subject. But, if they asked, he gave his opinion, as he doubtless gave it to his papist brother at home; and as he would probably have given it had he met his papist grandfather in Stanton St John. It is revealing that he did not waive the point, even when in the company of such an illustrious and powerful man as Manso. Had he been less stubborn, Milton would have probably been showered with material rewards and been received by the King of Naples himself. But he would not tell a lie.

Shortly after he left the old man Milton penned him a fulsome Latin tribute in verse. He pays tribute to Manso for his friendship to great poets in the past, to Tasso and to Marini. He thanks him for his care and attention. And he makes it clear what the subjects of their conversations had been: Manso would not scorn the idea of the Muses visiting the frozen north where Milton comes from.

> O mihi si mea sors talem concedat amicum . . .

'O may my fate send me such a friend . . . who knows so well how to honour Phoebus's followers, if ever I bring back to life in my songs the kings of my native land, and Arthur, who set wars raging even under the earth, or tell of the great-hearted heroes of the round table, which their fellowship made invincible, and – if only inspiration would come – smash the Saxon phalanxes beneath the impact of the British charge.'

Manso had evidently urged the young genius to write a great epic, a national epic

> and what resounds
> In fable or romance of Uther's son
> Begirt with British and Armoric knights;
> (*PL* I. 579–81)

and it remained for a long time Milton's ambition to dissect

> With long and tedious havoc fabled knights
> In battles feigned . . .
> or to describe races and games,
> Or tilting furniture, emblazoned shields,
> Impreses quaint, caparisons and steeds,
> Bases and tinsel trappings, gorgeous knights
> At joust and tournament;
> (*PL* IX. 30–1; 33–8)

In *Paradise Lost* he dismisses such subject matter, but as a young man, talking to the friend of Tasso, that surely seemed the very stuff of which great poetry was made. He had not yet undergone the full and (to many readers) equally tedious dissection of his own religious opinions which was to leave him so detached from the Christian religion as it was practised or believed in by the generality of the human race, that he could use its central stories as mythologies, just as he had once considered using the story of King Arthur.

He concludes his poem to Manso by looking forward to his own fame. If one can be sure of anything, he writes, 'and if rewards really do lie in store for the righteous, I myself, far away in the ethereal home of the heavenly gods, the region to which perseverance and a pure mind and ardent virtue carry a man, shall watch this earth and its affairs . . . and, with all my soul calmly smiling, a bright red blush will spread over my face, and I shall joyfully applaud myself on ethereal Olympus'.

On this characteristic note he bids farewell to the grand old man of the Italian Renaissance. In poems to Lawes, to Edward King, even to the imagined royalist invading his garden during the early years of war – 'Captain or colonel, or knight in arms' – Milton flatters his subject by saying that their claim to fame will turn out to have been their association with him. In all cases, of course, his presumptuous prophecy has turned out to be true.

In Naples Milton would have found post waiting for him from England. It was here that he heard progress of political events at home, and in particular of Charles I's ill-starred attempt to persuade the Scots to accept episcopal liturgy and order by force of arms – the so-called Bishops' War.

It seems grotesque now, when all the episcopalian churches have abolished their ancient liturgies, and when the Presbyterian Church of Scotland has done its best to conform to episcopalian practices such as the observance of a liturgical year, that there should have been a war over the Solemn League and Covenant. For men like Lovelace, or Sir Jacob Astley, it was an opportunity to rally behind their unfortunate monarch. For men of Milton's persuasion it was a sign of yet more arbitrary, Medici-style imposition of royal authority in matters of conscience.

Milton evidently saw things at this juncture from an Italian perspective. He could see that in all the Italian states there was a high standard of debate, learning, poetry, and art. But politically, Italy was much more repressive than England. Enlightened Italians praised what they took to be English liberty. It was shaming to hear them speak thus while he thought of his King imposing a liturgy by force. 'And though I knew that England was then groaning loudest under the prelatical yoke, nevertheless I took it as a pledge of future happiness, that other nations were so persuaded of her liberty.'[28]

This pledge of future happiness was to prove entirely illusory. But at the time the equation seemed easy enough to make. The Italians did not enjoy liberty; theirs was the most prelatical of European states; *ergo* if one abolished the bishops in England, liberty would be set up, or restored . . . So he reasoned. He did not rush home, for the reasons we have stated. But for the next eight months he was preparing himself as a prophet, the man who would save his nation by providing it with the Perfect Idea to get it out of difficulties.

Leaving Manso, he returned to Rome, where he heard rumours that English spies had been listening to his conversation and that his life was in danger from the papists. Probably there was something in all this cloak-and-dagger stuff. Milton quite plainly was not a papist. And the papist cause in Italy depended on persuading the Italian authorities that English Protestants needed to be converted. Here was an English Protestant who was a great poet, a cultivated talker, an accomplished musician, a brilliant linguist. His Protestant views were firm and clearly argued. But he was an inoffensive, charming, handsome man; a very bad thing from the point of view of English Jesuits who would have liked Italians to think that all but papists had more or less abandoned the Christian religion in England. Perhaps the Fellow of New College, Gawen, was behind these underhand threats to Milton's life. They did not stop him going out and mixing with new friends, such as Cardinal Francesco Barberini, the Pope's nephew. If not at the Cardinal's palace then elsewhere,[29] he heard the immortal Leonora Baroni sing, and he wrote a Latin ode on the diva.

In October, probably, he attended a splendid concert at the Cardinal's residence. Milton described it, in a letter to Lucas Holstenius, as a concert of truly Roman significance, 'magnificentia vere Romana', and he was flattered when the Cardinal made his way through the crowds and saluted his handsome young English guest; he asked Milton to call on him privately the next day, and this was clearly a success. The Cardinal seemed to have all the time in the world for him, and he was surprised to find the interview lasted much longer than he had expected.

This Lucas Holstenius was Cardinal Francesco Barberini's secretary and librarian. Milton had met him in the Vatican library. He was a German from Hamburg, where Thomas Young had lived for a time; but, unlike Young, a convert to Catholicism.

But – gradually – he was on his way home. It was impossible to imagine going back to London without further sojourn in his beloved Tuscany, and thither, sometime in the spring, he went. We know that he was in Florence in March 1639 because on the 17th of that month there is record that he read a Latin poem in the Svogliati Academy. He did so again the next week on the 24th, his friends Bonmatthei, Gaddi, and others in attendance. There followed a discussion of Aristotle's *Ethics* and the reading of some Italian poetry.

He revelled in his Tuscan friendships, and yet he still found time to write a long letter to Lucas Holstenius at the Vatican, thanking him for all his hospitality. Quietly, at the back of his mind, he was taking leave of the Italians. But before he left Florence there was to be one more momentous encounter. Italy was the 'home of humane studies and of all civilised teaching' in Milton's view. He had met and befriended these wits and seen abundant evidence of their civilization. He had turned over old manuscripts, gasped at the architecture and paintings, luxuriated in their musical concerts, and met some of the great men of the age, Cardinal Franceso Barberini and Manso. But, as he always knew, there was another side to it all; a side represented by the threats to his life and safety in Rome, a side represented by the old man out at Fiesole whom Milton was taken to visit on his second stay in Florence: Galileo. He was deeply revered by Milton's friends in the Svogliati and the Apatisti; Coltellini had written a poem in praise of the astronomer which, years later, he published. He praised the way, after Galileo's imprisonment and torture, he turned to spiritual studies:

The great Tuscan Lincean no longer surveyed the spots upon the sun, nor cared any more to study Jove and Saturn and the Bear. He put down his crystal lens and closed his eyes, and from the lowly earth, filled with the desire to behold lovelier things than these, with the wings of love he raised himself above the stars, the eyes of his mind fixed upon God.

Thus Coltellini, in a mannered conceit, finds virtue in Galileo's very blindness.[30] For Milton, there was doubtless much delight in meeting Galileo, but the grotesqueness of his position must have horrified him. Here was a man who had been imprisoned simply for pursuing an academic truth. The astronomer's old friend Maffeo Barberini, now Pope Urban VIII, pursued him with the vigilance and cruelty that might have suited the persecution of a traitor. And Galileo had been forced to recant his belief in the Copernican theory of the universe.

This crazy state of things, Milton must have been only too conscious, was only a step away from the view of theology and statecraft promulgated by William Laud. If your ears could be sliced off for not wearing a surplice, and a neighbouring kingdom could be invaded because it did not wish to use the communion service written by Laud, where would it end? All the prizes of the Renaissance, the achievements of the humanists, Catholic and Protestant, heretic and orthodox, were in danger of being destroyed if this attitude could silence the pursuit of the truth. So it is later, six years later, that he is to declare publicly his passionate belief in liberty of speech.

I could recount what I have seen and heard in other countries, where this kind of inquisition tyrannizes; when I have sat among their learned men, for that honour I had, and been counted happy to be born in such a place of philosophic freedom, as they supposed England was, while themselves did nothing but bemoan the servile condition into which learning amongst them was brought; that this was it which had damped the glory of the Italian wits; that nothing had been there written now these many years but flattery and fustian. There it was that I found and visited the famous Galileo, grown old a prisoner to the Inquisition, for thinking in astronomy otherwise than the Franciscan and Dominican licensers thought.[31]

The meeting with Galileo, then, brought into sharp focus what Milton felt called to do when he returned home: to summon with every fibre of being, and all the eloquence at his disposal, the means to save and defend the ancient liberty.

Strikingly, when Milton remembered Galileo in verse it was as an astronomer, not as a figure persecuted. Even though Galileo was almost certainly blind when Milton met him, Milton, for poetic purposes, forgets that. His tribute, so unlike Coltellini's, conveys the excitement of science itself when, in Book I of *Paradise Lost*, he speaks of the moon

> whose orb
> Through optic glass the Tuscan artist views
> At evening from the top of Fesole,
> Or in Valdarno, to descry new lands,
> Rivers or mountains in her spotty globe.
>
> (287–91)

With mixed feelings, then, he left his Florentine friends. For their wit, learning, and hospitality, he was very grateful. But he did not envy them their prelatical overlords. To Dati he wrote, years later,

Very sad to me also, I will not conceal from you, was that departure, and it planted stings in my heart which now rankle there deeper, as often as I think with myself of my reluctant parting, my separation as by a wrench, from so many companions at once, such good friends as they were, and living so pleasantly with each other in one city, far off indeed, but to me most dear.[32]

Leaving the Florentines he went for a few days to Lucca: 'ad paucos dies'.[33] It was from this city that the Diodati family sprang. Pacing its broad walls and enjoying the splendid view of the Apulian alps, Milton could comfort himself with the thought (sadly untrue as it turned out) that, even though he wept to be parted from a group of clever Italians, there was one clever Italian eagerly awaiting his return to London: Charles Diodati.

With such thoughts in mind, he sped on northwards during the lovely

Italian April, through Bologna, through Ferrara, until he came to Venice. Even his eagerness to be home could not prevent him from spending a month there. All time spent in Venice is too short.

It was here that he shipped home the precious collection of books which he had put together during his previous year in Italy.[34] They were not all works of theology, history, or philosophy. His nephew tells us that they contained, 'a chest or two of choice music books of the best Masters flourishing about that time in Italy, namely, Luca Marenzo, Monte Verde, Horatio Vecchi, Cifa the Prince of Venosa and several others . . .'[35]

One of the delightful things about being alive at this juncture in the twentieth century is that it is only lately that the full glories of Venetian music as performed in the seventeenth century have been revealed to us. Thanks to the ardours of musicologists and the skill of performers, we can now hear the music of Monteverdi performed authentically; sounds which have been closed up for centuries are now heard once more; and we can listen to the exact tones which would have delighted the ears of Milton. A convincing case has even been made to suggest that, when he came to write *Samson Agonistes*, Milton was strongly influenced by the musical dramas of Monteverdi such as *The Coronation of Poppaea*.[36] He almost certainly met Monteverdi, the aged choirmaster and organist at St Mark's, and heard operas at San Cassiano. But the fact that he packed music in trunks and sent it on to England shows that he was by now firmly on the move.

It was inevitable, given his friendship with the Diodatis, that he should want to pass home through Geneva, where Giovanni Diodati, Charles's uncle, was a professor of theology. Dr Johnson says that when he went to Geneva, 'he probably considered [it] as the metropolis of orthodoxy', and this satire has been accepted unquestioningly by later commentators. It is true that Milton briefly flirted with Presbyterian notions of church government, but since he never accepted the Calvinistic doctrines concerning election and grace, and since he had a horror of political tyrannies of all colours, there is no reason to suppose that he saw in the Genevan system anything like a heaven on earth. Doubtless the Calvinists were cleaner and more respectable than the Italians, but there is no evidence that Milton formed any attachments to the Swiss as strong as he had made with a Neopolitan marquis, a Cardinal's secretary in Rome, or the cultivated young priests in Florence.

What, then, did he talk about with Giovanni Diodati? We do not know the exact date when Milton learned of his friend's death, the previous

August. Some say the news must have reached him in November in Naples; others think it was during his second visit to Florence that he heard the news. My own suspicion is that he did not learn of Diodati's death until he met his uncle in Geneva. It must have been a shattering blow, and the pain of being absent from London gnaws at him as he pours out, in his most passionate poem, regret for his lost friend. Was his Italian journey so necessary, he asks himself in 'Epitaphium Damonis', that he had to be absent from his friend's side? How much rather he would have preferred to be at home, and held Diodati's hand and closed his dying eyes! 'Epitaphium Damonis' brings with it the sense, more powerful even than in 'Lycidas', that Milton's youth is finally over. King's death had merely made Milton think of his own. Diodati's passing brings a sense of profound personal loss. There were many friendships and intimacies in Milton's life, but none quite like this. It is analagous to the feeling Tennyson had for Arthur Hallam:

> My Arthur whom I shall not see
> Till all my widowed race be run.

Milton's life, from now on, has some of this quality of widowhood. From the learned old Dr Diodati he took his leave, and passed home along the same route through France that he had taken fifteen months before. The door of Paradise was shut. It was a bleaker, more turbulent England to which he returned; nor, as he had hoped, did he have the laughter of friends to help him face the impending crisis.

CHAPTER 6

ANTI-EPISCOPAL

He never came up in the rear, when the outworks had been carried
and the breach entered. He pressed into the forlorn hope. At the
beginning of the changes, he wrote with incomparable energy and
eloquence against the bishops. But, when his opinion seemed likely
to prevail, he passed on to other subjects, and abandoned prelacy to
the crowd of writers who now hastened to insult a falling party.
There is no more hazardous enterprise than that of bearing the
torch of truth into those dark and infected recesses in which no light
has ever shone. But it was the choice and pleasure of Milton to
penetrate the noisome vapours and to brave the terrible explosion.
Those who must disapprove of his opinions must respect the
hardihood with which he maintained them.

Lord Macaulay, *Edinburgh Review*, August 1825

MILTON returned to London in the high summer of 1639 to find his
country in a state of uneasy expectation. The King had been made to
look a fool by the Presbyterian Scots. The Pacification of Berwick in
June had been, in effect, a triumph for the Covenant, a fact which must
have given bright hope to those of a Presbyterian turn of mind south of
the border. The detested Lord Strafford was away with the army in
Ireland. London must have been full of talk, charged with the atmosphere of conflict.

Milton, however, who had not seen his family for fifteen months, was
bound to be absorbed initially in their doings and needs. It seems that he
took lodgings just off Fleet Street in St Bride's churchyard, 'at the house
of one Russel, a tailor'.[1] Here, doubtless, he sorted through his books,
while making occasional journeys out to Horton to see his father,
brother, and sister-in-law. With what joy old John Milton must have
opened that trunkful of music by Monteverdi and the Venetian compos-
ers! What traveller's tales there were to tell. Milton's family, from their
side, had sad stories to relate. Doubtless they were able to tell him in
greater detail the end of Charles Diodati's life. Christopher and

Thomasine Milton, for their part, had lost an infant son, buried the previous March. And it seems more than likely that Milton's sister Anne, Mrs Thomas Agar, had died in the poet's absence.

At any rate, it seems to have been concern for her children that took Milton to London, rather than share the comfortable Buckinghamshire retreat of his father. Perhaps, too, after so long away, he could not countenance the idea of being anywhere but London. Whatever the reason, Thomas Agar proposed that Milton should take charge of his two young nephews, Agar's stepsons, John and Edward Phillips, aged eight and nine years old. Johnson mocks famously at the man 'who hastens home because his countrymen are contending for their liberty, and when he reaches the scene of action, vapours away his patriotism in a private boarding-school'.[2] The facts of the case are less absurd. Milton, it is true, was to take in other pupils, mainly the children of friends, mostly gentry or aristocracy. The initial impulse was one of simple devotion to his family. The little boys needed someone to look after them; their uncle John came to the rescue. There is no evidence, of course, that this piece of kindness deflected him from his purpose, which was nothing less than to wage war on the bench of bishops and the whole idea of episcopacy. The elder boy, Edward Phillips, continued to live for a while with his father Thomas Agar. John Phillips, for what reason we are not told, moved in with his uncle almost at once. The lodgings were quite quickly abandoned for a nice little house, but it was there that he first started on the programme of his nephews' education.

Milton never again lived anywhere that could be called spacious. His houses were usually poky, people were always on top of him, and he appears to have been generous about filling every nook for which he was responsible with dependants. It was a generosity akin to Johnson's own. Milton was probably only too anxious to be doing the necessary reading for his anti-episcopal pamphlets. He was also, as we know, thinking continually of his conversations with Manso, and the vision imparted to him by the aged Neapolitan marquis, that he could write a great national epic. It is not every man in this position who would be prepared to devote a lot of energy and time to two little boys. But we can be grateful for his fondness for his nephews. Edward Phillips became his most vivid biographer. He lacks, of course, Aubrey's gossipy touch, Johnson's bombast or Masson's learning, but it is to him that we owe the glimpses of Milton's domestic privateness; the mysterious first marriage; the atmosphere of the little academy; his business and absorption in books; the genesis of *Paradise Lost*; the daughters and their sufferings. Both

Phillips brothers left accounts; both are maddeningly uninformative. We long for more. But at the same time, no biography of Milton gives off a more powerful feeling of authenticity.

Soon enough, uncle and nephews had moved into the little house off Aldersgate Street, and there the programme of education began.

And here by the way, I judge it not impertinent to mention the many authors both of the Latin and the Greek, which through his excellent judgment and way of teaching, far above the pedantry of common public schools (where such authors are scarce ever heard of) were run over within no greater compass of time, than from ten to fifteen or sixteen years of age. Of the Latin, the four grand authors, *De Re Rustica*, Cato, Varro, Columella and Palladius; Cornelius Celsus, an ancient physician of the Romans; a great part of Pliny's Natural History; Vitruvius his Architecture; Frontinus his Strategems; with the two egregious poets, Lucretius and Manilius. Of the Greek: Hesiod, a poet equal with Homer; Aratus his *Phaenomena* and *Diosemeia*; Dionysius Afer *de situ Orbis*; Oppian's *Cynegeticks & Halieuticks*; Quintus Calaber his poem of the Trojan War continued from Homer; Apollonius Rhodius his *Argonauticks*: and, in prose, Plutarch's *Placita Philosophorum*, and Περι Παιδων ᾿Αγογιας; Geminus's Astronomy; Xenophon's *Cyri Institutio* and *Anabasis*; Aelian's *Tactics*; and Polyaenus his Warlike Stratagems. Thus by teaching he in some measure increased his own knowledge, having the reading of all these authors as it were by proxy; and all this might possibly have conduced to the preserving of his eyesight, had he not, moreover, been perpetually busied in his own laborious undertakings of the book or pen.[3]

These undertakings were remarkably varied, as we know from the jottings in the Trinity Manuscript which contains 'Lycidas'. We know that, in addition to the *Arthuriad*, Milton was doodling with the idea of an epic about King Alfred. He was also thinking of a scriptural drama, possibly on the model of Grotius's early works, perhaps inspired by the more recent experience of seeing the 'melodrammas' of Monteverdi in Venice. *Adam in Banishment* is one idea, and there are two pages of notes for a drama called *Adam Unparadised*. *The Flood* and *Abram in Egypt* were other possibilities, the latter an interesting one, since it suggests that Milton's mind was turning towards marriage. Here he was, an Abraham with two little Isaacs in his charge, but no Sarah to comfort him. Abram in Egypt, as readers of the Book of Genesis will recall, outwits Pharaoh by trying to pass off his wife Sarai as his sister:

> . . . I know that thou art a fair woman to look upon:
> Therefore it shall come to pass, when the Egyptians shall see thee, that they shall say, This is his wife; and they will kill me, but they will save thee alive.

Say, I pray thee, thou art my sister: that it may be well with me for thy sake; and my soul shall live because of thee.[4]

This primitive story clearly found some sort of echo in Milton's bosom, perhaps not unconnected with the fact that he was more or less the adopted father of his sister's children. Perhaps he felt a longing for progeny. Perhaps, on the other hand, he was struck by the abiding image of Abram bravely leaving his father's house to become the father of a great nation, an exile from the security of Ur of the Chaldees.

Whatever the truth of the case, Milton was entering a new phase of life. People speak of Milton at this period of his life as a 'pamphleteer' and his anti-episcopal writings as 'pamphlets'. But this, of course, gives an entirely false impression, implying the flimsiness of occasional literature. The five ecclesiastical tracts published in the single year 1641–2 take up some 400 large (and admittedly over-annotated) pages of the Yale edition of his works, and the first of them, *Of Reformation touching Church Discipline in England and the Causes that hitherto have hindered it* is less a pamphlet than a substantial piece of historical argument.

It needs an act of supreme historical imagination to be able to recapture an atmosphere in which Anglican bishops might be taken seriously; still more, one in which they might be thought threatening. But the imaginative leap so required is greatly helped by reading *Of Reformation*. Some critics have a distaste for Milton's prose. 'He plays with it awkwardly, flinging up huge sentences, like baroque palaces, to the sky, abandoning them unfinished, starting another, adorning them with gallant jewelled phrases', as Rose Macaulay put it, going on to regret 'the coarse brutality which all too easily beset' Milton the prose-writer.[5] Her distinguished great-uncle, Lord Macaulay, perhaps was closer to the truth when he wrote:

It is to be regretted that the prose writings of Milton should, in our time, be so little read. As compositions, they deserve the attention of every man who wishes to become acquainted with the full power of the English language. They abound with passages compared with which the finest declamations of Burke sink into insignificance. They are a perfect field of cloth of gold. The style is stiff with gorgeous embroidery. Not even in the earlier books of *Paradise Lost* has the great poet ever risen higher than in those parts of his controversial works in which his feelings, excited by conflict, find a vent in bursts of devotional and lyric rapture. It is, to borrow his own majestic language, 'a sevenfold chorus of hallelujahs and harping symphonies'.[6]

He could have added that Milton the prose-writer has all the contemptuous humour of Swift. If this were a work of criticism, many pages would have to be devoted to expounding the truth of Lord Macaulay's observation. In our generation enormous interest has concentrated on the views Milton entertained, and the identification which can be made between certain thoughts and expressions in his controversial writings and those of fellow-travellers or crypto-revolutionaries. In a passage already quoted from *De Doctrina Christiana*, Milton insisted that he did not belong to the 'radical underground'. 'I had not even read any of the works of the heretics, so called, when the mistakes of those who are reckoned for orthodox, and their incautious handling of Scripture, first taught me to agree with their opponents whenever those opponents agreed with Scripture.'[7]

But that, in a way, is only part of the point. The really important thing about the issue of the bishops, for the purposes of a biography of Milton, is that they inspired some of the best writing Milton ever produced. The occasion was less than the result. He wrote *Of Reformation* for the most urgent and serious of reasons: having searched the Bible and the old writers for years he has reached a crisis in his own person:

The pleasing pursuit of these thoughts hath oft-times led me into debatement with myself how it should come to pass that England (having had this grace and honour from God to be the first that should set up a standard for the recovery of lost truth and blow the first evangelic trumpet to the nations, holding up, as from a hill, the new lamp of saving light to all Christendom) should now be last, and most unsettled in the enjoyment of that peace whereof she taught the way to others . . .[8]

He was never to waver in his loyalty to the principles which gave rise to this 'serious question'. Pathetically, like all political issues, and even more those of ecclesiastical politics, the causes about which he minded so passionately are dead. Almost all the Churches of the Reformation have fizzled out, and are ignominiously clustering together for shelter before their final eclipse. The Church of Rome which they were founded to undo, has, meanwhile, eagerly embraced all their austere iconoclasm and evangelical zeal, proclaiming as if discovered yesterday, things for which Ridley would have been burnt or for which Prynne would have lost more than his ears. No one, it seems, more than the present Congregation of Rites in Rome could have more distaste for 'deformed and fantastic dresses in palls, and mitres, gold and gewgaws fetched from Aaron's old wardrobe, or the flamen's vestry'.[9] The unthinkable has happened. Institutional Christianity, which in the seventeenth century was the very fabric on which society reposed, has crumbled to bits in our day, no one more eager to discard its doctrines than its own theologians, no one more venomously opposed to its old liturgies than the compilers of its own missals and prayer-books.

Milton's prose, unlike almost all the other prose of these episcopal conflicts, pro or anti, survives on its own merits. But it represents more than the 'huge sentences like baroque palaces' of Rose Macaulay's description. The style is only part of what makes his prose deserving of 'the attention of every man who wishes to become acquainted with the full power of the English language'. For, if we read the whole of his prose, from *Of Reformation* to *De Doctrina*, the Latin and the English, the public and the private, we are struck again and again by the extraordinarily personal quality of the arguments and revelations. Unless we are historians, we do not peruse for pleasure the works of many ecclesiastical controversialists in the seventeenth century. And if we did, we would not find many passages as good as Milton. The positioning of the communion table is a dull enough subject in itself, unless one can read of 'the table of communion now become a table of separation' which 'stands like an exalted platform upon the brow of the choir, fortified with bulwark and barricado, to keep off the profane touch of the laics, whilst the obscene, and surfeited priest scruples not to paw, and mammock the sacramental bread, as familiarly as his tavern biscuit'. Once again, sentiments which express in the most moderate terms the views of modern Roman Catholic liturgists. Much more striking than the quality of the writing itself is the fact that Milton uses the controversial writing as a vehicle for self-revelation, self-exploration. His Satan is the great archetype for the hero of all Romantic poems, from the time of Blake onwards. But it is his unwavering interest in himself, as a pamphleteer as much as a poet, which makes Milton the great archetype of all Romantic poets, the ego which Wordsworth and Shelley are never wholly able to escape.

'The pleasing pursuit of these thoughts hath oft-times led me into a serious question and debatement with myself', confesses the unidentified author of *Of Reformation*, subtitled, 'two books written to a friend'. He never pretended to a dispassionate view. Even in his most public utterances, he is having debatement with himself.

Almost certainly the 'friend' to whom *Of Reformation* is addressed was his old childhood tutor Thomas Young, a Scot to whom recent developments in the so-called first Bishops' War can have done little to endear him to Episcopalianism. Although accepting preferment in the

Established Church, Young was a convinced Presbyterian. Nothing he told Milton about Presbyterianism could make it sound worse than prelacy under Laud. Young would have appreciated Milton's comments of the late troubles, 'that laughed such weak enginery to scorn, such poor drifts to make a national war of a surplice-brabble, a tippet-scuffle, and engage the untainted honour of English knighthood, to unfurl the streaming red cross or to rear the horrid standard of those fatal guly dragons for so unworthy a purpose, as to force upon their fellow-subjects that which themselves are weary of, the skeleton of a mass-book'.[10] And he would have been pleased by the second tract, *Of Prelatical Episcopacy*, which asserts that 'through all [the Scriptures] can be nowhere, either by plain text, or solid reasoning found any difference between a Bishop, and a Presbyter, save that they be two names to signify the same order',[11] an opinion happily endorsed nowadays by almost all Anglican theologians.

But Young was most specifically grateful to Milton when he entered the lists, in July 1641, with *Animadversions upon the Remonstrant's Defence against Smectymnuus*.

Smectymnuus, as everyone knew, was the *nom-de-plume* of five Presbyterian divines, one of them Thomas Young. The name Smectymnuus is arrived at by arranging their initials in order: Stephen Marshal, Edward Calamy, Thomas Young, Matthew Newcomen, and William Spurstow. With a mentality like this, in happier periods of history, they would doubtless have been crossword champions. As it was they had the temerity to deliver what they thought was a very well-argued attack on the writings of Bishop Joseph Hall, a Laudian divine who had been having some success in 1640 and 1641 with such titles as *Episcopacy by Divine Right* (based on an idea suggested by Archbishop Laud)[12] and *An Humble Remonstrance*. The Smectymnuans did not like to see Bishop Hall hogging the market in ecclesiastical controversy, and replied with *An Answer to a Book Entitled An Humble Remonstrance*. Not to be outdone, the Smectymnuans wrote a further book called *A Vindication of the Answer to the Humble Remonstrance*, to which, on 28 July, the indomitable prelate wrote *A Short Answer to the Tedious Vindication of Smectymnuus*.

It is striking that Milton thought it was worth keeping this row going, and that he sought to perpetuate it in such a rough and vulgar way. 'Evidence of Milton's good manners in society could be multiplied', wrote Tillyard plaintively, 'But the puzzle is: how can they be squared with his deplorable methods of controversy? . . . Milton is much ruder than custom positively demanded . . .'[13] It is probably pointless to try to

whitewash Milton's evident delight in the rough and tumble of pamphleteering skirmishes. Bishop Hall was an admirable man, a copious
and rewarding author both of poetry and of prose. Yet, his very readable
satire *Virgidemiarum* (1598) can have few admirers today and the cruel
fact is that almost no one would have heard of Hall had he not been
immortalized by Milton's grotesque sense of humour. Hall's *Defence of
the Humble Remonstrance* is reprinted as a sort of catechism, each
question raised by the prelate, answered by Milton. The measured
arguments of his first anti-episcopal writings have been abandoned here
for the delights of mere abuse.

Remonstrant: No one clergy in the whole Christian world yields so many eminent
scholars, learned preachers, grave, holy and accomplished divines as this
Church of England doth at this day.
Answer: Ha, ha, ha.

Milton complains to Hall: 'You would enforce upon us the old riff-raff
of Sarum, and other monastical relics, since you live upon their unjust
purchases, allege their authorities, boast of their succession, walk in
their steps, their pride, their titles . . .'

What? he arranges Hall to say, Would you have no churches re-
edified?

Answer: Yes, more churches than souls . . .
Remon: No seduced persons reclaimed?
Answer: More reclaimed persons seduced.
Remon: No hospitality kept?
Answer: Bacchanalia's good store in every bishop's family, and good gleeking
[trickery].

So it goes on, as he imagines the bishop 'in his new washed Surplice, we
esteem him for sanctity little better than Apollonius Thyanaeus in his
white frock, or the priest of Isis in his lawn sleeves, and they may all for
holiness lie together in the suds'.[14]

Of course, you cannot taste the delights of delivering abuse without
suffering in your own turn. Milton had been deliberately provocative,
and someone would inevitably hit back. But this is why controversialists
take up the pen in the first place: they want to be noticed. Milton, who
had been idolized in Italy, could not tolerate the oblivion of London. He
was quite determined to draw attention to himself, and when he had
done so he was evidently satisfied. The final two anti-episcopal pamphlets are the finest, and they are the most autobiographical of the five.

In the opening section of *The Reason of Church Government Urged against Prelaty* (the first of Milton's pamphlets, incidentally, not to be published anonymously) he applies himself patiently once more to the old arguments about whether the threefold order of bishops, priests, and deacons are of scriptural origin; and he takes issue with Archbishop Ussher of Armagh, and old Bishop Andrewes, whose elegy he had so piously composed as an undergraduate. Some of Andrewes's writings on the subject had recently been published at Oxford, 'said to be out of the rude draughts of Bishop Andrewes. And surely they be rude draughts indeed, in so much that it is marvel to think what his friends meant to let come abroad such shallow reasonings with the name of a man so much bruited for learning'.[15] But, after reiterating the old arguments against the notion of a Christian priesthood (as distinct from the one priesthood of Christ) and asserting that all the bishops of the Primitive Church were *elected* (something he had been reiterating since *Of Reformation*), the pamphlet takes a more personal turn. First, in Chapter VII, he asserts a notion of liberty which is to know its full flowering in the *Areopagitica*. The bishops have claimed that there is a danger of sects and divisions springing up in the Church. Milton shows how extraordinarily remote he is from any such sects by claiming that they are 'partly the mere fictions and false alarms of the prelates, thereby to cast amazements and panic terrors into the hearts of weaker Christians'. But, he continues, 'If God come to try our constancy we ought not to shrink, or stand the less firmly for that, but pass on with more steadfast resolution to establish the truth though it were through a lane of sects and heresies on each side'. He cannot, in other words, praise a fugitive and cloistered virtue in the Church any more than in individuals. The Reformation is incomplete, and it will only come closer to completion if the Church is prepared to pursue the truth, however painful the road.

In the second book of *The Reason of Church Government*, Milton can restrain himself no longer and he turns to passages of pure self-revelation:

I should not choose this manner of writing wherein knowing my self inferior to my self, led by the genial power of nature to another task, I have the use, as I may account it, but of my left hand . . .

One wonders what the pamphlet-reading public made of this. They had rushed to buy the latest onslaught on the bishops. They found a long account, by someone who had never published a line and who must have been largely unheard-of, concerning his life, his upbringing, and his ambitions:

For although a poet soaring in the high region of his fancies with his garland and singing robes about him might without apology speak more of himself then I mean to do, yet for me sitting here below in the cool element of prose, a mortal thing among many readers of no empireal conceit, to venture and divulge unusual things of myself, I shall petition to the gentler sort, it may not be envy to me . . .

How very typical of Milton to think that poetry's chief merit over prose is that it allows the writer to speak more of himself! Undaunted, he continues:

I must say therefore that after I had from my first years by the ceaseless diligence and care of my father, whom God recompense, been exercised to the tongues, and some sciences, as my age would suffer, by sundry masters and teachers, both at home and at the schools, it was found that whether aught was imposed me by them that had the overlooking, or betaken to of mine own choice in English, or other tongue, prosing or versing, but chiefly this latter, the style by certain vital signs it had, was likely to live.

For the time being, the bishops and the whole anti-episcopal argument happily abandoned, Milton settles down to a leisurely contemplation of his own merits. People had thought he was a brilliant poet in England, he has told us, but it was nothing compared to what they thought of him abroad. Endearingly, Milton says that he knew he was brilliant before he went to Italy, but not *how* brilliant. And it was after this encouragement, and the enthusiasm of friends at home, that

I applied myself to that resolution which Ariosto followed against the persuasions of Bembo, to fix all the industry and art I could unite to the adorning of my native tongue . . . That what the greatest and choicest wits of Athens, Rome, or modern Italy and those Hebrews of old did for their country, I in my proportion with this over and above of being a Christian, might do for mine: not caring to be once named abroad, though perhaps I could attain to that, but content with these British Islands as my world . . .[16]

His second book then continues, with arguments about the bishops. But it had been a striking transition, one which readers would be unlikely to forget. Who, some hostile critics would be inclined to ask, does he think he is?

Someone thought to answer this question by replying to his *Animadversions* against Bishop Hall, in a production called *A Modest Confutation of a Slanderous and Scurrilous Libel*. No names were actually exchanged: Milton's *Animadversions* had been anonymous; the reply was anonymous, but there was no doubt that a certain amount of crude research had been done for the purpose of putting Milton in his place. The lounging about the streets and theatres, which in 'Elegia prima' Milton told Diodati formed so happy a part of his adolescence, has here been translated into a youth spent 'loitering, bezelling and harlotting'. And the fracas with Chappell, Milton's first tutor at Christ's, has been got hold of and distorted. 'Thus, being grown impostume in the breast of the University, he was at length vomited out thence into a suburb sink of London . . .'

It was all rather feeble stuff, but it was grist to Milton's mill; at least he had been recognized. In a way, the more scurrilous and inaccurate the attacks made upon him, the better. He could reply to them more eloquently and at greater length. In the final anti-episcopal pamphlet, *An Apology Against a Pamphlet called A Modest Confutation etc.*, he writes initially that he had not intended in any of his arguments to be personal. He was not pamphleteering in his own right but (echoing majestically that liturgy he professed to loathe and abominate), 'I conceived myself to be now not as mine own person, but as a member incorporate into that truth whereof I was persuaded . . .'[17] 'I will not deny but that the best apology against false accusers is silence and suffrance', but he can hardly resist answering this 'babbler'.

Is there not precedent for doing so? 'No worse an author than Gregory Nyssen, who mentioning his sharpness against Eunomius in the defence of his brother Basil, holds himself irreprovable . . .'[18] It seems odd that he should find justification for anything in the works of the Fathers, since he had complained less than a year before about the 'knotty Africanisms, the pampered metaphors; the intricate and in-volved sentences of the Fathers; besides the fantastic, and declamatory flashes; the cross-jingling of periods which cannot but disturb'.[19] But not for nothing had he learnt, in his Cambridge *Prolusions* and debating exercises, to twist and turn arguments for his own purposes with unscrupulous casuistry.

Warming to his theme, which is himself, he answers his detractors in punctilious detail.

I must be thought, if this libeller (for now he shows himself to be so) can find belief, after an inordinate and riotous youth spent at the university, to have been at length vomited out thence. For which commodious lie, that he may be encouraged in the trade another time, I thank him; for it hath given me an apt occasion to acknowledge publicly with all grateful mind, that more then ordinary favour and respect which I found above any of my equals at the hands of those courteous and learned men, the Fellows of that College wherein I spent some years: who at my parting, after I had taken two degrees, as the manner is, signified many ways, how much better it would content them that I would stay.[20]

There is a certain amount of over-egging the pudding here, but it was fundamentally true. Milton had left Cambridge because he wanted to, not because he was sacked. Whether he was treated better than his equals (and therefore, by implication, thought more brilliant) is something we can never know. The 'cursing Shimei, a hurler of stones' has not been fully answered yet, however. He has accused Milton of leading a riotous life. Well, then, Milton will give a clear account of how he spends each day:

. . . up, and stirring, in winter often ere the sound of any bell awake men to labour, or to devotion; in summer, as oft with the bird that first rouses, or not much tardier, to read good authors, or cause them to be read, till the attention be weary, or memory have his full draught. Then with useful and generous labours preserving the body's health, and hardiness; to render lightsome, clear and not lumpish obedience to the mind, to the cause of religion, and our country's liberty, when it shall require firm hearts in sound bodies to stand and cover their stations, rather than to see the ruin of our protestation, and the enforcement of a slavish life. These are the morning practices . . .[21]

We can be grateful indeed to the cursing Shimei for having provoked these revelations. They are fascinating, and beautiful. It sounds like the perfect life, a domestic existence of reading and scholarship, starting early, ending early, and interrupted only by light exercise and visits from friends. If a reader, then or now, saw something incompatible between Milton's cultivation of private virtue and his apparent concern for the liberty of his country, he has failed to understand the entire purpose of the five anti-episcopal pamphlets. Milton was opposed to the bishops and what they were doing because they were attempting to tell other people how to think. Their judgements were not, in his submission, based on the unwavering pursuit of intellectual truth. They were political. And, as soon as you allow bishops to dictate the truth for political reasons, you are only a shade away from making Galileo the prisoner of the Inquisition. The private mind, pursuing virtue and learning on its own, with few companions in domestic quietness, is therefore one of the clearest signs that a nation enjoys liberty. One recognizes how supremely true Milton's insight was when we see that, in modern dictatorships, it is invariably people living the sort of quiet lives he describes who are the first to be labelled as dissidents and whisked off to prison. Free minds are the great fruits of the Renaissance, or, as

Milton would call it, the Reformation. And they are what terrify governments more than weapons or physical force.

So it is, after hilarious reminiscences about the absurd amateur dramatics of the young clergymen in the Cambridge of his day, 'writhing and unboning their clergy limbs to all the antic and dishonest gestures of Trinculos', that he turns to the beautiful notion, Stoic perhaps more than Christian, 'that he who would not be frustrate of his hope to write well hereafter in laudable things, ought himself to be a true poem, that is, a composition, and pattern of the best and honourablest things; not presuming to sing high praises of heroic men, or famous cities, unless he have in himself the experience and practice of all that is praiseworthy.'[22]

Milton was as far as it was possible to be from the Protestant notion of 'Christ my righteousness' or justification by faith only. He believed in self-edification, self-purification, and, in his moral views at least, had no time at all for the Christian doctrine of the redemption.

So it is that he describes, in a famous passage, his painstaking self-preparation for the life of a great poet:

> . . . and the ceaseless round of study and reading led me to the shady spaces of philosophy, but chiefly to the divine volumes of Plato and his equal Xenophon. Where if I should tell ye what I learnt, of chastity and love, I mean that which is truly so, whose charming cup is only virtue which she bears in her hand to those who are worthy.

It was this sublime and very unChristian way of aspiring to virtue which Milton had genuinely come to believe might be achievable on a universal scale if the Church of England would only adopt a Presbyterian system of government. 'Christianity had been but slightly taught me', as he proceeds to admit, but he kept himself chaste from his youth up, hoping to accompany 'the Lamb, with those celestial songs to others inapprehensible, but not to those who were not defiled with women, which doubtless means fornication: for marriage must not be called a defilement'.

What kind of Christ did Milton believe in? The question must have been asked by all his readers. In the course of defending a rather silly joke he had made in an earlier pamphlet, about a bishop having smelly feet, Milton says,

> I beseech ye friends, ere the brick-bats fly, resolve me and yourselves, is it blasphemy, or any whit disagreeing from Christian meekness, when as Christ himself speaking of unsavoury traditions, scruples not to name the dunghill and the jakes, for me to answer a slovenly wincer of a confutation, that it would needs

put his foot to such a sweaty service, the odour of his sock was like to be neither musk, nor benjamin?[23]

The point is well made, but in his own manner one is tempted to answer the rhetorical question. Yes, it *is*, quite manifestly, 'any whit disagreeing from Christian meekness' to write and speak in this way. It is all the more hilarious for being so. Few paragraphs he ever wrote show more clearly his fundamental lack of sympathy with Christianity if he could honestly believe that there was anything Christ-like about mud-slinging pamphlets. The texts, Luke 14: 35, Matthew 15: 17, and so on, are there, of course, to justify the assertion that Christ scrupled 'not to name the dunghill and the jakes'. But it is doubtful whether Christ would have spent his morning perusing Plato and Xenophon, and his afternoons accusing bishops of having sweaty socks.

In this way, in the quietness of Aldersgate Street, while his country cascaded towards the first Civil War, Milton spent his days with his nephews. He was still toying with the preface to his great drama of *Adam Unparadised*. Who should speak the Prologue? Moses? The Angel Gabriel? One day he had a different idea, and decided to open the drama with a speech, not by a virtuous, but by a fallen archangel. Edward Phillips recalls the moment[24] when his uncle read to them 'the beginning of the said tragedy' – a speech which was to be used, years later, in the fourth book of *Paradise Lost*:

> O thou that with surpassing glory crowned,
> Look'st from thy sole dominion like the God
> Of this new world; at whose sight all the stars
> Hide their diminished heads; to thee I call,
> But with no friendly voice, and add thy name,
> O sun, to tell thee how I hate thy beams
> That bring to my remembrance from what state
> I fell, how glorious once above thy sphere;
> Till pride and worse ambition threw me down
> Warring in heaven against heaven's matchless king . . .
>
> (32–41)

There is something, of course, some hidden demon in the pamphleteering Milton which enabled him to invest with supreme sympathy the scornful, carping, and yet majestic voice of the Prince of Darkness. 'Pride and worse ambition' are at war in Milton with the desire to 'be a true poem'. His epic was far off. The drama from which it sprang was to be discarded. Wars, not against 'heaven's matchless king', but against

Charles I, were about to provide distractions which, in various ways, would last twenty years. Among them, mingling with the ambition to sing, at last, songs 'inapprehensible among those not defiled with women', there was a sense that 'marriage must not be called a defilement'.

CHAPTER 7

MARY POWELL

The really delightful marriage must be that where
your husband was a sort of father, and could teach
you even Hebrew, if you wished it.

George Eliot, *Middlemarch*

On 23 February 1642 King Charles I sent his wife and daughter to the
Low Countries for their own safety. Both were in tears, and when the
Lion stood out to sea, the King galloped along the cliffs of Dover to keep
her in sight until the ship vanished. It was one of the earliest marital
separations caused by the Civil War.[1] Milton's royalist brother Christopher was parted from his wife Thomasine for three years after 1643.

After the Queen's departure it was really only a matter of time before
the hostility between the King and Parliament led to war. Throughout
the three kingdoms, there was agitation. The King refused to allow
Parliament to pass a militia ordinance putting the military into their
control. But, in his absence, they defiantly issued it none the less. The
King moved north to rally support, while Parliament prepared themselves by training armed bands in London. The rebellion was still raging
in Ireland, and the Scottish question had still not been settled. But for
Londoners that summer, home affairs must have seemed more important.

London, naturally, was alive with contrasting factions, and all the
agitations of war. The Lord Mayor, for instance, was sympathetic to the
King and refused to rally support for the parliamentary cause – a refusal
for which, in July, he was to be impeached.[2]

Earlier, in May, Edward Hyde, the future Earl of Clarendon, had
slipped out of London carrying the Great Seal, in effect rendering the
deliberations and pronouncements of the Long Parliament henceforth
illegal. Two or three days after 21 May he paused with it at Oxford before
proceeding on his journey to York where he joined the King.

A week or so later, quite by chance, Milton was taking the same road out of London. It is hard to imagine that he was unaffected by the events of the previous few months. A Bill had been passed to exclude bishops from the House of Lords; and this was only one of many indications that Parliament was about to introduce England forcibly to the 'glorious liberty of the sons of God'. It must have been impossible to think that his own pamphlets had not had something to do with the matter. It was worth having returned from Italy after all.

We might have expected Milton, who was an accomplished swords-man and fancied himself with a musket, to have been arming for the approaching struggle. But his justification for not doing so is that he could better serve the cause of his allies in other ways: 'Since from my youth I had been wholly devoted to humane studies and was always stronger in mind than in body, and since I esteemed less highly the work of the camp, in which any ordinary stronger man would easily have excelled me, I betook myself to those pursuits in which I could be more effective.'[3]

It is unimaginable that someone of Milton's lofty and fastidious nature would have settled happily to the rough life of a soldier's camp. It would seem that he went in for a little sword and musket practice with a sort of Home Guard in the City of London, but his assertion that in the summer of 1642 he 'betook himself to pursuits in which he could be more effective' is pure flannel. Perhaps, with hindsight, he believed it to be true. But he could scarcely have described what actually happened between May and the end of September 1642 in *Defensio Secunda* without gross indiscretion.

Nobody has any hard evidence about these months, even though they are among the most crucial of his whole life. We have it on the authority of Edward Phillips, who was living with Milton at the time, that, as Whitsuntide approached, Milton resolved to go 'into the country'.[4]

Probably, for all the political agitation going on in London, the household in Aldersgate Street had pursued its tranquil but vigorous routine. Milton had read, taught the little boys, and seen to the affairs of the household over the previous twelve months as well as seeing five pamphlets through the press. Almost certainly, as the holiday and the fine weather approached, Milton felt in need of a rest from this boarding-school atmosphere which he had imposed upon himself. He decided on a visit to Oxford. The Bodleian Library had been given each of his pamphlets; he would go to make sure that Rouse, the librarian, had got them; he was bad at answering letters.[5] In addition, Milton could look at books and manuscripts unavailable in London. *En route* he could visit his father, who had moved house yet again and was now living with brother Christopher and Thomasine in Reading.

Did the Miltons discuss the state of the nation? It is rather improbable. Christopher, by now a practising barrister and a father of two little girls, Sarah and Anne, had moved to Reading in the previous year with his wife and his father, who was now in his late seventies. As we know from what happened during the previous year, Christopher's sympathies were markedly royalist. As for old Mr Milton, there is no reason to suppose that he was of a political cast of mind. Probably they all regarded the poet's political sympathies with the pained tolerance which families so often afford to their more opinionated or 'intellectual' relations. Their quarrels cannot have been violent because they all kept in such close touch throughout the war.

Almost undoubtedly there would have been some good music. Old Mr Milton probably never tired of hearing about the musical tradition of Umbria. Perhaps, as he played, Milton gazed a little wistfully at Christopher and Thomasine, happy together with their three-year-old Sarah and their baby Anne.

Very probably, too, he discussed money with his father. Milton's income at this date came almost entirely from his father's investments, one of which was a loan of £300, being paid back annually at eight per cent interest – that is £24 per annum – by Mr Richard Powell of Forest Hill, near Oxford. The payments had been regular enough in the previous years; Milton even received them in Italy. But, over the past months, Powell's money affairs had fallen into chaos. Probably Mr Milton knew the family of old. They were more or less neighbours of old Richard Milton, the poet's grandfather, who had lived all his life in Stanton St John, a few miles down the road from Forest Hill. Now, the young squire had evidently written asking if he could extend the loan. What was to be done? Mr Milton suggested, if John was to be in Oxford anyway, that he stroll over to Forest Hill to visit the family and see if the muddle could not be sorted out. Young Powell was obviously a spendthrift; but by all accounts he was a pleasant enough fellow and it was spendthrifts, not wise men, who kept scriveners and their like in business.

Another thing they almost certainly discussed was the future of John and Edward Phillips. It is odd that Phillips tells us he went into the country, 'no body about him certainly knowing the reason'.[6] The likeliest explanation for this is that he did not want to disturb the boys by revealing to them their uncertain position in his household. Perhaps there was pressure from old Mr Milton that the little boys should come to Reading. Christopher and Thomasine, with children of their own, were almost certainly better equipped to bring up poor Anne's boys than their bachelor uncle. If any such suggestion was made, it was obviously highly disagreeable to Milton who had grown fond of the boys and their companionship. And yet, perhaps there was something in the argument. He was fond of them, but did they receive enough female attention and affection? Was he doomed to remain a bachelor uncle for ever? 'Marriage must not be called a defilement.'

Parting from his father with these thoughts in his head, Milton must have taken up lodgings in Oxford soon after Whitsun. There he probably looked up Rouse, Bodley's librarian. Rouse was aged sixty-seven at this date and he was to cause a stir three years later when Charles I, with the signature of Fell, the Vice-Chancellor of the University, asked to borrow the *Histoire Universelle du Sieur d'Aubigne* from the Bodleian. That library has never lent books and Rouse refused to allow his monarch to be an exception to this rule. In the republic of letters, all men are treated with equal contempt by librarians. There is something in that of which Milton would have approved.

Perhaps, then, after a few days in Duke Humphry's Library enjoying the treasures in Rouse's care, he remembered about the Powells of Forest Hill and decided to go and look them up.

The walk from Oxford was a pleasant one in clear June weather. The trees had freshly come into leaf on the shady slopes of Shotover, and, his books momentarily laid aside, he was in holiday mood. 'We cannot', as he himself observes, 'always be contemplative, or pragmatical abroad, but have need of some delightful intermissions, wherein the enlarged soul may leave off awhile her severe schooling; and like a glad youth in wandering vacancy, may keep her holidays to joy and harmless pastime: which as she cannot well do without company, so in no company so well as where the different sex in most resembling unlikeness, and most unlike resemblance cannot but please best and be pleased in the aptitude of that variety'.[7]

The Powells were obviously a large, jolly family, and there is abundant evidence that Milton, like so many men of an inward and studious disposition, had a taste for extrovert and jolly companions. Edward Phillips tells us that 'Once in three weeks or a month he would drop into the society of some young sparks of his acquaintance'.[8] There were plenty of young sparks at Forest Hill; plenty of music, probably; and, in spite of the young squire's financial difficulties, plenty to eat and drink, and plenty of laughter. But none of this can have refreshed Milton's tired spirits more than meeting the eldest daughter of the house. She was called Mary and she was seventeen years old, only a little over half Milton's age.

We know nothing of their courtship, except that it was extremely brief.

Instantly in love, Milton's deeply passionate nature hastened on to marry this pretty young teenager whom he hardly knew. Here indeed was a 'most unlike resemblance'. There was a marriage settlement in which the Powells agreed to pay £1,000 as dowry; money which, as Milton knew very well, they did not really have. There is no reason to suppose that it was in any sense an arranged marriage or that Milton 'bought' Mary Powell. The most likely explanation is the simplest and the most romantic. He was profoundly and physically infatuated with her; perhaps she with him. Perhaps the recent sight of Christopher and Thomasine, happy with their young children, helped to precipitate this famous, sudden, and ill-fadged union.

Whatever the motives were, the little boys in Aldersgate Street must have had the shock of their lives when their uncle returned, scarcely a month after leaving London, with a bride not five years older than young Edward Phillips and a horde of noisy relations in tow. Richard Powell the younger, the bride's brother, was only twenty-one; James, the next boy, eighteen; Anne, her younger sister, just sixteen. Probably the seven younger ones did not come up to London, but there was company enough here, with 'Feasting held for some days',[9] to disturb the quiet routines of the schoolroom. Then they all went away again to Oxford-shire, and the house was quiet.

Mary had grown up surrounded by perpetual rumbustuousness. One imagines it was Milton's wit, his good looks, and his musical ability which attracted her. But perhaps, too, she was beguiled by the idea of a quieter life, more full of repose than the squeals of infants and the barking of dogs and the shouting of servants and her mother's chatter which had echoed in her ears endlessly since she was born. It must have been tempting to take the chance to be, for the first time in life, a unique person, not merely a third in a family of eleven siblings.

Edward Phillips tells us, however, that when the relations went home, she suffered an unpleasant shock and that 'having been used to a great house and much company and joviality', Mary found it hard to settle down to the quiet passages of a 'philosophical life'.[10]

Her husband's idea of pleasure, since infancy, had been to sit silently with a book. She, perhaps, had never sat silent in all her seventeen years, nor been without the companionship of constant chatterers. It is easy to imagine that she felt chilled and frightened; and that Milton was quickly irritated by her.

Yet, although it is so easy to imagine, there is no hard evidence of what actually happened. It is quite clear from Phillips's account that he did not know what went on between his uncle and nymph-aunt during that sad summer. Schoolboy speculations about the love-life of their teachers are not always the most reliable. It would be a foolish biographer of Samuel Johnson who relied solely, for his account of the great lexicographer's married life, on the scurrilous reportage of Garrick.

On the other hand, Phillips's is the earliest and closest evidence which survives of Milton's relationship with Mary Powell in its initial stages, and it is on the foundation of the Edward Phillips account that all the others have been fabricated. So, from Anthony à Wood, we hear that 'she, who was very young, had been bred in a family of plenty and freedom, being not well-pleased with her husband's retired manner of life, did shortly after leave him and went back in the country with her mother'.[11]

But if any evidence is less reliable than that of a twelve-year-old pupil, it would be that of a hostile mother-in-law. That there was little love between Milton and Mrs Powell is readily believable. It is from her, nine years later, that we learn that 'Mr Milton is a harsh and choleric man'. But this we learn only, it must be added, when she was trying to sue him for 'widow's thirds'.

The mother certainly plays a noticeable part in the gossip. Wood tells us that when Mary was reconciled to Milton, she pleaded 'that her mother had been the chief promoter of her frowardness',[12] and this would tally with Aubrey's version.

What is the truth of the matter?

Marriages, and what makes them a success or a failure are impenetrably difficult things to interpret. It requires the imaginative intrusiveness of Henry James to be able to fathom them; a gift singularly lacking in the malicious and crude pen of Robert Graves whose novel *Wife to Mr Milton* presents such a laughably improbable account of the case. He cribbed the idea of writing the book from the much better *Mary Powell* (written by Anne Manning), but it was really George Eliot's *Middlemarch* which provides the clue to Graves's fantasy. Dorothea Brooke, it will be remembered, dreamed of being married to Milton, and ended up with the unspeakable Mr Casaubon.

But there is really no evidence at all that Mary Powell's marriage was
like Dorothea Brooke's. Aubrey, certainly, tells us that 'she found it very
solitary: no company came to her, often-times heard his nephews
beaten, and cry'. But it is easy to make too much of this. It all goes back, if
it has any origin in fact at all, to Phillips's schoolboy speculations. Very
possibly she felt lonely. But it is unthinkable that, coming from a large
family at that date, she would have been unused to boys being thrashed.
Aubrey is running Milton into one with his old headmaster, who was
famed for the severity with which he administered corporal punishment.

It can hardly be doubted that liking the company of young sparks
'once in three weeks or a month' is very different from settling down to
married life with one. Perhaps Milton failed to make a sufficient
adjustment. People talk glibly of the honeymoon period of marriage, but
very often the first few weeks are the most painful for both parties. When
the door finally shuts on the young people and they are alone together for
the first time, fear and disillusionment can quickly set in; and the person
who had been their lover becomes suddenly a stranger. Such feelings,
strong at first, have time to evaporate in most cases; but not in Milton's,
and for peculiar reasons.

It is sometimes assumed that every passage in the divorce pamphlets
is charged with autobiographical significance. But this is surely evidence
which has to be approached with the very greatest circumspection.
When, in *The Doctrine and Discipline of Divorce*, he vividly conjures up a
picture of domestic hell with phrases like 'a drooping and disconsolate
household captivity', it is possible to imagine sharp intakings of breath,
silences at meals, and slamming of doors, in the little house in Aldersgate Street. It is possible, but is it legitimate?

Milton's marriage, very evidently, got off to a poor start. But there is
more to consider than merely the question of how the young people got
on. Very possibly, the schoolboy Phillips was right to sense *froideur*
between his uncle and his bride. But soon, national events of much
greater moment were to play their part in tearing the young Miltons
apart. For the first time, and with the most cruel irony, the great prophet
and poet of the new Reformation was directly affected by the conflict;
and it was to cost him the companionship of his teenage wife.

We are told by Phillips that 'her friends [i.e. her relations] possibly
incited by her own desire, made earnest suit by letter, to have her
company the remaining part of the summer'. Notice that 'possibly'. Even
Phillips does not vouch for the fact that Mary *wanted* to go home so soon
after her wedding and her arrival in London. But it seems likely that the

boy would have been aware of letters coming to the house and the Miltons discussing them. Why did the Powells want her home? Evidently the Civil War was on the point of breaking out and London – or so people went on believing throughout 1642 – was going to be in the thick of it. The Powells were partisans of the King; London, almost in spite of itself, was to be made a parliamentary bastion. Milton's own political and religious views can scarcely have been a secret from the Powells. Is it a wonder that they should have wanted the girl home? Or that she should hesitate about where her loyalties lay?

The Powells probably knew the Milton family of old, as has already been said; they probably thought of the Miltons as a perfectly reliable old Catholic Oxfordshire family. Mary had chosen to become attached to the one member of that family who seemed fond of the new ideas that were floating about at that time. He had apparently written against the bishops. Who knew where *his* allegiance would lie in the coming conflict?

One can see how the family would have built up the pressure in the letters mentioned by Edward Phillips and how, once she had gone home, Mary Milton would have been trapped. If the Civil War had never broken out that summer, history would almost certainly have remained innocent of any knowledge that the opening weeks of Milton's marriage were a bit of a disappointment. The fact that she went home does not necessarily imply that she wanted to be parted from her husband for more than a few weeks. Every speculation about Milton's 'unhappy marriage' springs from a series of historical accidents; and from the curious fact that, until the diligence of the late W. R. Parker established it, no one knew in which year the Miltons were married. It was always assumed that they were married in 1643, which makes the dating of the earliest divorce pamphlet mysterious (Milton would have had to start writing it before he was married) and the reasons for Mary's defection seem purely personal. Obviously, she would not have gone home unless she wanted to do so. But the tradition is all based on hearsay. That 'her mother had been the chief promoter of her frowardness' is just as strong a tradition as the notion that she ran away from her husband because he was ill-tempered, or thrashed the little boys. The strongest likelihood is that she was lured home by possessive relations and, in effect, kidnapped.

All over England that summer, sporadic fighting had broken out. No one was able to predict that 'sporadic fighting' was all that the Civil War would ever amount to. Royalists were leaving London in droves, as the

Powells were doubtless aware, in the very month that Mary began her married life there. On 22 August, when Mary was perhaps back with her family in Forest Hill, or perhaps on her way, the King raised his standard at Nottingham and war had officially begun.

Milton was expecting Mary back by 29 September, Michaelmas. It must have been irksome, not to say hurtful, that she had submitted to return to her family so soon. Almost certainly, in so doing, she damaged his affections for her. To marry a man and then, after only a few weeks, to allow oneself to be taken off by one's noisy relations was a silly and superficial thing to do. Milton must have wondered whether he had done the right thing in marrying her. But there is nothing in Edward Phillips's account to make us suspect that any serious rift had by this stage occurred. It is one thing for a young bride to be a little lonely when she first settles down to married life away from her family. It is quite another for her to consider, on the strength of this, that she wants to be separated from her husband. And nothing in Mary Powell's behaviour at this stage or later suggests that she did want such a separation. In her absence, we may assume, Milton continued to thrash his nephews until they had mastered Oppian's *Cynegetica and Halieutica*. For relaxation he read Harington's translation of Ariosto. His copy survives for us, and we know which part he was perusing at this date because he has written, after the forty-second book, 'Questo libro due volte Io letto, Sept. 21. 1642'. How characteristic of Milton to write, in an English translation of Ariosto, an Italian footnote.

In only one week, he would have thought at this date, she would be home. Meanwhile, he read *Orlando Furioso*. The forty-second book is the one in which Bradamante is pining for her absent lover Ruggiero; and Renaldo is in the very different position of having fallen out of love with Angelica:

> Now that same great mislike and hate retorned
> Of faire Angelica whom late he loved,
> Now he despised her and greatly scorned
> To thinke that he for her one foote had moved . . .[13]

Were Milton's the feelings of the pining lover or the scornful man who felt he had made a fool of himself? We do not know. But he was a proud man; he was an inward, spiritual man. It is hard for women who attract the passionate devotion of spiritual men, because with one part of themselves they despise the very object of their passion, and if there is any danger of their pride being wounded, they easily fall out of love. It is hard not to suspect that this was happening as Milton angrily awaited the return of his young bride. But, of course, had she returned, such feelings could have been assuaged easily by the normal marital affections. It is only because she stayed away that the story became interesting; and she only stayed away because her mother said that it was not safe to travel to London which was a hotbed of Roundheads.

Edgily, Milton waited. Kind friends rallied to distract him, among them John Hobson and his wife Margaret. Hobson, ten years older than Milton, had married Lady Margaret Ley less than a year before in St Giles, Cripplegate. She was the daughter of the Earl of Marlborough, a former Lord Chief Justice and President of the Council. He had resigned just before the Eleven Years' Tyranny began, in March 1628, and he had died almost at once. 'The sad breaking of that Parliament/ Broke him',[14] as Milton put it in a sonnet addressed to Lady Margaret. With her, doubtless, he felt at home; he could indulge his taste for good-looking, aristocratic women. She was, moreover, the daughter of a parliamentary hero. Her husband, unlike Milton's family or the family into which he had married, saw eye to eye with him politically. Indeed, John Hobson early enlisted in the parliamentary army with the rank of captain.

From day to day, probably, Milton's mood changed. Sometimes he thought of Mary with tender longing; sometimes with hurt fury. Michaelmas came and went.

It was not purely physical infatuation, for his part, which made him marry her. He could not allow himself to believe such a thing, that merely a beautiful face and a pretty singing voice could be enough to turn a mind which had been admired by Manso and Gaddi and Bonmatthei. He wrote to her, begging her to return. He even sent down a special foot-messenger. And he wrote (a guess, but I believe it) 'Sonnet IX' at this period. Had they not spoken together of how they both longed for a quiet life? He could teach her, as he taught the boys. But she could provide him with so much more than the boys, so very much more . . .

> Lady, that in the prime of earliest youth,
>   Wisely hath shunned the broad way and the green,
>   And with those few art eminently seen,
>   That labour up the hill of heavenly truth,
> The better part with Mary and with Ruth
>   Chosen thou hast . . .

He writes to the Mary whom he hopes, in the superficial gaiety of her youth, he can educate her into becoming. She has a quiet and natural

innocence, a desire for godliness and sobriety. What chance does she
have to exercise virtue in the broad way and the green of Forest Hill? She
must not allow her foolish relations to dissuade her from returning to
London. Even when her mother scolds her, he has noticed that she is
quiet and submissive:

> . . . and they that overween,
> And at thy growing virtues fret their spleen,
> No anger find in thee, but pity and ruth.

As a sound and serious Protestant stoic, Milton could have had no doubt
that the noisy merriment of Forest Hill, in which the men were always
half-drunk, and the women never quite literate, was no place in which to
be fashioning one's soul, day by day, hour by hour, up to the fulness of
the measure of the stature of Christ, and the other great ancients. Mary,
who was so young, and so impressionable, appealed to the teacher in
Milton as well as to the man. She had traces of quiet sobriety which were
promising material.

> Therefore be sure
> Thou, when the bridegroom with his feastful friends
> Passes to bliss at the mid-hour of night,
> Hast gained thy entrance, virgin wise and pure.

Milton, I suspect, was not allowing himself to recall that it was quite
largely the mirth and jollity of *her* 'feastful friends' which enabled him to
fall in love with her in the first place. But at the same time this sonnet
suggests (if I rightly guess the occasion of it) that there was a vein of
seriousness in Mary's talk which, from the first, added to her attractiveness. So, he sent the sonnet off to Oxfordshire. Nor can he have been
unaware that the threat of the 'coming bridegroom' in the parable might
have more than scriptural application. At any moment, judgement was to
be visited on the king. The foolish virgins were the ones who thought
that he would get away with it.

'But,' we are told, 'the messenger came back not only without an
answer, at least a satisfactory one, but to the best of my remembrance
reported that he was dismissed with some sort of contempt.'[15]

This was very serious indeed. Mary was now being kept at Forest Hill
by her family. But worse was to come. Forest Hill is less than five miles
from Oxford and, as the autumn advanced, the road between London
and Oxford became impassable. For Charles I had made the university
town his capital.

Few wars have ever started which people did not believe, in the first year, would be over by Christmas. So it was with the first Civil War in England. In October there was the indecisive Battle of Edgehill. The Earl of Essex, general of the parliamentary army, claimed it as a victory, but his cavalry had been no match for that of Prince Rupert. Minor skirmishes were going on all over the country. As Lucy Hutchinson wrote in the biography of her husband, 'Before the flame of war broke out in the top of the chimneys, the smoke ascended in every county'.[16] And it was assumed, rightly, that the King would try to take possession of London.

Not much evidence survives to make us think Milton took a very active part in national events at this time. He was interested in the establishment of civil liberties, but it is doubtful whether he thought these could be established by one group of horsemen charging at another group of horsemen on a hill outside Banbury. He was usually aloof, in a high stoical way, from the emotions of the mob. But perhaps most people at this date did not feel that the Civil War was quite real. Some blood had been shed, but not much. Most of what had taken place had been sabre-rattling. In the eyes of parliamentarian optimists, of whom Milton was the most eloquent, the revolution had been all but effected already. They were not expecting, at this stage, a republic. The very fact that the King had been reduced to waging war on his subjects was a sign of his constitutional weakness, not his strength. Loyalists who had pictures of Essex, the parliamentary leader, would have been familiar with the legend under the engraving: 'Robert Earle of Essex, his Excellence, Generall of ye Army, Imployed for the defence of the Protestant Religion, the Safety of his Maties Person and of the Parliament the preservation of the Lawes and Liberties of the Subjects.'

That, very succinctly, explains why men were at arms. Milton, to judge from what he wrote and did not write at this date, would have agreed with it. When Charles I came to his senses, consented to the limiting of his power by parliamentary means, consented to the abolition of the bishops, consented to the abolition of Star Chamber and Ship Money and their attendant iniquities, the country could look forward to the completion of the Reformation and a thorough purging in the commonwealth of the last vestiges of popery and absolutism.

Charles, meanwhile, felt that as soon as he could take possession of the ports and of London, crush the rebels, restore order to the churches, strengthen the power of the bishops and establish once and for all his authority to levy tax as he chose and to assert his royal justice as he saw fit, then the country could return to the peace and tranquillity it had known during the eleven years when Parliament was not sitting.

The degree to which the King failed to see that he had already been defeated partly explains the duration of the war. And it is further explained when one considers that it was one of the most half-hearted wars in history. It only occupied the attentions of a small proportion of the population. It did not divide the nation entirely between ardent supporters of one side or another. On the contrary, most either did not know that it was going on, or were angry with both sides for being unable to resolve their differences peaceably.

These things partially explain, I think, Milton's behaviour at this date. He does not appear to have followed the fortunes of the war very closely in 1642; and, as far as we know, he was not writing any more political prose. What survives from 1642 is his poetry. Some time during this year, as we have seen, he had toyed with the notion of his drama *Adam Unparadised*, inspired by the example of Grotius and Monteverdi – a strange combination! He had read the boys the opening speech by Satan. It seems clear that at this date he was thinking of himself as a great dramatic poet, if we are to judge from his beautiful and semi-serious sonnet 'When the assault was intended to the City'.

Charles, having established himself at his headquarters in Oxford, marched on London in November. I imagine the attractive entrance to the little house in Aldersgate Street being kept firmly shut and bolted at this period. Trained bands of volunteers patrolled the streets in the cold misty weather, shopkeepers and merchants and lawyers turned soldier for the purposes of the emergency, intent not only on keeping the City for Parliament, but, almost more important, preserving shop-fronts and houses from revolutionary fanatics and common thieves as well as from Cavalier marauders.

The weather was thickly misty[17] and the parliamentary armies dispersed. At Brentford the royalists attacked the regiment of one Colonel Hollis, but they failed to achieve the complete victory they had hoped for because of the arrival of two other parliamentary regiments, those of Brooke and Hampden, to relieve their comrades. Essex, with the greater part of the parliamentary army, had returned to London just in time to be ready for this attack. Mobilizing the trained bands, he marched them out of the City towards Chiswick on 13 November and surrounded the royal army.

The skirmish which took place at Turnham Green was a profound anti-climax. Clarendon tells us of the panic caused by the approach of the royal army, turning to scorn when the trained bands actually confronted the exhausted royalist remnant, staggering to meet them through the dripping fog. 'They had then before their eyes the King's little handful of men and then began to wonder and blush at their own fears; and all this might be without excess of courage; for without doubt their numbers then, without the advantage of equipage (which to soldiers is a great addition of mettle) were five times greater than the king's harrassed, weather-beaten and half-starved troops.'[18]

The trained bands, however, were not as trained as they should have been, and, in spite of superior numbers and the advantage of fighting without the exhaustion of a season's campaign behind them, they let the King escape. Probably, had they caught him, he would have died a natural death. Only the most hardened fanatics would, at that date, have dreamed of chopping off his head. Mrs Hutchinson was not alone in thinking that after Turnham Green, since they had the King surrounded, 'the war had been ended, but that, I know not how, three thousand of parliament's forces were called away by their procurement who designed the continuance of the war; and so the king had a way of retreat left open, by which he got back to Oxford'.[19]

Milton, at some stage during this potentially alarming crisis, wrote his sonnet addressed to a Cavalier marauder, reminding him how, in times past, invading armies have spared the houses of poets. Alexander the Great, 'the great Emathian conqueror' told his troops not to raze Pindar's house to the ground when he despoiled Thebes; and, as we learn from Plutarch, an attack on Athens by the Spartans was warded off when someone recited some lines from the *Electra* of Euripides.

It is with Euripides, by implication, that Milton half-ironically compares himself: the great playwright. Turnham Green was scarcely Athens; and the exhausted fighting men in their torn old leather jerkins, uneasily clutching pikes and muskets, can scarcely have summoned up a picture of Alexander the Great's conquering armies. Nevertheless, tradition has it that Milton actually pinned these lines on his door for the plunderers to read:

> Captain or colonel, or knight in arms,
> > Whose chance on these defenceless doors may seize,
> > If deed of honour did thee ever please,
> > Guard them, and him within protect from harms,
> He can requite thee, for he knows the charms
> > That call fame on such gentle acts as these,
> > And he can spread thy name o'er lands and seas,
> > Whatever clime the sun's bright circle warms.

> Lift not thy spear against the muses' bower,
> The great Emathian conqueror bid spare
> The house of Pindarus, when temple and tower
> Went to the ground: and the repeated air
> Of sad Electra's poet had the power
> To save the Athenian walls from ruin bare.

The muses' bower was it, now? So we can imagine the cockney passer-by, the muffin or the night-soil man, observing to himself in November 1642. He had always thought it was some sort of school.

Milton, in this triumphantly successful sonnet, once more confidently announces that he is to be famous in ages yet to come. The 'Captain or colonel', like old Mr Milton, Harry Lawes, and others, is to be grateful, famed only because of his association with a poet as great as Euripides. 'Milton', as Lord Macaulay wrote, 'admired Euripides highly, much more highly than, in our opinion, Euripides deserved.'[20]

Whatever the justice of that aside, it is striking that Milton casts himself here in so firmly a poetical role. He is about to enter a phase of life in which his prose output and his work for the cause of the revolution was to be more in evidence than his poetry. But it was as a poet, first and foremost, that he continues to think of himself.

Charles I withdrew to Oxford and all roads to Forest Hill became after that truly impassable. There were no messages from the Powells. Even if he wrote his 'Captain or colonel' sonnet in a spirit of semi-jest, the little affair of Turnham Green showed with pathetic clarity that he and the rest of his relations (including his relations by marriage) were on opposite sides in a war. One of the thoughtless louts who had been staying in Aldersgate Street only a few months before – Richard Powell or James – might have come marching into the City and attempted to overthrow the parliamentary government. So, too, might Milton's brother Christopher. But that was painful in a different way. The Powells had snatched Mary back in the nick of time. And the fact that she had consented to be snatched was now a sign to Milton that the marriage had been a disastrous mistake.

But he was about to make an even greater mistake. It was one thing to imagine himself as Euripides. It was quite another to think that the Presbyterians, now dominant in Parliament and the army, were going to fall happily into the mould of fourth-century BC Athenians, embracing a glorious intellectual freedom, a liberty of conscience and morals and mind of a sort unknown in Christian times.

CHAPTER 8

MISS DAVIS AND THE LIBERTIES
OF ENGLAND

Who order'd, that their longing's fire
Should be, as soon as kindled, cool'd?
Who renders vain their deep desire? –
A God, a God their severance ruled!

Matthew Arnold, 'Isolation.
To Marguerite – Continued'

IN 1643 England came closer to being in a state of total anarchy than at any stage in its history. Neither the King nor Essex and the parliamentary leaders could raise the necessary cash for paying their increasingly disgruntled troops, and it was hard to see how either side could afford to perpetuate the war much longer. Pym, in February, eloquently said that he 'had too much confidence in his own cause not to believe that, if the arguments in which he relied were heard, without the distraction caused by the presence of armed forces, they would bear down all opposition'.[1] Nevertheless, after the third peace proposal with the King that year broke down, Pym, who had begun his rise to parliamentary greatness by attacking excise duties, attempted to get a bill through the Commons to revive the tax which he had so much reviled the King for trying to levy in 1628. The motion was rejected by the Commons.

It was poverty, on both sides, which led to an ungracious wooing of the Scots, a wooing in which Parliament eventually succeeded. By the end of that year the legislation of the country was being determined, in effect, by a dozen peers (most days no more than five sat in the House), perhaps a hundred MPs and the sixty or eighty Presbyterian divines, many of them Scotch, who sat in the nearby Jerusalem Chamber as a consequence of the so-called Westminster Assembly. This motley collection of people, only half of whom had been elected to speak for their fellow-Englishmen (and nearly all of whose members were dispersed in their constituencies, never to return to Westminster) was the body which Milton was to address proudly as the 'supreme Senate'.

This was the period in which he could write, 'Methinks I see in my mind a noble and puissant nation rousing herself like a strong man after sleep, and shaking her invincible locks'. It was good that he saw this nation in his mind. But what were the symptoms of this nobility, this puissance, in the England of 1643? Perhaps it was the moment in May when Colonel Cromwell burst in on a very old clergyman called Wilson in Huntingdon, physically molested him and tried to make him say that he was a malignant; and when his son, another clergyman, protested, 'Cromwell became so furious and impatient that he told him he would spoil his preaching, and presently caused him to be hanged up, and bored his tongue with a hot iron'.[2]

Or perhaps Milton was thinking of the special committee of the House of Commons, set up on 23 April to look into the idolatrous monuments in Westminster Abbey, who sent a working party round the Abbey and St Margaret's, Westminster next day to smash as many windows and monuments as they could. Perhaps, rather, he was thinking of the enlightened figures who, at the expulsion of the Capuchins from Somerset House in March, had thrown the Rubens altar-piece into the Thames. Or perhaps he had seen the party of horse riding close to his house in the City on Thursday 8 July, 'who marched the streets in great pomp and triumph; first four in buff coats, next four in surplices with the Book of Common Prayer in their hands, singing in derision thereof, and tearing it leaf by leaf, and putting every leaf to their posteriors, with great scorn and laughter'.[3] Was it scenes like this which made him describe London as 'this vast city; a city of refuge, the mansion house of liberty', capital of a nation which he saw as 'an eagle mewing her mighty youth, and kindling her undazzled eyes at the full midday beam; purging and unscaling her long abused sight at the fountain itself of heavenly radiance'?[4]

While the King refused to accept any parliamentary proposal for settlement, the royal army darted about the country in a series of time-wasting, ill-conceived, expensive, and untactical military operations. While Parliament, for the sake of enlisting a Scotch army of over 21,000 men, willingly embraced the Presbyterian system of government ('For the quarrel is whether Jesus shall be King or no')[5] in the panic-stricken realization that the vast majority of English Protestant opinion was against them. London was, as it were, worth a metrical psalm. Rutherford, one of the Scots who was to earn Milton's most withering scorn, would preach to the Commons that, 'the Lord hath intrusted Christian rulers with the most precious thing he hath on earth, he hath given his bride and spouse to their tutory and faith'; but to other people's way of looking at things – the Independents, the Ranters, the Quakers, the Brownists, the Muggletonians and the horde of other crackpots which the civil broils seemed to be throwing up so prodigally, all this smacked of Erastianism. How could a government, whether of King or Parliament, be entrusted with the spouse of Christ? This was as bad as the worst excesses of the Archbishop.

Laud, incidentally, languished in the Tower. Prynne, his arch-enemy, whose ears had been sliced off because of his views on the liturgy, was to have his revenge. Parliament put him in charge of prosecuting the ruined prelate. Like his king, diminutive of stature and proud of heart, a stubborn and charmless figure in life, Laud achieved a kind of sanctity in the mode of his dying.

Cromwell alone, in the few years which elapsed after this, was to have the strength or the enterprise or the political vision to make use of this seething and unruly situation, in which malcontents, maniacs, and murderers had, as they will always have when there is a revolution in the state, as powerful a voice as the men of reason.

What was it then, that could prompt Milton to take so comparatively optimistic a view of things in 1643 as to be able to interpret all this chaos as God, shaking 'a Kingdom with strong and healthful commotions to a general reforming'?

Are we to picture him as that rather sinister figure, the intellectual playing at parlour politics? Was the author of *Areopagitica* no better than leftists in the 1930s, who could turn a blind eye to Stalin's atrocities on the grounds that you can't create an earthly Paradise without murdering tens of thousands of your fellow-countrymen? Or are we to read the pamphlets of this year, with their perpetual dwelling on the ancient liberties of Rome and Athens, as a sort of schoolmasterly fantasy, the product of a mind scarcely aware of the sordid political realities of the day? Or, alternatively, are they great statements of faith: expressions of what he believes the troubled times could lead towards, given time; hopes for what might be achieved with the right leadership and guidance? All these images flash in and out of our minds when we consider Milton in 1643, including the cruel thought that there can be no more supreme example of his egotism than the fact that he chose, with the nation collapsing into turmoil, and public order almost gone, to urge Parliament to turn its immediate attentions to reforming the divorce laws:

an issue, as no biographer of Milton could fail to observe, which was directly relevant to his own predicament at this hour.

And yet, we have the testimony of *Defensio Secunda* that he genuinely had the public good in mind.

Since then I observed that there are, in all, three varieties of liberty without which civilized life is scarcely possible, namely ecclesiastical liberty, domestic or personal liberty and civil liberty, and since I had already written about the first, while I saw that the magistrates were vigorously attending to the third, I took as my province the remaining one, the second or domestic kind . . . For in vain does he prattle about liberty in assembly and market-place who at home endures the slavery most unworthy of man, slavery to an inferior.[6]

In Milton's view, then, his plea for divorce was integral to the general struggle going on at that time for liberty of a more general character. And it is only fair to admit that the euphoric passages from *Areopagitica* which I have quoted were written, not merely after the desecration of Westminster Abbey, but after the Battle of Marston Moor. It was at this battle that Cromwell had delivered the first decisive blow against the royalists; and it was after Marston Moor that the Independents began to get the ascendancy over the Presbyterians. But in order to trace the course of Milton's euphoria, it is necessary to go back to the beginning of 1643.

Mary, his bride of a few weeks, had vanished the previous autumn like a dream, and without, as far as we know, being able to renew contact. Her family returned Milton's entreaties for her to come back to London, and dismissed his messenger with insults. There is record that, until 1644, her father continued to keep up the repayments of his debt to his son-in-law; but there is no evidence that the two communicated over this. The marriage had passed, like a bitter-sweet episode. And now, the war had developed, the King was in Oxford, and numbered no more besotted admirers in his train than the Powells, who lived a little way out of Oxford in Forest Hill.

To Milton, for all these reasons, it must have seemed that his marriage was irrevocably over. There is no evidence about how he felt. Biographers have usually felt free to say how wounded and angry he was. There have been hints, and more than hints, that the marriage was not consummated; and plenty of ink has been confidently spent describing the psychosexual crisis caused by Mary's 'desertion'. But, of course, there is no evidence for any of this. There is not even evidence that she did, technically, desert him. They were separated by the war, like so

many married couples. But unlike others – unlike Charles I and Henrietta Maria, or Milton's brother and sister-in-law – they were separated in a way which made it look unlikely that they could ever come
together again. It is true that a man who falls in love quickly might fall out
of love quickly. We do not need to picture an enchantress to consider
reasons why this Renaldo should have forgotten the charms of his
Angelica. Mary was gone; out of sight, out of mind. He was saddled with
the marriage-bond which according to the laws of the church, and
therefore of the state, could not be dissolved.

The injustice of this rankled, but we are not to picture him silently
brooding about this and about nothing else for the whole of 1643.
Nevertheless, it must have affected his thinking, as he perused his books
and continued his researches, his teaching, his social and family life
during the first six months of the year. Were there, in fact, strong
scriptural grounds for divorce? What had the early reformers, what had
the Fathers, what had this author and that writer said on the subject? His
eye would naturally fall on passages relevant to the theme in the course
of his general reading. But there was much else to occupy his thoughts.

There was, for instance, his family. His father, his brother, and his
sister-in-law (she was far advanced in another pregnancy) were still at
Reading, and they were caught there when it was besieged by the Earl of
Essex on 15 April. Reading surrendered twelve days later. Royalist
propagandists claimed that, in order to disguise the extent of the carnage
even from his own troops, the Earl buried the slain in mass graves
outside the town.

Christopher Milton, as a musketeer in the royal army, did not stay to
be taken prisoner. He had to follow his own destiny, which was to
separate him from Thomasine and the children for three years. She fled
to London. Old Mr Milton came to live with his son John in Aldersgate
Street where, Edward Phillips recalls, with evident affection for his
grandfather, 'the old gentleman [lived] wholly retired to his rest and
devotion, without the least trouble imaginable'.[7]

Milton loved his father, and remained devoted to him, whatever their
political differences might have been. Music must have been a great
bond at this date, and we notice that, surely with the son's help and
encouragement, the old man, now nearly eighty, published some of his
own music in this year. 'I trust in God then to my soul . . . by I. Milton'
was one of the items in William Slater's *The Psalms of David* (1643).

As well as looking after his father, Milton was adding to his collection
of pupils, and by now had something resembling a school. He never

actually had a 'wonder-working academy', as Johnson unkindly calls it, but he almost certainly had between half a dozen and ten pupils at some stages. 'It is well known he never set up for a public school to teach all the young fry of a parish, but only was willing to impart his learning and knowledge to relations, and the sons of some gentlemen that were his intimate friends.' As with everything else in his life, the teaching arrangements were highly selective and exclusive. He always flourished best in small groups, as in the Florentine Apatisti.

But we should not imagine him as some kind of recluse in Aldersgate Street. The barricade which he had put up against the 'Captain or colonel, or knight in arms' was doubtless meant partly to amuse and impress his friends. Lady Margaret Hobson has already been mentioned. Lady Barrymore and Lady Ranelagh were also intimates of Milton's at this date, as well as sages like Samuel Hartlib. His favourite company appears to have been educated gentry and lawyers. But there is no reason to suppose that he lost touch with Harry Lawes (who presumably continued to come to play music with old Mr Milton), or with Alexander Gil the younger, nor with Thomas Young (more of him later).

Milton also appears to have befriended a doctor and his family called Davis. Alas, we know all too little about him. If only he had had a name as odd as Hartlib, we might hope that it would shriek out at us from some parish register, some will or litigation. But this shadowy medic's claim to historical fame flickered into light only when Milton conceived the idea of marrying one of his daughters, 'a very handsome and witty gentlewoman, but averse . . . as it is said, to this motion . . .'[8]

'Did Mary have something to forgive which took place during her absence?'[9] asks a modern historian: a very modern question. History draws the veil. I shall neither ask the question, nor stay for an answer. Miss Davis has her place in the story but it is not quite yet.

As we began the chapter by noticing, England was 'rousing herself like a strong man after sleep, and shaking her invincible locks'. As we observed, without the alliance of the Scots at that point in the war, the parliamentary army could not have continued in the field. In February the parliamentary treasurer of the army, Sir Gilbert Gerard, announced that he had not a penny left to pay the troops.[10] The Scots, for their part, seized it as the perfect opportunity for establishing their own religious autonomy. They did so, not by merely extracting an agreement that Presbyterianism be the national religion of Scotland; they imposed it on the English too as a condition of their alliance. 'All things are expected of God and the Scots', said Robert Baillie, with no discernible irony.[11]

Milton would be memorable if he had written none of his great poems, for having coined some of the best anti-Scotch phrases in the language. But I suspect that his prejudice against our northern neighbours developed during 1643, rather than being, like Dr Johnson's, innate. Thomas Young, although his influence on Milton's early life has been grossly overestimated and exaggerated, was a figure whom Milton had revered and liked. He had gone to the trouble of defending Young in his *Apology* for the Smectymnuans. And, more important, in his anti-episcopal tracts of the years before war broke out, Milton had, broadly speaking, developed a Presbyterian view of church government. We know what he thought of bishops 'belching the sour crudities of yesterday's popery',[12] arrayed in 'deformed and fantastic dresses in palls, and mitres, gold and gewgaws fetched from Aaron's old wardrobe'.[13] There can be no doubt that he would have been glad to see the back of them.

Most certain it is (as all our stories bear witness) that ever since their coming to the see of Canterbury for near twelve hundred years, to speak of them in general, they have been in England to our souls a sad and doleful succession of illiterate and blind guides: to our purses and goods a wasteful band of robbers, a perpetual havoc, and rapine: to our state a continual Hydra of mischief and molestation, the forge of discord and rebellion: this is the trophy of their antiquity, and boasted succession through so many ages.[14]

Although no Calvinist, Milton had been impressed by the orderliness of the Genevan system – the seventeenth-century equivalent of making the trains run on time – and he must, in principle, have welcomed the coming of the Westminster assembly, which spent its days poring over the Thirty-nine Articles and wondering which ones to discard.

Milton, however, would take a wider view. The religious and political viewpoints in his mind are inseparable. When he had exclaimed, 'O, if we freeze at noon after their early thaw, let us fear lest the sun for ever hide himself and turn his orient steps from our ingrateful horizon', he would have taken it for granted that a reform of the Church would entail, be part of, a wholesale reform of the body politic. He had the optimistic, if irrational, belief that the liberty of the Gospel, if allowed by Protestant divines to hold sway in the Church, would bring to pass an era of civil liberty. And he therefore devoted himself to expounding a sort of social programme for the fruits of this liberty. He had already spoken of reformation and religious change. Now, with the Assembly of Divines actually in the process of taking over the government of the country, or at any rate influencing it, he chose to implore them to introduce domestic liberty, educational reform, and freedom of the Press.

The pamphlets are not fairly seen as 'armchair politics'. Although pamphlets of all colours were flying from the presses at this date in profligate clouds in the absence of Laud and Charles I's censors, it did not mean that liberty of the Press or liberty of speech really existed in the sense that it does today. Libels were easier to get away with than nowadays; but you could not necessarily reckon on being allowed a point of view. Unlike us, they regarded ideas as more in need of protection than persons. Perhaps to publish fanatical abuse under a pseudonym or under no name at all took no more courage, than, today, it would take to daub a political slogan on a wall. But writing something as full and as learned as *The Doctrine and Discipline of Divorce* was a different matter.

It is true that, in the first edition, Milton did not put his name on the title-page, but no one who had read his earlier tracts attacking the bishops could have much doubt about its authorship. There could have been few pamphleteers of that date who had been busying their heads with what Paulus Fagius wrote in his commentary on Deuteronomy.[15] But there was one and one only who could have written, 'O perverseness! that the Law should be made more provident of peacemaking than the Gospel! that the Gospel should be put to beg a most necessary help of mercy from the Law, but must not have it: and that to grind in the mill of an undelighted and servile copulation, must be the only forced work of a Christian marriage . . .'[16]

Since divorce is one of the very few things which Christ appears from Scripture specifically to have forbidden, it required all Milton's ingenuity as a controversialist to be able to argue, from a Christian point of view, that divorce was a good thing. But the logic-chopping exercises which he had so much despised at Cambridge had not been wasted on him.

There was, moreover, a large body of opinion on his side.[17] The first divorce pamphlet is striking more for the vehemence of its expression and the trenchancy with which its case is argued, than for its novelty.

Ever since early Christian times the problem of divorce had been with the Church. Christ himself appeared to sanction it on the grounds of adultery, but to forbid the remarriage of the divorced person. St Paul adds the further exception of divorce between a Christian and an unbeliever, the 'Pauline exception' allowed to this day in the Roman Church. The early reformers – Tyndale, Calvin, Melanchthon, Bucer, Osiander, Paraeus, all sanctioned divorce; and it was one of the charges brought against Bishop Hooper (burnt by Bloody Mary) that he was an advocate of divorce.

But now that, with the help of the Scotch divines, Parliament was gradually outlawing the episcopacy and all that had gone with it, the whole question of the marriage law could be reopened and discussed, Milton hoped, freely.

In Milton's view, marriage was chiefly a matter of mutual compatibility and companionship rather than primarily a matter of sex. The Anglican view, that a marriage could only be annulled if it had not been consummated, suggested that sex was the be-all and end-all of married life. 'And with all generous persons married thus it is, that where the mind and person pleases aptly, there some unaccomplishment of the body's delight may be better born with, than when the mind hangs off in an unclosing disproportion, though the body be as it ought; for there all corporal delight will soon become unsavoury and contemptible.'[18]

Sex, in Milton's view, looks after itself. A single person may resolve to live chastely. It will be easier for him to do so than for a married man saddled with an incompatible companion. If they love one another, sexual attraction is likely to follow; any measure of sexual incompatibility 'may be better borne with'. If they have come to hate each other, then sex will not save them. And the frustrated man who has come to hate his wife will find it impossible to control his lust. Milton draws a strong and terrible picture of such marital collapse, leading to sordid visits to brothels and casual adulteries: he depicts

that same God-forbidden loneliness which will in time draw on with it a general discomfort and dejection of mind, not beseeming either Christian profession or moral conversation, unprofitable and dangerous to the Commonwealth, when the household estate, out of which must flourish forth the vigour and spirit of all public enterprises, is so ill-contented and procured at home, and cannot be supported; such a marriage can be no marriage whereto the most honest end is wanting: and the aggrieved person shall do more manly, to be extraordinary and singular in claiming the due right whereof he is frustrated, than to piece up his lost contentment by visiting the stews, or stepping to his neighbour's bed, which is the common shift in this misfortune, or else by suffering his useful life to waste away and be lost under a secret affliction of an unconscionable size to human strength . . .[19]

There is tenderness, imagination, and sympathy in that last sentence, the *waste of life* being almost the worst feature of rigidly forbidding divorce in all circumstances. Far from being a virtue, putting up with marital unhappiness is, in his view, morally dangerous. The enforcement on unhappy couples of 'a drooping and disconsolate household captivity without refuge or redemption'[20] brings worse sins and unhappinesses in its train: sins of adultery, sins of resentment and anger, sins of despair. 'Who shall answer for the perishing of all those souls perishing by stubborn expositions of particular and inferior precepts, against the general and supreme rule of charity?'[21]

It is this supreme rule of charity which, he argues, is Christ-like. Christ had taught that the Sabbath was made for man and not man for the Sabbath. Marriage, too, was an institution made for mankind, and when it ceased to bring the peace and joy which God intended, it was no virtue to persist in it for purely legalistic reasons. As he concludes 'God the Son hath put all other things under his own feet; but his commandments he hath left all under the feet of charity'.[22]

In the pamphlet Milton sees marriage as a civil contract drawn up for the good and comfort of society; and he therefore claims divorce as a civil and political right. The so-called canon law drawn up by Lombard and Gratian 'rendered the pure and solid Law of God unbeneficial to us by their calumnious dunceries'.[23]

Liberty of divorce, we claim not, we think not but from this Law; the dignity, the faith, the authority thereof is now grown among Christians, O astonishment! a labour of no mean difficulty and labour to defend.

Moses had allowed divorce, and was not Moses the giver of God's law?

It must be your suffrages and votes, O Englishmen, that this exploded decree of God and Moses may scape, and come off fair without the censure of shameful abrogating: which, if yonder sun ride sure, and mean not to break word with us tomorrow, was never yet abrogated by our Saviour. Give sentence, if you please, that the frivolous Canon may reverse the infallible judgement of Moses and his great director.[24]

With great boldness, then, on 1 August 1643 Milton published his pamphlet. Many of his biographers have assumed that there is a direct connection between the disappearance of Mary Milton and her husband's interest in divorce; indeed, it is so obvious that such a connection exists that it is hardly worth mentioning. But, although he writes from the heart, he is not merely writing about himself. It is very conspicuous, for instance, that the kind of marital discord and horror described in *The Doctrine and Discipline of Divorce* could not possibly be those of a man who was married, in effect, for only three weeks. Even if he had fallen out of love with Mary as soon as her relations went home, or even on the wedding day itself, there would scarcely have been time for either of

them to suffer from 'a drooping and disconsolate domestic captivity'.
The phrase fits better, of course, the position assigned by legend to
Mary in the matter. But any such speculation is vain. Milton was an
egotist; one of the most supreme egotists who has ever lived. But that is
not to say that he had no imagination or that he had not observed the
married life of people other than himself. The really striking thing
about Milton's ideas on the subject is that he never once suggests
desertion as a plausible ground for divorce. Other writers on the subject
had thought desertion a reasonable ground; it seems an obvious one.
This is surely a sign that he very deliberately avoided discussing the
matter from his own point of view. If he mentioned desertion, there
would be those who thought Mary had deserted him, and that he was
merely asking Parliament to change the laws of England to suit his own
convenience. It was a general issue, and one of political relevance; he
could not risk it being dismissed *ad hominem*.

Nor were his erudite and profoundly considered reflections over-
looked. *The Doctrine and Discipline of Divorce* sold out by the end of the
year, and when it was reprinted Milton thought to justify some of the
furore it had caused by admitting his authorship of it and dedicating it to
'the Parliament of England with the assembly'. He urged them to see
divorce as a political matter. 'Advise ye well, supreme Senate, if charity
be thus excluded and expulsed, how ye will defend the untainted honour
of your own actions and proceedings: he who marries intends as little
to conspire his own rule as he that swears allegiance: and as a whole
people is in proportion to an ill Government, so is one man to an ill
marriage . . .'

The Preface makes it clear that the first divorce pamphlet had a
disquieting reception, ranging from harsh disapproval to an unthinking
enthusiasm for the idea of divorce which failed to take in the strictures of
Milton's argument. Such a figure as Mrs Attaway, a sectarian preacher
who did not get along with her husband, was an immediate and
enthusiastic admirer of *The Doctrine and Discipline of Divorce*. She eloped
with a fellow enthusiast, William Jenny, holding herself to be as free
from sin as Christ was when He was in the flesh. John Robins, a Ranter,
authorized his disciples to change their husbands and wives, setting
them a good example by changing his own. These were far from isolated
instances.

But were they the kind of audience that Milton had been hoping to
attract? His old tutor, Thomas Young, evidently fell out with him over
the issue. He knew which side his bread was buttered, becoming Master

of Jesus College, Cambridge the following year, when the Anglican heads of houses were deposed. In a sermon to the House of Commons on 28 February 1644, Young advised them not to do anything which would advance the cause of legalizing 'bigamy'. Prynne, later in the year, on 16 September, was to assail Milton indirectly when he regretted 'the late dangerous increase of many Anabaptistical, Antinomian, Heretical, Atheistical opinions as of the soul's mortality, divorce at leisure etc., lately broached, preached, printed in this famous City, which I hope our grand Council will speedily and carefully suppress'.[25]

For Milton, this must have caused dismay. On the one hand, crackpot enthusiasm for his ideas on divorce; on the other, a rigid legalism which he could scarcely have expected from the fathers of the glorious completing of the Reformation which he thought was taking place. The fact that some maniacs misinterpreted him seemed to have earned him the reputation of a libertine. Divorce on demand; divorce at leisure? He had never contemplated such a thing. Was he to be held responsible for the ranting of Robins or the gadding of Mrs Attaway?

What though the brood of Belial, the draff of men, to whom no liberty is pleasing, unbridled and vagabond lust without pale or partition, will laugh broad perhaps, to see so great a strength of Scripture mustering up in favour, as they suppose, of their debaucheries; they will know better, when they shall hence learn, that honest liberty is the greatest foe to dishonest license. And what though others out of a waterish and queasy conscience because ever crazy and never yet sound, will rail and fancy to themselves that injury and license is the best of this Book?

Milton's expectations of people, above all his expectations of legislators, had been absurdly rosy. He thought that lawgivers would be able to see the moral beauties which he had celebrated in *Comus*.

Love virtue, she alone is free.

It is a fundamental truth for Milton that virtue can only shine in places where one sees it free to be unvirtuous. Just as the cruel marriage laws imperilled souls, so civil liberty would be an enabling of private virtue. Why, why, why, he must have wondered with that lofty naivety which still characterized him, could the fools of both extremes not *see* what he was trying to say:

I did but prompt the age to quit their clogs
By the known rules of ancient liberty,
When straight a barbarous noise environs me
Of owls and cuckoos, asses, apes and dogs.

'Ancient liberty', of course, means pre-Christian liberty. Defending Milton's sympathy for the Regicides, Aubrey was to write,

whatever he wrote against monarchy was out of no animosity to the King's person, but out of a pure zeal to the liberty of mankind which he thought would be greater under a free state than under a monarchal government. His being so conversant in Livy and the Roman authors and the greatness he saw done by the Roman commonwealth and the virtue of their great captains induced him to.[26]

This is most profoundly true. Milton was much more at home in BC than AD. Nothing in his poems, although he was technically a Christian of sorts, suggests the very slightest warmth of feeling about the person of Christ. Unlike Herbert, Milton never brings to God 'the cream of all his heart' still less does he call God 'my dear'. He brings to God a fearless and impersonal pursuit of the truth and a mind overbrimmed with reading. His God is a 'great task-master'; more recognizable in the Mosaic lawgiver than in the Galilean carpenter; but yet more recognizable still in that immovable *gravitas* and virtue which had been cultivated by Cicero and Seneca.

Milton, of course, would have felt no conflict between his Christianity and his classicism, any more than, in a Bernini altar-piece, Christian saints would have shunned the company of Bacchic putti. Milton, too, was a Renaissance man, believing with an almost unimaginable simplicity in the manifest workings of divine providence, identifying that providence with the God which Plato sought and Cicero expounded.

Reason was God-given. Cardinal Newman was never less Miltonic than when he asked 'What is reason itself but a product of the Fall?' Freedom of mind and expression was, therefore, to Milton, not merely something worth claiming for political ends, but a sacred gift which no government had the power to stifle. It is from this belief that his optimism about the early stages of the new reformation (what has been called the English Revolution) sprang.

We, 340 years on, can analyse the progress of that revolution with the secular, dispassionate, and academic eyes of historians. It was not possible to do so in 1643 or 1644. Carlyle's very obvious point about the seventeenth century eludes us all the time because it is so simple and so very hard to grasp fully with our imaginations. As the reader looks back on it,

gradually a very stupendous phenomenon may rise on his astonished eye. A practical world based on belief in God; such as many centuries had seen before, but as never any since has been privileged to see. It was the last glimpse of it in our world, this of English Puritanism: very great, very glorious; tragical enough to all thinking hearts that look on it from these days of ours.[27]

Nothing but divine providence could explain the reversal of the social and political order which took place after 1640. They had prayed for the abolition of the bishops, and the bishops had been abolished. For Milton, initially, this was a great sign that God was at work. Milton could therefore approach the Assembly of Divines and the Parliament with confidence that it was merely a matter of time before liberty was established in the land: true liberty, 'the known rules of ancient liberty'. To contradict this inexorable process would therefore seem to Milton not merely politically unenlightened but blasphemous.

He was mistaken, of course, in his countrymen. The only people who heeded him were cranks and scandalmongers. The Presbyterians on whom he had placed so much hope were not merely deaf to his plea; they were as hostile as Laud would have been.

> License they mean when they cry liberty;
> For who loves that, must first be wise and good;
> But from that mark how far they rove we see
> For all this waste of wealth, and loss of blood.

In July, at Marston Moor, the parliamentary army won the first decisive victory of the war, thanks largely to the military genius of Cromwell who described his victory in characteristic terms:

England and the Church of God hath had a great favour from the Lord in this great victory given unto us, such as the like never was since this war began. It had all the evidences of an absolute victory, obtained by the Lord's blessing upon the godly party principally [i.e. his own Eastern Association]. We never charged but we routed the enemy. The left wing, which I commanded, being our own horse, saving a few Scots in our rear, beat all the Prince's horse. God made them as stubble to our swords. We charged their regiments of foot with our horse, and routed all we charged. The particulars I cannot relate now; but I believe of 20,000 the Prince hath not 4,000 left. Give glory, all the glory, to God.[28]

With the knowledge of retrospect, we know it to be one of the greatest turning points in Cromwell's fortunes. His victory was crucial to the history of the divisions within the parliamentary side, as much as a purely military supremacy over Prince Rupert's disgraced army. From now on, we can see, the Independents were to develop their strength over the Presbyterians. The way is opening for the men who would not be satisfied with a modified monarchy and an ordered Church based on

Presbyterianism rather than episcopacy. Waiting in the wings were the republicans who did not, strictly, believe in Church government at all.

It is hard to trace with accuracy the movement of a man's mind, particularly a mind like Milton's which, while being no flibbertigibbet, changed radically and often; changed as a result of deeply read, deeply held opinions. But one comes close to understanding the paradox with which this chapter begins by noticing the dates of Marston Moor and *Areopagitica*. The initial reactions of hostility to the divorce pamphlets must have disappointed Milton. Marston Moor, however, confirmed that God was, after all, working his purpose out, making the royalist foot-soldiers as stubble to the well-trained cavalry of a Huntingdonshire squire. When Milton replies, then, to Presbyterian attacks, he does so not with disillusionment but with exultant confidence and fervour that the Reformation is indeed being accomplished; that 'ancient liberty' has after all, a chance of being extended.

It was an unfortunate young divine of the name of Herbert Palmer who specifically provoked Milton's wrath, on 13 August 1644, by preaching a sermon to the House of Commons about the regrettable laxity of the times. One example he gave was Milton's divorce pamphlet: 'If any plead . . . for divorce for other causes than Christ and his apostles mention (of which a wicked book is abroad and uncensured, though deserving to be burnt, whose author hath been so impudent as to set his name to it and dedicate it to yourselves) . . . will you grant toleration for all this?'[29]

Milton could have replied at once, and in detail, to the various objections raised by his first divorce pamphlet. He did not do so because the issue touched upon by Palmer's sermon was of more general application. Liberty of speech and liberty of the Press were at stake (for, of course, Palmer was not alone in his views). If these presbyters were to set themselves up as inquisitors of what should or should not be read, England would be in a worse case than she had been in the worst days of Archbishop Laud's censors. At least in Laud's time, there had been merely twenty-six bishoprics to contend with.

> . . . whenas now the pastor of a small unlearned parish on the sudden shall be exalted archbishop over a large diocese of books, and yet not remove, but keep his other cure too, a mystical pluralist.[30]

But it was not merely the system of censorship proposed which Milton found objectionable. It was the whole principle of censoring the Press at all. The very people who had been persecuted by Laud now came forward as willing persecutors, egged on by Scots, 'some who of late were little better than silenced from preaching shall now come to silence us from reading . . . and will soon put it out of controversy, that Bishops and Presbyters are the same to us, the name and thing . . .'[31] It was a sentiment which he was to sharpen into verse. But, for the present purpose, his passionate prose would serve.

Areopagitica is Milton's finest prose work. It was provoked by the Commons passing an ordinance for the regulation of printing in June 1644. But this was merely the occasion for the most eloquent manifesto for the known rules of ancient liberty ever to be penned. The victory of the Independents at Marston Moor in July unquestionably gave him further confidence. Such men as Richard Overton, William Walwyn, or Henry Robinson, all radical Independents, shared the opinions expressed in the pamphlet. Milton would have been aware of the strength of feeling in London about what he said. Its great central doctrine had far wider implications than merely the laws relating to printing. Speaking to the Parliament of England as if it were a democratic assembly of ancient Athenians on the Areopagus (hence the title) he bids them imitate 'the old and elegant humanity of Greece' and he compares himself with Isocrates. 'And out of those ages, to whose polite wisdom and letters we owe that we are not yet Goths and Jutlanders, I could name him who from his private house wrote that discourse to the Parliament of Athens, that persuades them to change the form of democracy which was then established'.[32]

Back to BC! The short historical survey of the history of censorship which follows is worthy of Gibbon. It is really only when we come to Christian times, and above all, of course, to Christian Rome, that 'the books of those whom they took to be grand heretics were examined, refuted and condemned in the general councils'.

Milton's powers of synthesis and analysis are nowhere more apparent than here. His separation from Mary Powell made him think generally about divorce. And his general reflections on divorce excited the anger of Parliament who wished to censor them; and censorship aroused his thoughts about freedom; and the notion of freedom was really an occasion for expressing his belief in the final lines of the masque he had written for the Earl of Bridgewater: 'Love virtue, she alone is free'. Here, once more, he reverts to this spiritual certainty:

I cannot praise a fugitive and cloistered virtue, unexercised and unbreathed, that never sallies out and sees her adversary, but slinks out of the race, where that immortal garland is to be run for, not without dust and heat. Assuredly we bring not innocence into the world, we bring impurity much rather: that which purifies us is trial, and trial is by what is contrary. That virtue therefore which is but a youngling in the contemplation of evil, and knows not the utmost that vice promises to her followers, and rejects it, is but a blank virtue, not a pure; her whiteness is but an excremental whiteness; which was the reason why our sage and serious poet Spenser, whom I dare be known to think a better teacher then Scotus or Aquinas, describing true temperance under the person of Guion, brings him in with his palmer through the cave of Mammon, and the bower of earthly bliss that he might see and know, and yet abstain. Since therefore the knowledge and survey of vice is in this world so necessary to the constituting of human virtue, and the scanning of error to the confirmation of the truth, how can we more safely and with less danger scout into the regions of sin and falsity than by reading all manner of tractates, and hearing all manner of reason? And this is the benefit which may be had of books promiscuously read.[33]

It is a passage worth quoting at length because it seems to represent such a rich pondering on his own promiscuous reading, from the early years (right back to the early days of first reading *The Faerie Queene* when he was a schoolboy in Bread Street), through the tedious years of reading scholastic philosophers at Horton and Hammersmith, and doubtless hearing them debated at Naples, Florence, and Geneva. It was an urbane, cosmopolitan, Stoic view, undeterred by the parochialism of the moment.

There was an almost grotesque contrast between Milton's ideal vision of an enlightened Protestant government and the bigotted legalists who tried to prop up the makeshift arrangements necessary at that stage of the Long Parliament's history. But there were new movements in the wind. God, surely, was blowing that wind. And it was surely with Cromwell in mind, and the rising power of the Independents, that Milton had the confidence to write, 'Now once again by all concurrence of signs, and by the general instinct of holy and devout men, as they daily and solemnly express their thoughts, God is decreeing to begin some new and great period in his Church, even to the reforming of the Reformation itself: what does He then but reveal Himself to his servants, and as his manner is, first to his Englishmen?'

There is not much irony here. One comes nowhere near understanding the political atmosphere of the early 1640s without noticing that its most eloquent piece of rhetoric combines the logical serenity of Aristotle with the most ludicrous superstitious rant; a fiery Protestantism which makes even the basest expressions of modern fanatics in Ulster seem pale; a lunatic jingoism; a cleverness, a rhetorical agility, and a literary lightness worthy of Hamlet.

The point about God and his Englishmen, though, is that the freedom of the English religion did not need to be shackled to the bigotries of the Scots. There is much in *Areopagitica* which anticipates the splendid anger of his poem 'On the New Forcers of Conscience under the Long Parliament':

> Men whose life, learning, faith and pure intent
> Would have been held in high esteem with Paul
> Must now be named and printed heretics
> By shallow Edwards and Scotch What-d'ye-call . . .

These are the men, like Thomas Young, his former mentor, the Smectymnuan whom he had so gallantly defended, and with whom he was now totally disillusioned. He looked forward to the time when the true Protestants, the true Reformation

> May with their wholesome and preventive shears
> Clip your phylacteries, though baulk your ears,
>   And succour our just fears
> When they shall read this clearly in your charge
> New *Presbyter* is but old *Priest* writ large.

Meanwhile, Milton's little school flourished, and it was probably above all with the young that he dreamed of his new liberal commonwealth actually being established, founded on Aristotle's *Politics* and Spenser's fairy land. While old John Milton snoozed in one part of the tiny house in Aldersgate, or played Monteverdi on the chamber organ, the younger John Milton gave attention to the little boys. For, in the intervals of translating Martin Bucer's pamphlet on divorce, and reissuing his own, Milton gave his mind to his theory and idea of education.

It seems that there were about half a dozen boys under his supervision now. The *Life* by John Phillips tells us, 'He had from his first settling taken care of instructing his two nephews by his sister Phillips, and, as it happened, the son of some friend: now he took a large house, where the Earl of Barrymore, sent by his aunt the Lady Ranelagh, Sir Thomas Gardiner of Essex and others were under his tuition'.[34]

It is not certain at what date, exactly, Milton moved house yet again, but the influx of pupils and dependants probably made it essential. The new house was not far away from Aldersgate, just up the road in the Barbican. It must have been some time in 1645, after his school had swollen in numbers, and after he had written the pamphlet *Of Education*.

Milton must have felt, surrounded by clever, slightly aristocratic and admiring youths, that he was very close to reviving the Platonic academy of fourth-century Athens. His reputation for harshness, muddled, as I have already suggested, in Aubrey's memory with that of Alexander Gil, would have meant nothing to him. All boys – until much more recently than the seventeenth century – were thrashed. Contemporary visitors to the Aldersgate academy would have been shocked or delighted not by its sternness but by its liberality, the liberality of intellectual discipline, the promiscuity, to use his own word, of books read. Edward Phillips tells us (he should have known, he was a boy there) that 'neither his converse, nor his writings, nor his manner of teaching ever savoured in the least any thing of pedantry; and probably he might have some prospect of putting in practice his academical institution, according to the model laid down in his sheet on education'.[35]

Of Education represents the third great area of liberty which Milton sought to be established in England. His 'sheet', however, does not concern the education of the masses. Doubtless he still held to his notion, expressed in 1641, that the bishops' lands and revenues should be used to finance schools. But that was for 'all the young fry of a parish', and not for the rather select group of youths under Milton's charge. They were potential leaders of men, and they deserved a better education, we are to infer, than was laid on for him at St Paul's or Christ's.

He wrote the pamphlet at the request of the Prussian exile Samuel Hartlib, who had been in Cambridge during Milton's undergraduate days and who was acquainted with most of the great names on what was becoming the revolutionary side in the Civil War – Prynne, Fairfax, Cromwell . . . It is a remarkable document, and any child who absorbed the range of reading which it prescribes would be a remarkable creature, certainly by the standards of the seventeenth century. For Milton was anxious that as well as a thorough knowledge of literature and philosophy (and not just the mainstream authors: he was in favour of twelve-year-olds being set to read Manilius and Nicander) a child would acquire a knowledge of practical arts. Law would be mastered; a little basic medicine ('how to manage a crudity');[36] agriculture, mathematics, and what he would call natural philosophy and we would call science. Languages were to be taught, of course, including Hebrew, 'whereto it would be no impossibility to add the Chaldee and the Syrian dialect'.[37] These, in addition to mastering logic, 'until it be time to open her contracted palm into a graceful and ornate rhetoric taught out of the rule of Plato, Aristotle, Phalereus, Cicero, Hermogenes, Longinus.'[38]

Sad to say, we have all grown so illiterate that this list is daunting enough to seem comic to the modern ear. It must be said that *Of Education* was written to impress a foreigner, and it is the expression of an ideal. 'First to find out a spacious house and ground about it fit for an academy, and big enough to lodge a hundred and fifty persons . . .'[39] That ideal was never realized in Milton's lifetime, and it sends a chill down the spine of any modern reader who recalls what life was like – is like, indeed – for children sent to such 'spacious houses' to be instructed in the ways of classical and athletic excellence which Milton thought so desirable. What misery the idea has caused, how many Dotheboys Halls, IAPS, Headmaster's Conference establishments have sprung up in such 'spacious houses' in the last 200 years, and with how little educative effect. The pursuit of Milton's educational ideals resulted in generation upon generation of what Matthew Arnold called Philistines being trundled out of their boarding-schools, and very far from viewing the Chaldee or the Syrian dialect as 'no impossibility'. Yet, even if the boys in Aldersgate could not foresee the horrors which lay in wait for their successors two and three hundred years later ('unsweating themselves regularly . . . to smooth and make them gentle from . . . distempered passions')[40] they doubtless learnt far more than boys in any average school. Milton, of course, was intent on stuffing their heads with all the learning of his grown-up life: a digest of some twenty years' solid reading.

Most striking and revealing of all is not so much the syllabus as the idea behind it; an idea which reveals Milton as the true father of modern educational ideas. 'The end . . . of learning is to repair the ruins of our first parents . . .'[41] No one, mercifully, took any notice of this dreadful idea for at least two and a half centuries, but it has now become axiomatic that education is conducive to virtue and that social evil is largely the result of improper education. He could have little conception that it was only by virtue of being self-educated that Milton had had time to read so much. His own 'education', in spite of school and university had, as 'Ad Patrem' makes clear, all happened at home. So, when he conducts us 'to a hillside, where I will point ye out the right path of a virtuous and noble education; laborious indeed at the first ascent, but else so smooth, so green, so full of goodly prospect that the harp of Orpheus was not more charming',[42] we can have no doubt that he believed quite literally that education could undo the work of original sin and create a new Paradise. Just as Cromwell's torturing of aged clergymen seemed to Milton a certain sign that God was revealing himself, as his manner is, first to his Englishmen; so, by reading Varro in agriculture and Theophrastus on physiology and Lycurgus on Greek law, it might be possible to undo the Fall of Man.

That was the idea. That it was a pipe-dream, he admitted to Hartlib in his conclusion: 'I am withall persuaded that it may prove much more easy in the assay than it now seems at distance, and much more illustrious: howbeit not more difficult than I imagine . . .'[43]

Not all day, however, can have been spent poring over books, nor telling the boys (what must have been of more immediate concern to their teacher) 'that sublime art which in Aristotle's *Poetics*, in Horace, and the Italian commentaries of Castelvetro, Tasso, Mazzoni and others, teaches what the laws are of a true epic poem'.[44]

Dr Davis was also occupying Milton's attention at this time; even more, Dr Davis's daughter. As the year wore on, and turned into 1645, Milton became increasingly obsessed with divorce. His eyes were paining him – the trouble seems to have begun some time during August 1644 – but he still toiled on, collecting ammunition against his detractors. As a matter of fact, there is nothing much new (by way of information) in either of the divorce pamphlets of 1645, *Tetrachordon* or *Colasterion*, but their rudeness is hilarious.

Colasterion, published on 4 March 1645, replies to an unfortunate *Answer to the Doctrine and Discipline of Divorce* by a lofty assault on its author's ignorance of Greek and Hebrew and on the 'low and homespun expression of his mother English'. To be homespun, in Milton's world-view, is to be contemptible. His tone is nowhere more forceful, or more self-revealing: 'I mean not to dispute philosophy with this pork, who never read any'.[45]

Tetrachordon is only less belligerent in tone because its purpose is more expository. In it, he reiterates the case for divorce on four scriptural heads (hence its title) and he improves on *The Doctrine and Discipline* in style, ease, and forcefulness. Fundamental to his view is the pamphlet's insistence that 'no ordinance human or from heaven can bind against the good of man', as even 'heathens could see'. He would have done better to write 'as *especially* heathens could see'. He attempts to overthrow the traditional notion, propagated since the early days of the Church, that Christians were under ecclesiastical obedience in moral matters, and to replace it with the idea of natural law, based on personal liberty, which even the dictates of Christ could not supercede. Any reader of *Areopagitica* does well to note the order in which he places his authorities. 'We should, in the judgement of Aristotle, not only' –

and then, added, as if an afterthought '– but of Solomon and our Saviour' . . . Nor can there be much doubt, in the same pamphlet, that in telling the story of St Jerome's dream, he thinks Cicero a better teacher than the saint; the Greek tragedians quoted by the apostle more congenial than the apostle himself; and the Athens of Plato a much more wholesome and sensible place than the Rome of Leo X. This attitude, combined still with the quaint notion that Jehovah was intimately interested in English politics and the military operations of the New Model Army, permeates *Tetrachordon* as much as it had *Areopagitica*.

The examples of marital unhappiness in this pamphlet, unlike his earlier pronouncements on the subject, bear a very distinct resemblance to his own case, for he seems to speak of those who marry in great haste and thoughtlessness and, after an initial infatuation, are trapped in an impossible position. Here he does not speak, as he had done earlier, of a husband and wife living together in a state of misery. His tones are vaguer. He speaks merely of the possibility of making the most terrible mistakes and having to live with those mistakes for the rest of life:

> there is nothing in the life of man through our own misconstruction made more uncertain, more hazardous and full of chance than this divine blessing with such favourable significance here conferred upon us, which if we do but err in our choice the most unblamable error that can be, err but one minute, one moment after those mighty syllables pronounced which take upon them to join heaven and hell together unpardonably till death pardon, this divine blessing that looked but now with such a human smile upon us, and spoke such gentle reason, straight vanishes like a fair sky and brings on such a scene of cloud and tempest, as turns all to shipwreck without haven or shore but to a ransomless captivity.[46]

Poor Milton! It is very hard not to think that this represents the way his own marriage seemed to him, the pathetic three weeks of it, as he looked back from the perspective of three years, during none of which he had so much as seen or heard from his wife. After *The Doctrine and Discipline of Divorce* appeared, Richard Powell had even stopped sending repayments of his loan to his son-in-law and Milton was attempting to litigate against him. There really could not have seemed much future in his marriage. As far as Mary was concerned, he must have forgotten what it was like to be in love with her. He was in love with Miss Davis. And the version of his marriage which was easiest, at that date to believe, and easiest to tell Miss Davis, was that he knew that he had made a mistake as soon as the words of the marriage vow were out of his mouth: 'one moment after those mighty syllables pronounced'.

Meanwhile, as he thought himself into this position, what was happening outside London?

The miracle which Cromwell discerned at Marston Moor – when 'God made them as stubble to our swords' (a miracle not unconnected with the fact that he used his cavalry regiment to hack down infantry, while Prince Rupert's horsemen galloped exotically over half a county) – continued to wear down the royalist armies. Simultaneously with the miracle, Cromwell's own career advanced and blossomed. Cromwell's success in the field was matched by a comparative failure by the parliamentary 'moderates' like the Earl of Essex, who was defeated in Cornwall. The clash of interest between these old moderate characters and the Independent faction was becoming more marked; and at each stage of the debate the opinions of Colonel Cromwell and the destiny of England seemed more intertwined.

'If we beat the King ninety-nine times, yet he is King still, and so will his posterity be after him,' [argued the Earl of Manchester at the first parliamentary Council of War]; 'but if the King beat us once we shall all be hanged, and our posterity made slaves.' 'My Lord,' retorted Cromwell, 'if this be so, why did we take up arms at first? This is against fighting ever hereafter. If so, let us make peace, be it ever so base.'[47]

Peace, of course, was the last thing which Cromwell wanted at this stage of his career, but the conflict with Manchester throws into sharp relief the fact that power was passing out of Parliament's hands into those of the Independent faction in the army. It is in this light that we are to read the Self-Denying Ordinance which Cromwell forced through both houses in February 1645, making it impossible for members of either House to hold commissions in the army; or, in other words, giving the sack to peers like Essex and Manchester. Fairfax now became the general of the parliamentary army. Cromwell, like all men who 'live by the will' had an unerring nose for the seat of real power. 'Why did we take up arms at first?' he asked sneeringly. The answer was, of course, to defend the ancient rights and privileges of Parliament. But, now that Parliament had ceased to be powerful, he had ceased to be interested in it.

In the first six months of 1645 Cromwell's military genius was shown to the full. In April his chief task was to prevent the King (in Oxford) from joining Prince Rupert: so he spent most of the time harrying the royal army in Oxfordshire. The Powells cannot fail to have been aware of what was going on. On 24 April, when they had almost certainly heard of, if not read, Milton's divorce pamphlets, Cromwell routed three regiments of the King's Horse at Islip, a village not five miles up the road from Forest Hill. He killed 200 and took away a further 200 prisoners, moving north a little way to Bletchingdon House which he briefly besieged; then south again to Bampton and Faringdon, all the time playing havoc in a small way with the exhausted pockets of royalist troops that he encountered. It was not like a cat playing with a mouse; it was more like a tiger playing with a mouse. For the royalists, it was, for the most part, a series of agitating setbacks, each more depressing than the last. But for Cromwell, it was a series of rehearsals for the great fight.

Northamptonshire was the scene of the last great battle of the first civil war. Prince Rupert assembled a grand array in the presence of the King. None but Cromwell could have dared to hope that God would bring about such complete victory for the parliamentary side:

'I can say this of Naseby . . . When I saw the enemy draw up and march in gallant order towards us, and we a company of poor, ignorant men, to seek how to order our battle – the General having commanded me to order all the horse – I could not, riding alone about my business, but smile out to God in praises, in assurance of victory, because God would, by things that are not, bring to naught things that are. Of which I had great assurance and God did it.'[48]

With our knowledge of Cromwell's supreme expertise at small-scale cavalry operations in an English setting and landscape, in which he had been relentlessly training his Ironsides for six months, his claim to be 'a company of poor ignorant men' may seem a trifle disingenuous. But like all the worst hypocrites, Cromwell actually believed his own lies.

Prince Rupert's failure at Naseby did indeed seem miraculous. It was a defeat from which the royal cause never properly recovered. 'As a Christian', the King feebly wrote to his nephew, 'I must tell you that God will not suffer the rebels to prosper, nor His cause to be overthrown'. Alas, Colonel Cromwell was demonstrating the opposite to be the case: leaving you either with the near despair of Job and the Psalmist at the unexplained problem of triumphant evil; or if you took a more optimistic view (as Milton did at this date) a clear sense that God was at last intervening in English affairs without ambiguity. As in wars before and since, God has a cynical way of being on the side of the most brilliant generals.

For royalists like the Powells, it was of more than theoretical interest. The inevitable defeat of the King meant, apart from anything else, yet more financial hardship. Did they know – how could they? – that six days after the Battle of Naseby, Milton had sent copies of *The Doctrine and Discipline of Divorce* and *Areopagitica* to Bodley's librarian in Oxford?

Someone appears to have told the Powells about Miss Davis. It was some relations of Milton's called Blackborough who lived 'in the lane of St Martin's le Grand'. They were upset by his worrying devotion to Miss Davis and they decided to put a stop to the whole silly business.

Milton was often in the habit of dropping in on the Blackboroughs. One afternoon, in the summer of 1645, as he walked into their parlour in St Martin's Lane, he was told that there was someone waiting for him in the next room. He evidently did not guess who it was, but since the Blackboroughs only watched from a discreet distance, we do not know what words passed between them, as he went next door and found himself face to face with Mary. We have only the vignette which Edward Phillips supplies: Mary, grown to a lovelier womanhood, Milton still remarkably youthful in appearance: the rustling of Mary's skirts as she knelt before him, in tears of confusion, paying homage to her lord and her lover.

BARBICAN

She ended weeping, and her lowly plight,
Immovable till peace obtained from fault
Acknowledged and deplored, in Adam wrought
Commiseration; soon his heart relented
Towards her, his life so late and sole delight,
Now at his feet submissive in distress,
Creature so fair his reconcilement seeking,
His counsel whom she had displeased, his aid,
As one disarmed, his anger all he lost,
And thus with peaceful words upraised her soon.

Paradise Lost, X. 937–46

TRADITION likes to apply those lines to the second phase of Milton's married life. Evidently, though, the reconciliation was a little slower than the original courtship; and the Barbican house 'till such time as he was settled in'[1] was not thrown open to Mary all at once. There was much to be thought of; much adjustment, on both sides, to be made. Of all the incidents in Milton's life, it is from this one that he emerges with most grandeur and goodness of heart. For the last five years we have been used to the sneering, lofty, cross, and satirical voice of the pamphlets. The silence in the Blackboroughs' back parlour is just as eloquent.

Mary lodged for a while with the mother-in-law of Milton's brother Christopher, a Mrs Webber. Mrs Webber lived in St Clement's churchyard and she had been looking after Thomasine during Christopher's absence in the wars. There the two daughters-in-law of old Mr Milton lived together for a while. Soon, Mary and her husband would be together again.

Her beauty, at twenty-one, was more alluring than the pouting girl of seventeen, and probably had much to do with Milton's spirit of forgiveness towards her, if forgiveness towards *her* was necessary. But there were things to be discussed. She must realize that she could not simply run away the next time her mother suggested it.

The point scarcely needed making. As soon as the house in the

Barbican was ready, she came to join him; she found herself living with a father-in-law, now eighty-two; the little nephews, now grown out of recognition and on the edge of manhood, and one or two rather grand pupils she had not met before.

In the merciful way that it does, life continued. There she was to stay, Mrs Milton, until she died. Whether she was happy, history does not record. There is absolutely no reason to suppose that she was not as happy as any other married woman. Edward Phillips tells us that their first child was born 'within a year'. Her three years away had perhaps made her a better household manager, and she had more to fill her days while her husband was closeted with the boys, or the old gentleman, 'without the least trouble imaginable', played the chamber organ which was carted from place to place during Milton's frequent moves of house.

The younger Milton was by now suffering from considerable eye-strain which cannot have been helped by poring over proofs in September or October. The forthcoming work was not, this time, another pamphlet, but his collected poetry; the fact that he was so engaged at this date perhaps indicating a new serenity of mood. It was a moment for taking stock, for clearing the desk before the great work began.

His publisher was Humphrey Mosely, who had recently brought out the poems of Edmund Waller with great success. If it was ever seriously supposed that Milton might have become an adjutant-general in Sir William Waller's army, then it was perhaps through this connection that Mosely was lighted upon as a likely publisher.

Mosely suggested having an engraving done of the author as a frontispiece to the volume and he produced a character called William Marshall to do the job. He was an experienced portrait-engraver, and had done portraits for editions of Bacon, Donne, Shakespeare and others in the previous few years.

Milton did not consent to waste time sitting for Marshall; and he offered him, perhaps a trifle vainly, the beautiful painting, now called the Onslow portrait, to copy from. The straight nose, the sensual, slightly girlish mouth, the bright eyes and oval face would all have been easy enough to copy, even if no engraver could ever hope to convey the delicacy of the complexion, or the beautifully textured auburn hair. Perhaps, even though he had been told he looked ten years younger, his thirty-eight years were starting to show; perhaps the hair was not so brown and not so abundant as it had been when he was twenty-one. Perhaps the fact that he was genuinely busy justified this momentary piece of vanity.

Marshall set to work, evidently slightly disconcerted by the difference between the beautiful oil painting and the face of the man who had brought it round to his workshop. The result is ludicrously bad.

One thing is certain; Milton never looked like the Marshall engraving. His right arm, if stretched out, would measure about five feet, and appears to be hideously withered at the wrist. The left arm, in contrast, is only about two foot six in length and is desperately trying to hide itself in the folds of his mantle. His collar is deeply asymetrical and does not appear to clasp properly at the top. And the face! Straggly hair, an ugly frown, a double chin, and a disconcertingly asymmetrical mouth, above which grows half a moustache, vaguely reminiscent of the Laughing Cavalier. If Marshall had done it out of malice, the portrait would surely have been cleverer. It is simply a mess. Perhaps some domestic or manservant, not Milton himself, took the portrait round to Marshall; perhaps the engraver was purely incompetent.

It was sad that the first readers (among the 'general public') of 'Lycidas' and 'L'Allegro' were to be led, by Marshall's ineptitude, to suppose that the poet looked, not merely ugly, but slightly stupid. Milton's complaints to his publisher about this ludicrous appendage to his work were unavailing. They had paid for the engraving now and it would have to stand. Milton then devised a light, humorous way of getting his revenge. Would Marshall very kindly engrave a Greek motto to go under the portrait?

> Ἀμαθεῖ γεγράφθαι χειρὶ τήνδε μὲν εἰκόνα
> Φαίης τάχ' ἄν, πρὸς εἶδος αὐτοφυὲς βλέπων·
> Τὸν δ' ἐκτυπωτὸν οὐκ ἐπιγνόντες φίλοι
> Γελᾶτε φαύλου δυσμίμημα ζωγράφου.

(You would say, perhaps, that this picture was drawn by an ignorant hand, when you looked at the form that nature made. Since you do not recognize the man portrayed, my friends, laugh at this rotten picture of a rotten artist.)

It is a schoolmasterish joke, but a good one of its kind. It is hard to know who comes off worse in the end, though: Marshall, for his incompetence as an engraver, or Milton, our image of whom remains indelibly, however unfairly, affected by that incompetence.

Much more important than the frontispiece is the book itself. At last, a quiet interlude in Milton's domestic life had allowed him to retreat for a while from public controversy and publish to the world the first-fruits of his labour, the poems of John Milton the Londoner, 'Joannis Miltoni LONDINIENSIS POEMATA'. This was the vocation to which he had

devoted himself since childhood, and to which all else in his life had
been made subservient. It was for this, as he had explained semi-
seriously in 'Ad Patrem', that he abjured the professions and the
prospects of worldly success. It was in his capacity as a poet that he had
jokingly implored the 'Captain or colonel, or knight in arms' not to
vandalize the little house in Aldersgate; it was in his capacity as a poet,
with passionate seriousness, that he had, the previous year, defended the
freedom of the Press to the sages of the Presbyterian Areopagus at
Westminster. His whole existence as a human being was bound up with
his destiny as a poet. So this was no mere casual publication of juvenilia
to stop them gathering dust in a desk drawer.

Here, in a single volume, was gathered the most perfect specimen of
pastoral elegy written in any language since the days of Theocritus.
Here, as Sir Henry Wotton had seen all those years ago, was incompa-
rably the greatest masque in English; and here were a series of odes
without rival – 'On the Morning of Christ's Nativity', 'At a Solemn
Music', 'On Time'; and a selection of sonnets which alter the very sense
in which we understand the word *sonnet*. Here, moreover, were Latin
poems which had held the greatest wits of Florence enthralled, which
had charmed the ears of Manso; of cardinals and heretics; of Barberini
and Galileo.

How could this fail to be a day of the most momentous importance,
this 6th of October 1645? There were, however, no queues stretching
down from the 'sign of the Prince's Arms in St Paul's Churchyard'
that day. The poems excited far less attention than the pamphlets
had done. John Milton: oh, the *divorcer*. They had no interest in his
versifying.

Nevertheless, the road, now open to Oxford, which had allowed Mary
to pass up to London and the *Areopagitica* to go to the Bodleian Library,
could now take parcel post. Milton dispatched his poems to follow his
pamphlets. It seems that they did not get there. John Rouse, Bodley's
librarian, who had caused such a fuss nine months before by refusing to
lend the King a book, wrote to tell Milton that the *Poemata* had not
arrived. It inspired Milton to write one of his finest occasional poems,
undeservedly neglected because it is written in Latin.

The poem is called 'Ad Joannem Rousium' but it is addressed, in fact,
not to Rouse, but to the little book, the *libellum* bright with the
spontaneous innocence of his youthful days, as he wandered heedlessly
through the Italian or the English countryside. How far away those days
must have seemed as he penned the lines

Dum vagus Ausonias nunc per umbras
Nunc Britannica per vireta lusit . . .

What thief, he then goes on to ask, could have stolen the little book as it
made its way to Oxford? And what god or god-begotten man ('quis deus,
aut editus deo') will be able to put an end to the confounded civil war,
restore with his sacred power nourishing or genial pursuits, 'studia
alma', and summon back the homeless Muses who are now banished
from almost every corner of England:

Et relegatas sine sede musas
Iam pene totis finibus Angligenum . . .

The poem goes on to sing paeans of praise to the Bodleian Library and
describes Oxford, with what can only be sarcasm, as the divine home of
Phoebus, the sun. But, once arrived in Oxford, and this is the important
point, Milton thinks of his book being read alongside the authors whose
illustrious names were once the lights and are now the true glory of the
Greek and Latin race:

Illic legeris inter alta nomina
Authorum, Graiae simul et Latinae
Antiqua gentis lumina, et verum decus.

The ode is a timely reminder, lest we should think Milton at this date
entirely swallowed up with politics, domesticity, or school-teaching, that
he never ceased to see his prime vocation as being that of a poet: not
merely a poet, but a great poet, whose name would shine in ages and
empires yet unborn. And it is that future generation, he concludes (but
only half humorously) who will be thankful to Rouse for having spared
the volume and kept it for the Bodleian. And there it still lies, in
confirmation of his boast. Much as he believed in the Good Old
Cause – and his belief deepened, not diminished, with the years –
politics was not, to use Phillips's phrase, 'the grand affair perpetually of
his life'. That affair was study; and the purpose of the study was to make
himself into a great poet.

The ode, moreover, shows him to be experimenting in new forms. He
adds a note in Latin explaining the innovation:

This ode consists of three strophes and three antistrophes with a concluding
epode. Though the strophes and antistrophes do not exactly correspond either
in the number of their lines or in the distribution of their particular metrical
units, nevertheless I have cut the poem up in this way in order to make it easier to

read, rather than with a view to imitating any ancient method of versification. . . .
The metres are partly determined by correlation, partly free.

It was a technique which he was to use again when he came to write the
choruses of *Samson Agonistes*. Meanwhile, though Bodley's librarian had
his poems on the shelves, few others seemed interested in them. There
were three editions of Edmund Waller's poetry in 1645; but Milton, that
other poet on Mosely's 'list', had to wait fifteen years before the first
edition of his work looked like selling out.

Milton was longing for the war to end and for appropriate conditions of
peace to allow him to continue with his artistic purpose. But a domestic
crisis of nightmarish magnitude soon brought all thoughts of peace to an
end.

Mary Milton was seven months pregnant when the news reached the
Barbican, in May 1646, that Oxford was yet again under siege. The
parliamentary army had surrounded the city and taken possession,
temporarily of course, of royalist lands and houses round about, including the estates of Richard Powell Esquire of Forest Hill.

The King, his hair cut short, and wearing a false beard, had escaped
just in time. This – though no one could have guessed it at the
time – was the first stage of his journey to the scaffold. While he paused
at Little Gidding, *en route* for Newark, the Powells huddled in Oxford
listening to the thumping of cannon fire. The war was more or less over
and the King's side, incredibly, utterly defeated. Oxford surrendered on
24 June and three days later Richard Powell received a pass from Fairfax
which allowed him 'to repair unto London upon his necessary occasions'.

Once the soldiers, billeted at Forest Hill, had been paid and had
ridden away, there was really no reason why life should not have
continued for the Powells as normal. But what were they to live on?
Without a penny, the wastrel young squire 'repaired unto London' and
turned up on his son-in-law's doorstep in the Barbican, bringing in tow
his wife and three of his sons – George, Archdale, and William – and
two daughters, both, unimaginatively but pleasantly, called Elizabeth.

Milton would have been justified, surely, in turning them away. The
house was not very large (though more spacious than anywhere else he
had ever lived); he had work to be getting on with; and he had no reason
to be grateful to the Powells, who had stolen away his wife, written him
abusive letters, and failed to repay their still considerable debts to him.

Without hesitation, Milton took them all in. It is one of his great, magnanimous moments. He knew, few in our literature can describe better, the torments of domestic irritation. And few men have more valued their quiet. But in the testing moment, Milton emerges simply as a man of honest Christian charity and forbearance. Nothing else can explain his opening the doors of his house in the Barbican and letting in this rabble.

By now he had quite a household. His old father still pottered about, giving no trouble. Some of the pupils were growing up, but some remained. Edward Phillips had probably gone before the Powell invasion; and not a week before they all arrived another of the boys, Thomas Gardiner, was admitted to Emmanuel College, Cambridge on 11 July.

Then, on 29 July, a fast day, at about half past six in the evening, as we learn from the family Bible, Milton's first child was born: a child called Anne.

The next six months were dominated by domestic chaos. The baby was far from well, though her parents were not to foresee then that she would grow up lame and what we would label 'sub-normal'. Richard Powell, too, was failing. On 13 December Milton witnessed his will and on 1 January he died. He was buried in St Giles, Cripplegate. Only two and a half months later, on 15 March, Milton returned to the church, following the body of his own dear old father. Richard Powell was not fifty when he died. Old Mr Milton was eighty-three. Fatherless, Milton and his wife now faced the world together.

'Some natural tears they dropped, but wiped them soon', since Powell was scarcely in his grave before the litigation started. Richard Powell had still owed his son-in-law £1,372 when he died. But this was only a small part of the almost Gothic confusion in which he left his financial affairs. So, on 11 February, a month before his own father died, Milton had to go into court to be sued by Sir Robert Pye, an MP who disputed his right to any share in the Powell estate.

Jarndyce and Jarndyce was going strong even in the seventeenth century and here is not the place to explain in detail the way in which Pye claimed possession of Forest Hill and its surrounding lands on Powell's death.[2] After the suit had been filed in the Court of Chancery Milton was persuaded by his counsel to reckon his £1,372 as lost, and he renounced his claim on the Forest Hill estate. His counsel in the case was John Bradshaw. On the very day on which the case was heard, Bradshaw became Chief Justice of Chester. His name was to be written in blood in the history books, for it was he, a couple of years later, who presided over the trial of the King.

Milton versus Pye dragged on, of course, deep into the winter, but the interest of it, such as it was, was over by early autumn.

Some time in the spring Milton heard from an old voice from the past, Carlo Dati, his friend from Florence. Dati had written to thank Milton for 'Epitaphium Damonis' and he had sent two letters subsequently, but in the chaos of the Civil War the letters had evidently not got through. In Milton's reply, we glimpse how lonely he was in the Barbican. Surrounded by domestic turmoil, how far away those evenings seemed, when he would talk far into the night with his Italian friends.

'Those who are closely bound to me', he replied to Dati,

by the mere fact of proximity or by some other tie of no real importance, as by chance or by some legal claim, although they have nothing else to commend themselves to me are with me daily, they deafen me with their noise, and I swear, torment me as often as they please; whereas those endeared to me by congenial manners and temperament and taste are almost all separated from me by death or by the cruel accident of distance, and are usually snatched from my sight so swiftly that I seem compelled to spend my days in almost perpetual loneliness.[3]

Nor was the chief of his worries the raucous voice of Mrs Powell, with her perpetual fussing over pillow-cases and puddings. The terrible and depressing state of the nation somehow made it impossible to get on with any serious work 'in the midst of civil war, bloodshed and rapine'.

At some stage during August 1647, it would seem Mrs Powell and her five children found somewhere else to live, and the house in the Barbican reassumed an atmosphere of calm. But the silence was not a restful one. It had never been a restful house, never a particularly happy one. It was a house where two men had died in the space of a few months. His favourite pupil and nephew had left him there. A baby had been born, and had been ill, there. There had been endless quarrels with his mother-in-law. At the first opportunity he moved house yet again, this time to a smaller place in High Holborn, on the edge of Lincoln's Inn Fields.

Here, Edward Phillips tells us, 'he lived a private and quiet life, still prosecuting his studies and curious search into knowledge . . . till such time as, the war being now at an end, with complete victory to the Parliament's side, as the Parliament then stood purged of all its dissenting members and the King after some treaties with the army, *re Infecta*, brought to his trial'.[4]

CHAPTER 10

PROPAGANDIST

Gyant, quoth Guy, y'are quarrelsome I see,
Choller and you seem very neere of kin:
Most dangerous at the clubb belike you bee . . .

Percy's *Reliques of English Poetry*,
'Guy and Amarant'

In approaching this matter, the whole point really is,
what kind of God do you believe in? . . . Nothing can
possibly be right which makes God wrong.

The Letters of Father Andrew, SDC

THE only immediate consequence of the King's execution, as far as the
subject of this book goes, was that Milton was given an honorific but
irksome job in the new republican government: he became Secretary for
Foreign Tongues on 20 March 1649. But the long-term consequences
were much greater, for it was in the course of the next decade that the
tensions were to arise in Milton's view of the world which were to be
creatively reflected in *Paradise Lost*.

First, though, for the first time in his life, he had a job. He had almost
certainly hoped, during the early 1630s, for some kind of ecclesiastical
preferment, which would bring him and his poetry into the recognition
he deserved. But his scorn for the Laudian clergy and his father's private
income had nullified this ambition. Political preferment, in those days,
had seemed a far-off possibility. He had started to sympathize with the
party of rebellion to the King, and, in some discontentment, but with the
blessing of one of the most learned and famous of English diplomats, he
had gone abroad. In Italy, recognition of the kind he had hoped for from
the English, had come. Gaddi, Bonmatthei, Dati and the rest – and
above all the Neapolitan Manso, had confirmed his belief in his own
genius. And yet, even surrounded by Neoplatonists like himself who saw
the greatness of his writing, he felt uneasy. Not only was his life
threatened. Not only did he meet fellow-countrymen like Thomas

Gawen, or like the seminarians at the English College, actively and surreptitiously engaged in plotting to make England Catholic once more: he also came face to face with the intellectual consequences of Catholicism as a political system: he met Galileo.

If England was not to have a Galileo, if Milton's countrymen were not to be enthralled by priestly censors and inquisitors, if intellectual freedom was worth striving for, then he must go home and expose the dangers of the Catholic system, to which, inexorably, with his high doctrine of the office and function of the episcopate, William Laud approximated. The bishops must go, Milton had argued, and they went.

In all the bloody and chaotic years of the wars, which had caused a false start in his own marriage, and the division of his brother's family, Milton had watched, with what must have been a mixture of satisfaction and awe, the opinions he had striven towards gain general acceptance. No one could accuse Milton of watching the wind to see which way it would blow. The opposite is the truth. But during the 1640s the movement of national events seemed to be following the movement of his own mind. He had thrown in his lot briefly with the Presbyterians: England had become Presbyterian. He had quickly seen that 'New Presbyter is but old priest writ large'. No sooner had he had the insight, than the Independent party in the army, of which Cromwell seemed to be the most eloquent mouthpiece, appeared in the ascendant. He had argued for divorce, and that was still a plea which went unheeded. But his general plea for religious freedom was being granted. In his historical researches and writings towards the end of the war he had worked towards the position of seeing regicide as 'the only effectual cure of ambition that I have read'. And now, the King was dead, tried by a court over which Milton's counsel in Chancery, John Bradshaw, had presided; destroyed, if one simple cause can be found for so strange an event, by the magnetic and powerful destiny of Oliver Cromwell (though Bradshaw, of course, remained at this date President of the Council).

In all these things, which, ten years before they happened would have seemed quite unthinkable, it was surely not absurd to see the workings of divine providence. And a belief in divine providence – it is tautologous to say so but it needs to be insisted upon – necessarily involves a belief that things come about as a result of God's almighty will. On both sides, therefore, the King's death on a scaffold in Whitehall was, and remains, a religious event. John Evelyn wrote in his diary, 'the villainy of the rebels proceeding now so far as to try, condemn and *murder* our excellent King, the 30 of this month, struck me with such horror that I kept this day of his *martyrdom* a fast, and would not be present, at that execrable wickedness'.[1] This was a point of view which Milton very earnestly contested; but he contested it, not as an atheist would do, but because he accepted the terms on which the royalist horror was founded. God was at work in the world. The death of the King was either a holy martyrdom (for this is what all the royalists started to claim) or it was the righteous deposition of a tyrant, a divine act, just as God had raised up his hand against Og, King of Bashan, against Saul or against Ahab. 'To bind their kings in chains' had been Hugh Peter's text in his sermon on the royal execution. The English revolution, therefore, as it is now sometimes termed, was a fundamentally religious affair in which both sides were attempting to 'assert eternal providence'. ' "This man against whom the Lord hath witnessed", Cromwell had said in justifica-tion of the act. But the King had read the will of the Almighty in a different sense and had been equally sure that he had "a just cause and a Gracious God" '.[2]

Unlike the French Revolution, or the October uprising in Moscow in 1917, the destruction of the English monarchy was a religious act – the fulfilment of the divine will or blasphemy depending on your point of view. We miss the feel of Milton's position at this date if we choose to read his regicide pamphlets – *The Tenure of Kings and Magistrates, Eikonoklastes* or the *Pro Populo Anglicano Defensio* – in an aridly political light. Consider this from a modern historian:

We are facing here the problem of any revolutionary minority which claims to act on behalf of the people, whether this is expressed by Jean-Jacques Rousseau as forcing to be free or by the Bolsheviks as the dictatorship of the proletariat. In the twentieth century we are suspicious of the notion of dictatorship on behalf of democracy; but the fact that the problem has proved insoluble does not mean that we should dismiss it ... Milton's age was facing for the first time the problem of educating the electorate.[3]

This, of course, is the unmistakable voice of the former Master of Balliol College, Oxford, who has succeeded in educating, not an electorate, but generations of students of the seventeenth century. While conceding that 'Milton's advocacy of revolutionary dictatorship together with freedom among a wide ruling élite should not be equated with Stalin-ism', Christopher Hill's rhetoric inevitably suggests some such equation at the back of the reader's mind. For Carlyle, Cromwell's generation was indescribably poignant and grand because it was the last 'practical world based on belief in God'.[4] But for Dr Hill, *Eikonoklastes* is not the swan-song of an old world: rather it is the first blast of a trumpet which we will hear again in the company of Rousseau, Engels and Marx; the opening of a new page, which will stretch in happy line down the shelf, past Bentham and Herbert Spencer, Shaw and the Webbs, the faded orange bindings of the Left Book Club, until we reach the voluminous outpourings of Dr Hill himself.

Dr Hill has an excess of hindsight, a useful quality in an historian, but not the only useful one. Looking back, the English revolution probably can be made to have much in common with subsequent European strugglings towards republicanism or freedom. In historical terms, these can be weighed and argued about. No one has argued about them more stimulatingly than Dr Hill himself; and he has done so much to promote his own view of seventeenth-century history that whole generations of readers have forgotten how idiosyncratic and distinctive it is. Having been something of a heresy, Dr Hill's view of the English revolution, in many circles at least, is now an orthodoxy. Carlyle's view, that the essence of these years is a religious mystery, is not rejected; it has been so completely forgotten that it is not even considered.

From the point of view of the mind which created *Paradise Lost*, however, it is not safe to view 1649 as a quaint kind of limbering up for 1789, 1848, and 1917. It was the last date in history in which God acted without ambiguity. Milton, a seer as well as a poet, stirred with the event. He had not been seeking a political career. His appointment as Secretary for Foreign Tongues did not come about as a result of political lobbying. By vocation he was a poet, a scholar, and a teacher. Religious conviction had first pushed him forward into the political arena as a pamphleteer: a conviction that God was working his purpose out, completing the Reformation, and revealing Himself, as his manner is, 'first to his Englishmen'. Milton had small feeling, if any, for what might be called 'personal Christianity'. His Protestant faith had nothing in common with the evangelicalism of later generations. But it led him firmly to a vision of God's active involvement in human history:

For when God shakes a kingdom with strong and healthful commotions to a general reforming . . . true it is, that God raises to his own, men of rare abilities.[5]

It was this fact which explains Milton's appointment as Secretary for Foreign Tongues. God was raising to his own men of rare abilities indeed. Milton was bound to interpret his sudden political acceptance in this way. The only alternative was too horrifying to contemplate. Either it was God's will that King Charles had his head chopped off, or it was not. No one in 1649 appeared to think, as a modern theologian might believe, that God was in two minds over the question. The royalists could claim immediately that the Lord's anointed had been slain, that a blasphemy had been perpetrated. Milton, who lived 'as ever in my great task-master's eye' was convinced, in 1649, of the opposite truth.

Small wonder that, when he came to write the *De Doctrina Christiana* after the collapse of his political hopes, Milton should have appeared to lose faith in God's omnipotence. Not so at the beginning. We completely lose the flavour of the early years of Cromwell's Protectorate if we speak about the politics in purely secular terms. For thinking men the establishment of a republic was either a sombre manifestation of God's will or it was a blasphemy. For Milton, ready to serve the Good Old Cause as a way of serving his task-master was either 'in bold conspiracy against Heaven's king'[6] or he was a 'man of ability' being raised up because God was shaking the kingdom with 'strong and healthful commotions'. When the commotions ceased to be strong or healthful, it began to look as though he had, perhaps, been a rebellious archangel. It was a thought which 'full counsel must mature',[7] which could never be made explicit. But it is this, fundamentally religious and personal position which makes Milton's years as Secretary to the Council seem so interesting in the light of his greatest poetry.

What did the job entail? To outward appearances, it seems a fairly tame appointment, more worthy of the talents of a trained diplomat than of an artist. It was to be his task to sit in, as an interpreter and adviser, during meetings with foreign powers. He was to translate letters for the Council, and compose them, at their dictation. But unlike the real Council members, men like Bulstrode Whitelocke (a Horton man), Sir Henry Vane, Lord Lisle, Bradshaw (first President) and of course Cromwell and the rest, Milton had no vote. Why did they enlist *his* services, then? Would not some tame linguist have done as well, one without the added infirmity of poor eyesight?

Milton doubtless took the job out of a sense of duty and because, as the father of a young family, he was glad of the money. It was now apparent that his child Anne was mentally retarded, as well as having some minor physical handicap. Her sister Mary was still a young baby. He appears to have moved about quite frequently to different lodgings, sometimes with, perhaps sometimes without the babies; clearly his work as Secretary occupied regular hours and he had to be near Westminster. Perhaps Bradshaw, who had represented him in his unsuccessful

Chancery case against Sir Robert Pye, trying to claim his money from the Powell estate, realized that Milton needed the money.

What the Council needed, of course, was not an Anthony Eden but a Lord Beaverbrook; not a diplomat, but a propagandist. And in Milton they found the perfect man. Obviously, he earned his money in all kinds of ways. He clearly made an energetic and punctilious civil servant, and the record of his first year of work is impressive: an official Latin translation of Parliament's *Declaration*, establishing its new republican government; endless letters to foreign governments, ranging from negotiations with the Company of Merchant Adventurers at Hamburg about passports to quarrels between the Admiralty and the Moroccan governor of Tetuan. There was the task of setting the Public Record Office in order, which Milton supervised. There was, unpleasantly perhaps for the author of *Areopagitica*, a certain amount of censorship work. He had to investigate papers seized from Lady Mary Killigrew, John Lee, and the notorious pamphleteer Marchamont Needham, who subsequently became a friend. There were the books of Clement Walker and William Small. But, rightly, posterity has forgotten these piffling tasks. They could have been done by any literate Wykehamical scholar, and it is amazing that Milton ever wasted his time on them. What the Council actually wanted from him was rhetoric.

Before he was appointed – almost certainly, the reason that he was appointed – he had written a pamphlet, published on 13 February 1649, called *The Tenure of Kings and Magistrates; proving, that it is lawful, and hath been so through all ages, for any, who have the power, to call to account a tyrant, or wicked king, and after due conviction, to depose, and put him to death, if the ordinary magistrate have neglected, or denied to do it. And that they who of late, so much blame deposing, are the men that did it themselves.*

The title gives a fair summary of what Milton's thesis was. He took it as axiomatic that 'the power of kings and magistrates is nothing else, but what is only derivative, transferred and committed to them in trust from the people, to the common good of them all'.[8] This Wat Tylerish sentiment is delivered in characteristically disdainful tones: 'No man who knows aught, can be so stupid to deny that all men naturally were born free, being the image and resemblance of God himself, and were by privilege above all the creatures, born to command and not to obey . . .'[9] It is typical of Milton to wish to make non-republicans seem *stupid*.

He reserves his longest sentences and his most scathing abuse in *The Tenure* for the Presbyterians. He points out that it was the Presbyterian government of John Knox which deposed Mary Queen of Scots, and that it was the Presbyterian involvement in the Civil War which helped to defeat Charles I. But now the Presbyterians were bleating about the wrongness of the execution.

The relation between king and subject can be no other than regal authority and subjection. Hence I infer past their defending, that if the subject who is one relative, take away the relation, of force he takes away also the other relative; but the Presbyterians who were one relative, that is to say subjects, have for this seven years taken away the relation, that is to say the king's authority, and their subjection to it, therefore the Presbyterians for these seven years have removed and extinguished the other relative, that is to say the king, or to speak more in brief have deposed him; not only by depriving him the execution of his authority, but by conferring it upon others.[10]

It was Cromwell's old argument against the Earl of Manchester. 'If this be so, why did we take up arms at first?' Milton scornfully remembers how the Presbyterians had behaved in the war: 'Have they not hunted and pursued him round the kingdom with sword and fire? Have they not formerly denied to treat with him, and their now recanting ministers preached against him as a reprobate incurable, an enemy to God and his Church marked for destruction?' It was these people, Milton almost certainly knew, who were now suing and negotiating with Charles II. The fullness and gleefulness of his invective in attacking the ministers suggests that his feelings for Thomas Young, the Smectymnuan who had dared attack his divorce pamphlets, were now less than kind: his anti-clericalism often produces his strongest, and his most amusing writings, and the Presbyterian divines get off no lighter than the Laudian parsons who, ten or twelve years before, had for their bellies' sakes crept and intruded and climbed into the fold:

Ministers of sedition, not of the Gospel, who while they saw it manifestly tend to civil war and bloodshed, never ceased exasperating the people against him [i.e. Charles I]; and now that they see it likely to breed new commotion, cease not to incite others against the people that have saved them from him, as if sedition were their only aim, whether against him or for him. But God, as we have cause to trust, will put other thoughts into the people, and turn them from giving ear or heed to these mercenary noisemakers of whose fury, and false prophecies we have enough experience.[11]

So the pamphlet proceeds, moving from pungent epigram – 'It is the glory of a Protestant King never to have deserved death' – to unwieldy assaults on his former allies, 'a pack of clergymen by themselves to belly-cheer in their presumptuous Sion', who, during the Westminster

Assembly, had not stuck to religion as they should have done, but were forever 'progging and soliciting the Parliament, though they had renounced the name of priests, for a new settling of their tithes and oblations'.[12] Full of sentences as rude and as backwardly irrational as this, *The Tenure* deserves to be better known. And it was because of *The Tenure* that the Council took him on.

No sooner had the King been executed than (as we have said) the royalists began to speak of his death as a martyrdom. The propaganda effect of this viewpoint, whatever its justification in terms of historical fact, was immense. To canonize the previous government is a natural human tendency. When combined with a fear that a blasphemy had been committed, there was no difficulty in whipping up popular support for Charles I after his death. At the time of his trial, of course, as more than one historian has pointed out, not one royalist voice was raised in the King's defence. It was only Lady Fairfax, from the public gallery, who had the courage to interrupt Bradshaw's assertion that the King was tried in the name of the people of England with the words, 'not half, not a quarter of the people of England. Oliver Cromwell is a traitor'.[13]

By October 1649, however, the truth of her outburst was proven, with the publication of a spurious volume, purporting to be an *apologia pro vita sua* of the King, interlaced with prayers and devotions. It was called *Eikon Basilike*, the *Royal Image*, and it appeared on 6 October with an engraved frontispiece by, of all people, William Marshall, the same man who, four years before, had provided such an execrable portrait for Milton's own poems.[14]

On this occasion Marshall came up, not with a warty, lopsided poet with withered arms, but with a contortionist monarch who would have defied the deftest executioner, since he appears to have no neck, and his head does not really fit on to his shoulders. His thigh bones run into his ribs. He is depicted in a kneeling position. One hand affectedly clutches at his collar (perhaps because it appears to have worked its way round to his shoulders rather than meeting at the neck); the other, with fingers eighteen inches long and thick as bananas, holds a crown of thorns. The whole icon is filled with appropriately pious mottoes and emblems. A crown of glory, bright with seven stars, hovers outside the somewhat Inigo Jones-style window. And the sunbeam, labelled 'Caeli Specto', shoots out in a straight line from the martyr's eye, somehow emphasizing the rather uncertain perspective of Marshall's architectural draughtsmanship. The book on the altar in front of the saint carries the legend 'In Verbo Tuo Spes Mea'.

Milton has sharp words to say about Marshall's work: 'quaint emblems and devices begged from the old pageantry of some twelfth night's entertainment at Whitehall, will do but ill to make a saint or martyr'.[15] But, clearly, the Council was more concerned with the contents of the book, and its popularity. (Something like sixty editions were exhausted within the year.) The little King, so tactless, ruthless, and charmless in life, so little loved by his people, was loved in death.

In the very oblique 'Horatian Ode upon Cromwell's Return from Ireland', written in the next year by Milton's young friend Andrew Marvell, the poet acknowledged Charles's impeccable demeanour in his final hour, adding with peculiar fancy that it was like the discovery (related by Pliny) of a human head on the Capitol in Rome, said to be a good omen for the republic:

> He nothing common did or mean
> Upon that memorable scene;
> > But with his keener eye
> > The axe's edge did try;
>
> Nor called the Gods, with vulgar spite,
> To vindicate his helpless right,
> > But bowed his comely head
> > Down, as upon a bed.
>
> This was that memorable hour
> Which first assured the forced power:
> > So when they did design
> > The Capitol's first line,
>
> A bleeding head, where they begun,
> Did fright the architects to run;
> > And yet in that the State
> > Foresaw its happy fate!

With the tenderest wit and delicacy Marvell manages to acknowledge the virtues of the King, while rejecting a belief in the *Eikon Basilike*. The 'royal actor' was too good a man to have called the gods with the sort of 'vulgar spite' which the *Royal Image* attributes to him. Thus, he can dismiss the vulgar royalist propagandists by suggesting that Charles was too good a man to be a saint of their making; the bloodiness of his end was, at the same time, good for the nation.

The paradoxes inherent in Marvell's 'Horatian Ode' are doubtless ones which Milton enjoyed; but the opinions behind the ode needed to be made more painstakingly, more bluntly, if the deeply attractive *Eikon* was not to do damage to the republic. The Image must be broken. He did not, as he told his readers, take on the task of breaking it himself. It was a burden laid upon him, 'a work assigned rather than by me chosen or affected'.[16] With a boldness which most men would have shrunk from he accepted the Council's request, and he adopted the task of being the Image Breaker. That is what his reply – *Eikonoklastes* – means.

It was essential to him to establish, little as he delighted in descanting 'on the misfortunes of a person fallen from so high a dignity',[17] not only that the book under discussion was a fake, but that it was, after all, the right thing to have done to get rid of the King. He is unable, therefore, to allow himself the subtlety of Marvell's recognition of Charles's virtue. He calls to mind

those faithful and courageous barons, who lost their lives in the field, making glorious war against tyrants for the common liberty; as Simon de Montfort Earl of Leicester against Henry the third; Thomas Plantagenet Earl of Lancaster, against Edward the Second. But now with a besotted and degenerate baseness of spirit, except some few, who yet retain in them the old English fortitude and love of freedom, and have testified it by their matchless deeds, the rest, embastardized from the ancient nobleness of their ancestors, are ready to fall flat and give adoration to the image and memory of this man, who hath offered at more cunning fetches to undermine our liberties, and put tyranny into an art, then any British king before him.[18]

Eikonoklastes somehow lacks the fire of Milton's best pamphleteering. He answers the inaccuracies of *Eikon Basilike* point by point, like a civil servant sending back a report to his Minister. Of course, it is an easy matter for Milton to unpick the pastiche, and show that in the last prayers of the martyr 'he consulted neither with the liturgy, nor with the directory, but neglecting the huge fardel of all their honeycomb devotions, went directly where he doubted not to find better praying, to his mind with Pamela in the Countess's *Arcadia*'.[19] As we know from other places, Milton actually admired Sidney's *Arcadia*, but his discovery of this little piece of fraud is put to good double use: not only is Charles's prayer a palpable fiction, written by Sir Philip Sidney, it is also evidence .that he treated the Book of Common Prayer with the indifference which it deserved. In fact, of course, as Milton must have known, Charles was doggedly faithful to his beloved Prayer Book to the end; Bishop Juxon read him the services from it on the morning of his death. But, just as royalist propagandists had already mythologized the martyrdom – making of the execution a Christ-like *passio*, in which the King was buffeted and spat upon by the vulgar soldiery,[20] so Milton, in answering, is less interested in the sobriety of truth than in the demolition of a falsehood. His old adversaries in the episcopal and divorce controversies had fallen like nine-pins before his darting satirical blows, his sharp debating points. But here he was not dealing with blunderingly inadequate arguments: he was confronting a myth. Vainly he inveighs against 'an inconstant, irrational and image-doting rabble'.[21] In rhetorical terms his painstaking (and frequently faithful) attempts to remind the reading public of Charles's duplicity and arrogance were as effectual as throwing paper darts at an elephant. Milton never understood the 'irrational and image-doting rabble' – the human race to which most of us belong. He was an image-breaker: teaching the age to quit its clogs, and holding it in the deepest contempt when it failed to do so. Politically, of course, the English monarchy was to evolve along the lines expounded in *The Tenure of Kings and Magistrates*. Except, perhaps, for Oliver Cromwell, there has never been an absolutist monarch in England since 1649.

Eikonoklastes is addressed to English readers. But what did the rest of the world make of the fact that the English had chopped off the head of their King? In the year immediately after the event, Europe was shocked. It would come round; after a firm government had been established under the Protectorate of Cromwell, the Spanish were the first to recognize it as the official and legally established regime; most other European heads of state did the same. But it was all much less certain in 1649 and 1650. Accounts of the King's trial appeared in French, Dutch, German, Latin, Italian, and Polish. Poets exploded with tragedies, panegyrics, and epigrams:

> Irritez vous, mortels, ligues vos potentats,
> Fondez sur cet état avec tous vos états,
> Faites partout la paix pour lui faire la guerre.[22]

wrote St Amant, urging the potentates of Europe to stop fighting each other, and unite to crush the English. In May 1649 Isaac Dorislaus, who had helped John Cook to draw up the charge against the King, was murdered in the Hague; and a year later, Anthony Ascham, sent as ambassador to Spain, was also murdered. In neither case did the Dutch or Spanish government prosecute the murderers. The republic, then, needed an apology addressed to the continent of Europe.

In November 1649 the Council in London took steps (unsuccessfully) to prevent the importation of a book called *Defensio Regia* by Salmasius. And on 8 January 1650, the minutes of the Council recorded, as an order, that 'Mr Milton do prepare something in answer to the book of Salmasius, and when he hath done it to bring it to the Council'.[23]

Milton undertook the task, we can believe, with very mixed feelings. The sight in his left eye had almost completely gone; the sight in the right was fading. In addition, he felt ill, and his strength was failing. But he undertook the task with eagerness. When he wrote it, two sides of his nature came together for the first time: his patriotism, and his desire for a European reputation; the author of *Areopagitica*, and the disciple of Manso; the man who turned for home, but lingeringly, in 1639. Salmasius was thought to be one of the greatest scholars of his age. Edward Phillips, no very keen republican, writes with justifiable pride of his uncle's reply to Salmasius:

out comes in public the great kill-cow of Christendom, with his *Defensio Regis contra Populum Anglicanum*: a man so famous and cried up for his *Plinian Exercitations*, and other pieces of reputed learning, that there could nowhere have been found a champion that durst lift up the pen against so formidable an adversary, had not our little English David had the courage to undertake this great French Goliath to whom he gave such a hit in the forehead, that he presently staggered, and soon after fell; for immediately upon the coming out of the answer, entitled, *Defensio Populi Anglicani, contra Claudium Anonymum etc.* he till then had been Chief Minister and Superintendent in the Court of the learned Christina Queen of Sweden, dwindled in esteem to that degree, that he at last vouchsafed to speak to the meanest servant. In short, he was dismissed with so cold and slighting an adieu that after a faint dying reply, he was glad to have recourse to death, the remedy of evils, and ender of controversies.[24]

Milton's *Defensio*, by general consent, destroyed the arguments, if not the life of Salmasius. By the time it was published it was no longer necessary as a piece of propaganda. The triumphs of Cromwell at Worcester, Drogheda, and Dunbar and the recovery of English naval strength in the hands of the republic, had established the republic, for the time being at least. That does not diminish the heroism of Milton's *Defensio*. Not only is it a great *tour de force*, a dismissal of Polonius by Hamlet, but it is a work of personal heroism, too, written, as he tells the reader, 'piecemeal', since he is forced by the weakness of his body to break off every hour or so. To Edward Phillips, as to *Mercurius Politicus*,[25] it seemed like the defeat of Goliath by a puckish little David. To Milton, who destroyed his health in the writing of it, it must have felt more like the mixed triumphs of Samson.

Three years after he considered himself to be totally blind, Milton wrote one of his most delightful sonnets to his young friend and pupil,

Cyriack Skinner, a poem in which Milton demonstrates how fully he has made the sonnet fit his own purpose, removed, as it were, from the tradition of Petrarch and adapted to that of Horace. The carefully measured lines give all the light impression of conversation; and conversation with Skinner was, plainly, intelligent, fast moving, slightly gossipy, as Milton liked. Yet, the conclusion of a Miltonic sonnet is always inexorable and strong. To the young friend's casual question, of what supports him in his darkness, Milton replies with his characteristic, and unChristian Stoicism, that it is his certainty of having been in the right, his knowledge that writing the *Defensio* had hastened the coming of his total blindness:

> Cyriack, this three years' day these eyes, though clear
> To outward view, of blemish or of spot;
> Bereft of light their seeing have forgot,
> Nor to their idle orbs doth sight appear
> Of sun or moon or star throughout the year,
> Or man or woman. Yet I argue not
> Against heaven's hand or will, nor bate a jot
> Of heart or hope; but still bear up and steer
> Right onward. What supports me dost thou ask?
> The conscience, friend, to have lost them overplied
> In liberty's defence, my noble task,
> Of which all Europe talks from side to side.
> This thought might lead me through the world's vain mask
> Content though blind, had I no better guide.

By a paradoxical twist of fortune, fame, which he had dreamed of in his youth as something which would come to him as a result of his poetry, had come about because of his skills as a controversialist, gifts hardly thought about when he was writing 'Lycidas'. His poems were still unbought; his English poems, at least, were largely unheard-of.

That, of course, did not diminish his sense of himself as a poet. Rather, his going blind emphasized with cruel force the absence of any major poetic output since 'Lycidas' had been written. At thirty, he had viewed with horror the prospect of being cut off 'dead ere his prime', like Edward King. But the great works, the dramas of *Adam Unparadised*, the *Arthuriad*, the national epic, remained unwritten. There had been sonnets. There had been the delightful Latin ode to Rouse at Oxford, and the Latin elegy for his friend Charles Diodati – the 'Epitaphium Damonis'. But considering the heights of Milton's poetic ambitions and aspirations, there had been quite astonishingly little output. If one

compares Milton's *oeuvre* at forty-one or two with that of Chaucer,
Spenser, or Shakespeare (not to mention Wordsworth or Browning) at a
comparable age, it is extraordinarily slender. And the huge proportion of
it had been penned before he was thirty. Not only had he aggravated his
eye trouble, made himself blind, 'in liberty's defence', but he had
neglected his poetic vocation.

Milton was much absorbed in the parable of the talents. Perhaps as
early as his three-and-twentieth year he was judging his life in the light
of it; the 'task-master' at the end of that seventh sonnet recalling the
scriptural dispenser of talents who is described as a 'hard man', an
'austere man'.[26] In the parable the 'unprofitable servant' is cast away into
outer darkness for, as it were, putting his talent into cold storage. 'I was
afraid and went and hid thy talent in the earth'. In poetic terms this
clearly means, for Milton, not writing. Through the years at Hammersmith and Horton he had been afraid of putting pen to paper until he was
ready to write the perfect poem. 'Lycidas' had been forced out of
him – 'bitter constraint' had made him shatter the leaves of laurel and
myrtle before the mellowing year. Now the year was mellowing, and it
looked as if the tree had already withered. Just as, politically, Milton had
argued himself into a position where he was either siding with a God
who 'smote great kings' or rebelling with hideous blasphemy against the
Lord who anointed Charles I's head so, in his literary career, he began to
feel the chilly sense that he was not, after all, on God's side. He had
neglected 'that one talent which is death to hide', and God, like the 'hard
man' he revealed himself to be in the parable, had cast him into 'outer
darkness'. With the intensely moving paradox which lies at the heart of
his Christian stoicism, Milton shows himself to be above the taunts of
such a task-master. If God lacks the patience to see that he will one day
be fruitful, Milton does not. He will wait, 'until this tyranny be
over-passed'. He is sure that he has done right in serving the republic
and the cause of liberty. He is equally sure that he serves God aright
now. In earlier poems, Milton has reassured his friends and relations
that their names will survive to posterity because of their association with
him: his father, the 'Captain or colonel, or knight in arms', Harry Lawes,
will all be remembered as long as poetry is remembered. In his sixteenth
sonnet, written, one may assume, very shortly after he had gone blind,
Milton delivers (by implication) a similar reassurance to the Almighty.
In so far as God is the 'hard man' of the parable, he looks only for results,
for 'day-labour'. But Milton's constancy powerfully and movingly will
remind him of another type of service, such as angels and archangels and

poets can give. At the moment it is the turn of the English republic; but the day will come when God, as his manner is, will reveal himself to his Englishmen, and be glad of an Englishman, to 'justify his ways . . . to men':

> When I consider how my light is spent,
>   Ere half my days, in this dark world and wide,
>   And that one talent which is death to hide,
>   Lodged with me useless, though my soul more bent
> To serve therewith my maker, and present
>   My true account, lest he returning chide,
>   Doth God exact day-labour, light-denied,
>   I fondly ask; But Patience to prevent
> That murmur, soon replies, God doth not need
>   Either man's work or his own gifts, who best
>   Bear his mild yoke, they serve him best, his state
> Is kingly. Thousands at his bidding speed
>   And post o'er land and ocean without rest:
>   They also serve who only stand and wait.

While he stood and waited, it was only a triumphantly self-confident inner sense of his own righteousness which could stave off the disturbing thought that He whose 'state is kingly' had plunged the man who had neglected his divine vocation of poetry and defended the Regicides, into the most dense outer darkness.

So much for the outer circumstances of Milton's life in the first two or three years of the republic. Domestically, the Almighty was no less severe. First, there was trouble with his mother-in-law. In 1647, thanks to mediation by Bradshaw, Milton had obtained possession of some cottages in the village of Wheatley, near Forest Hill, in recompense for his loss of income from Richard Powell's unpaid debts to him. While he was hard at work on the *Defensio*, legislation was passed through Parliament to fine any person who had taken possession of property of royalist delinquents since May 1642. The point of this rather sweeping law was to prevent such delinquents enjoying their property while having technically placed it in the hands of some friendly republican. In August 1650 Milton had put in a petition to compound the Wheatley property but it had not gone through, and it took two or three petitions to get it passed; meanwhile, Milton had to pay a fine of £130, and Mrs Powell automatically lost her 'widow's thirds' which entitled her to a share of the income from the Wheatley property.

She accordingly set about suing Milton. She had lost almost all her income, and it is by no means clear that he was not secretly rather pleased. To judge from the evidence she submitted to the court, they did not get along very well together. She complained that 'Mr Milton is a harsh and choleric man, and married Mrs Powell's daughter, who would be undone if any such course were taken against him by Mrs Powell, he having turned away his wife heretofore for a long space upon some other occasion'.[27] Probably Mary had by this date turned against her mother; and there was something unreasonable about Mrs Powell expecting Milton to keep her, when she had four sons between the ages of twenty and thirty. Whatever the justice of the matter, it can hardly have contributed to the happiness of life to have all this litigation and wrangling going on while he laboured away, sight and health failing, at the defence of the republic.

Mary, meanwhile, was the mother of three children, and expecting a fourth. Anne, lame and slightly soft in the head, was six; Mary was three and a half; Milton's son John was only a little over a year old, when, on Sunday 2 May 1652, Mary went into labour. The child was called Deborah. Deborah, in the Book of Judges, judged over Israel. Hers is one of the most eloquent, and certainly the most ancient, pieces of epic song. She had sung of the stars in their courses fighting against Sisera; and the enemies of the Lord perishing.

Mary Milton perished, three days after Deborah's birth. She was only twenty-seven. Too much nonsense has been written about Milton's first marriage for it to be possible to disentangle what it was like; but that it was young, and sad in its ending, no one can doubt. Some six weeks after Mary's death Milton also lost his baby son John. The song of Deborah, crowing over the deaths of her enemies, must have echoed strangely in the ears of Milton as he sat alone, his wife of ten years taken from him, and his son; the wailing baby Deborah, whom he would never see: 'Out of Ephraim there was a root of them against Amalek; after thee Benjamin among thy people; out of Machir came down governors, and out of Zebulun they that handle the pen of the writer . . .'

CHAPTER II

HARD SEASON

. . . what may be won
From the hard season gaining?
'Sonnet XVII'

THE *Defensio Secunda* has been described as 'the greatest of Milton's prose works and one of the greatest of the world's rhetorical writings'.[1] One of the reasons for this must be that it allowed him to write about the subject which was, to him, the most consumingly important: himself, and his own personal destiny.

Needless to say, there had been a reaction to his assault on Salmasius. In August 1652 there appeared *Regii Sanguinis Clamor ad Coelum adversus Parricidos Anglicanos* ('The Cry of the Royal Blood to Heaven against the English Parricides'). It was a pamphlet actually written by an Anglican clergyman resident in England, Peter du Moulin. No one suspected this at the time, because the work was printed in the Hague; Milton persisted in believing it was the work of Alexander More. Indeed, four years after its publication, far from being seen as an enemy of the republic, Du Moulin was awarded a DD by the Cromwellian Vice-Chancellor of the University of Oxford.[2]

The title of his piece takes up a phrase from *Eikon Basilike* in which the royal martyr doubts not, 'but my blood will cry aloud for vengeance to heaven'. It contains much personal abuse of Milton himself. It speaks of him as an unheard-of creature 'whether man or worm, lately voided from the dung-heap'.[3] It accuses him of having been sent down from Cambridge, and it describes his defence of the Regicides as the crowing of some hellish gallows-bird.

Milton's reply in *Defensio Secunda* makes it perfectly clear that the year in which he lost his first wife, his son, and his sight was a time of deep and ultimately religious crisis. Salmasius had died a year before the *Defensio Secunda* appeared, but Milton still obsessively takes up the cudgels against him, even though he says that 'I shall not impute his death as a crime to him, as he imputed my blindness to me'. This is a very revealing error. Although the Preface to the *Clamor* hopes that Salmasius will give Milton the castigation he deserves, 'a monster horrible, deformed, huge[!], sightless', Salmasius's actual reply was not published till years later in 1660. Milton anticipates the association between his wickedness (supposed) at having supported the Regicides, and his blindness.

Word by word, with all the unmistakable punctiliousness of wounded vanity, Milton replies to the abusive sentence which, had he considered it rationally for a moment, he would have realized could not have been written by anyone who had ever seen him. How could anyone have ever described him as 'huge'?

'A monster, dreadful, ugly, huge, deprived of sight'. Never did I think that I should rival the Cyclops in appearance. But at once he corrects himself. 'Yet not huge, for there is nothing more feeble, bloodless and pinched.' Although it ill befits a man to speak of his own appearance, yet speak I shall, since here too there is reason for me to thank God and refute liars, lest anyone think me to be perhaps a dog-headed ape or a rhinoceros, as the rabble in Spain, too credulous of their priests, believe to be true of heretics, as they call them. Ugly I have never been thought by anyone, to my knowledge, who has laid eyes on me. Whether I am handsome or not, I am less concerned. I admit that I am not tall, but my stature is closer to the medium than the small. Yet what if it were small, as is the case with so many men of the greatest worth in both peace and war . . .[4]

The great argument, the Good Old Cause, the defence of liberty, has come down to a discussion of whether you would call Milton tall or small. Clearly, he *was* slightly smaller than average and minded about it intensely. He was vain, even when sightless, of his personal appearance, and emphasizes, as in the sonnet to Cyriack Skinner, that his eyes do not have the slightly sinister cloudy appearance of some blind men.

They have as much the appearance of being uninjured, and are as clear and bright, without a cloud, as the eyes of men who see most keenly. In this respect alone, against my will, do I deceive. In my face, than which he says there is 'nothing more bloodless' still lingers a colour exactly opposite to the bloodless and pale, so that although I am past forty, there is scarcely anyone to whom I do not seem younger by about ten years. Nor is it true that either my body or my skin is shrivelled . . .[5]

This sounds more like Sir Walter Elliot than some 'great deliverer' from the Book of Judges. There is something, precisely because of that, poignant and moving about these public displays of personal vanity.

'What are my eyes like – tell me. Have my cheeks really lost their colour?' questions such as this must have been fired at his friends, as his silky hands ran desperately over his forehead, or the sides of his mouth and eyes, trying to detect wrinkles.

Why did he mind so much? Of Sir Walter Elliot we do not ask the question. 'Vanity was the beginning and the end' of his character, and that was that. With Milton, things are a little more complicated. Vanity certainly played a huge part in his character. But more was at stake than the thought of exiled royalists in the Hague mocking his crow's-feet. The debate is not really one against Salmasius (who was dead) or More (whom he merely sets up as an Aunt Sally, to be attacked with a ferocity which is noticeably virulent even by Milton's ungentle standards). The debate is going on at a higher level than that. Cardinal Newman, as an adolescent boy, came to the conclusion that there were 'two and only two supreme and luminously self-evident beings, myself and my Creator'.[6] Milton could very easily have written the same. For him, a self-defence and a defence of the republic were both fulfilling the same function. In terms of propaganda, they were assuring the outside world, perhaps a little too certainly, that 'I have been aided and enriched by the favour and assistance of God'.[7] At the same time his dogged acceptance of God's will, his sense, indeed, that his blindness has brought him closer to God, has been belied by the sonnet 'When I consider how my light is spent'. He can write in the *Defensio Secunda* 'To be sure, we blind men are not the least of God's concerns, for the less able we are to perceive anything other than Himself, the more mercifully and graciously does He deign to look upon us'.[8] This seems like a paraphrase of Newman's almost identical perception about the two and only two supreme and luminously self-evident beings. Yet in the bitter little joke of the sonnet – 'Doth God exact day-labour, light denied'? (although of course the question is answered with a strong affirmation of God's providence) it suggests a fundamental questioning of whether God could really be on his side. His imprecations in the *Defensio* being assertions of his own innocence, seem like reproaches to the task-master:

I call upon Thee, my God, who knowest my inmost mind and all my thoughts to witness that (although I have repeatedly examined myself on this point as earnestly as I could, and have searched all the corners of my life) I am conscious of nothing, or of no deed, either recent or remote, whose wickedness could justly occasion or invite upon me this supreme misfortune.[9]

And so it is, lest the reader should be in any doubt, that he is telling the truth, that he feels it necessary to rehearse the story of his life. He describes his parents, his upbringing, his early headaches in childhood, which he now sees are related to his affliction, his successful career at school and university, his retirement at Hammersmith and Horton, his Italian journey, and the success that he met with there, social, and academic. It has been suggested that he deliberately suppresses the fact that he heard of Diodati's death in Naples; but, as we have already said, there is no evidence that he *did* hear of the death there. Geneva is the likeliest place for this. Italy, in the final months, was an awakening in precisely the way that Milton says it was. 'I thought it base that I should travel abroad at my ease for the cultivation of my mind, while my fellow-citizens at home were fighting for liberty.'[10]

Milton's life over the previous fifteen years, 1638–53, makes no sense if these words are not true. He meant them passionately. Italy had been the great moment of revelation for him. He had not been much caught up in politics in England during the 1630s. Having a sharp contempt for the clergy is not the same thing as being a revolutionary. Everything Milton writes about his awakening political conscience suggests that something important happened *in Italy*. And this, as we have already suggested, must have been the thought that the Bishops' War, and the oppressive policies of Archbishop Laud, would, if allowed to go unchecked, lead inevitably to the sort of Inquisition which had imprisoned Galileo. He had visited the old astronomer when he was old and blind. The Inquisition could be blamed for his decrepitude. Full of hope, his literary ambitions for the time being put to one side, Milton returned to England determined to fight in liberty's defence. And, less than twenty years later, although he vainly protested that he did not look a day over thirty, he too was blind, and 'that one talent which was death to hide' was lodged with him useless.

The *Defensio Secunda* is a remarkable account, before the bar of Heaven, of Milton's innocence. Unlike Thomas Browne, or Richard Baxter, Milton did not write any single book which could be called his autobiography; just as, unlike Donne, his poetry does not overtly and consistently play with images of himself. But his self-obsession is more all-pervading than almost any other writer's of that century, in which 'self-expression' of the modern sort first begins to emerge, in diaries, memoirs, and verse.

At the same time, and in the same pamphlet, Milton sinks to his most vulgar and hilarious attack in a decade of brilliant abuse. There is a marked contrast between the concentrated, almost awed seriousness with which he talks about himself, and the technique he adopts for getting rid of his adversary More, whom, he assumes, is the author of the attacks on himself. Not only is More a feeble poet – the schoolmasterly Milton finds two false quantities in one word of his iambic penta-meters – but he is also a common little wife-pawer, and fornicator. Although the *Clamor* was anonymous, Milton writes, it is in vain that he lurks unknown. More is half Scotch and half French, so what do you expect? He is not a man to trust with the servant-girls. With one of these young trollops, More was frequently seen nipping off to the garden-shed: doubtless to discuss gardening ('de re hortensi'). But unfortunately the Genevan elders who expelled More put a less chari-table explanation on his conduct. He went to stay with the great and learned Salmasius, when, lo and behold, Salmasius's wife became pregnant: so did More. She with a bastard child; More with 'this addle and windy egg from which burst that tympany, *The Cry of the Royal Blood . . .*'

In describing the set-up at Salmasius's house, Milton puts them all in the position of *farceurs* in some Chaucerian *fabliau*. He manages to make the reader believe that we have to do not with serious adversaries, but with a troop of clowns: 'non cum gravi adversario, sed cum grege histrionico'.

Modern readers of Milton, especially those who look in his writings for serious doctrine, must be scandalized by the relish with which he savages More; particularly when we know now that he got the wrong man. It has been said in Milton's defence that for him, his adversaries were not personal beings, but representatives of detested points of view. But if this were the case it would be scarcely necessary to resort to bawdy abuse. It would nowadays be thought extraordinary, even among the fiercest political or intellectual adversaries, if (in support of a serious and religious point of view) one party accused another of copulating in garden-sheds. A profound personal hatred motivated such fantasies; a hatred, not so much of the point of view expressed in the *Clamor* (he had already effectively demolished the royalist argument in his first three regicide pamphlets) but the tone of voice: that nagging, cruel taunt – that Milton was a ridiculous, ugly, unheard-of little man; and that his great heroes, Bradshaw and Cromwell and the rest had been presiding over a bloody and blasphemous mistake.

The pamphlet concludes, therefore, with the sort of thoughts which (judging by its title) one would expect to have occupied the whole: a paean of praise of Oliver Cromwell. Milton's personal misfortunes – his blindness, his dead son – are perpetual reproaches to the Almighty. But, if the republic succeeds, then it will be a clear sign that God was indeed looking after his England and his Englishmen. One man could guarantee this in Milton's eyes: Oliver Cromwell. 'For while you, Cromwell, are safe, he does not have sufficient faith even in God himself who would fear for the safety of England, when he sees God everywhere so favourable to you, so unmistakably at your side.'[11]

Milton's adulation of Cromwell is not at all to be dismissed as toadyism (which was foreign to his nature). It is inevitable that he would at first idolize the Protector (as he became in 1653) since Cromwell had not only been chosen (in a series of militarily unmistakable signs) by God; he belonged to that section of society to which Milton aspired to belong himself, and from which he chose nearly all his friends. Milton would not have married Mary Powell if he did not slightly idolize the gentry of the level which we would call squires. He had obviously been brought up by his father to entertain notions of the superiority of the country gentry to the city-bred middle class to which (perforce) he belonged. The Powells, as the local squires in a village where the Miltons, the previous generation, had been prosperous yeomen, had held out an irresistible lure, even had he not fallen deeply in love with Mary: her looks and her youth. When God addresses himself, as his manner is, to his Englishmen, one can be sure that the type of Englishmen Milton had in mind owned a few hundred acres and were merciful towards the poor of the parish, harsh to poachers, and handy with rod and line. The extent to which Richard Powell, with his loud, silly, extravagant ways, failed to live up to this ideal, earned him his son-in-law's contempt.

Cromwell, on the other hand, who belonged to roughly speaking the same class as the Powells, was nevertheless much richer and much more powerful. Indeed, he belonged to one of the richest families in England. As Milton put it, he was 'sprung of renowned and illustrious stock. The name was celebrated in former times for good administration under the monarchy and became more glorious as soon as the orthodox religion was reformed, or rather established among us for the first time'.[12] Cromwell's riches, the fact that he had already established himself as one of the most efficient of fen landowners, counts for much in Milton's view of him. He does not see the Protector, as some have done since, as a sort of proto-Marxist man of the people, thrown up by the inevitable forces of the hour. Instead, Milton recognizes that the powers of a slightly batty country squire, brilliant in the organization of land, his head buzzing with religious certitude, is precisely what the country needed to establish ancient liberties. He likened Cromwell to Cicero and the best of the Caesars; above all he admired that diffident and iron self-control which must have been with his hero since early manhood: 'Commander first over himself, victor over himself, he had learned to achieve over himself the most effective triumph, and so, on the very first day that he took service against an external foe, he entered camp a veteran and past-master in all that concerned the soldier's life'.[13]

Yet even in the sonnet written to Cromwell when he was Lord General in May 1652, there were the seeds of disenchantment. This was the month, it will be remembered, in which Mary Milton had died and Deborah had been born. But Milton still found the energy to contemplate Cromwell's rise to power

> . . . who through a cloud
> Not of war only, but detractions rude,
> Guided by faith and matchless fortitude
> To peace and truth thy glorious way hast ploughed . . .

It is conspicuously his worst sonnet, with a catalogue of Cromwell's battle triumphs at Dunbar and Preston and Worcester. But it contains the plea

> Help us to save free conscience from the paw
> Of hireling wolves whose gospel is their maw.

The hireling wolves referred to (a collation of phrases he had used fifteen years before to refer to the Anglicans and Roman Catholics) were a body of Protestant clergymen, selected by Cromwell himself and formed into a Committee for the Propagation of the Gospel. They suggested, in a document which came to be known as the Humble Proposals, that some form of religious settlement be reached, in which toleration was allowed to the sectaries, provided they were prepared to subscribe to a list of fifteen 'Fundamentals' – which included the authority of the Scriptures, the Trinity, original sin, and justification by faith only.

Milton, as it happened, was almost certainly moving away from these orthodoxies in his own mind at this date, but what he objected to was the principle of religious faith being placed in the hands of the magistrates. The liberty for which he had prayed and worked was denied by this unfortunate little group of clergymen, presided over by Cromwell's chaplain, John Owen. Of course, by the standards of the age, Cromwell had a very tolerant ecclesiastical policy. But Milton felt that it was not the magistrate's task to coerce or determine, merely to protect religion – a belief of course which is universal in the West today. The plea at the end of the sonnet to Cromwell is the first glimmering of disillusionment with the Protector. Milton could never be a hero-worshipper for long. He briefly (in *Defensio Secunda*) tried to justify the ending of the Long Parliament and Cromwell's seizure of absolute power. But clearly, in retrospect, it shocked him, and he had been appalled by the rule of the Major-Generals, the suppression of dissident groups such as the Levellers with a severity worthy of the most absolute tyrant, and the persecution of people like Colonel Overton (a Cambridge contemporary of Milton's) who was locked up quite early by Cromwell's KGB. When, in 1660, the Long Parliament was restored, he spoke of its members as the 'recoverers of our liberty', to whose care the country had been entrusted 'after a short but scandalous night of interruption'.

He came to see, in other words, that Cromwell was a tyrant and a thug; someone who nursed beneath the surface of his gentry manner a fanaticism and a lust for power less attractive, if anything, than the dishonest and weak leadership of Charles I. But of course, it was a perception which Milton could not allow himself to have fully. Cromwell's tyranny was 'a scandalous night of interruption', but the things he stood for were still the Good Old Cause; just as, although he doubted the providence, and ultimately the omnipotence of God, Milton devoted the rest of his days, one way or another, to the justification of God's ways to men. The only alternative, during the 1650s at least, was a disillusionment so black that blindness itself would be a brightness. During the summer of 1653 he translated Psalms, all deeply applicable to the sorry state which he did not allow himself to recognize that he was in:

> Pity me Lord for I am much deject
> Am very weak and faint . . .   .
>   Wearied I am with sighing out my days,
> Nightly my couch I make a kind of sea;
> My bed I water with my tears; mine eye
>   Through grief consumes, is waxen old and dark
> I' the midst of all mine enemies that mark.
>   (Psalm VI)

In the final couplet, by paraphrasing the desolation of the ancient poet, Milton was writing lines which matched his own wretched state. The Psalmist had written nothing about his eyes growing *dark*: the epithet was Milton's addition.

This was a hard phase for Milton, this four-year period after the death of his wife and after his blindness. In poetry he tried to make himself submit to God's 'mild yoke', but this did not stop him writing to a Greek correspondent, Leonard Philaras, who, it was thought, might be able to get help for Milton's condition from French doctors. He wrote to Milton asking for a description of his symptoms, and received a long reply:

> Since you tell me that I should not give up all hope of regaining my sight, that you have a friend and intimate in the Paris physician Thévenot (especially outstanding as an oculist) whom you will consult about my eyes if only I send you the means by which he can diagnose the cures and symptoms of the disease, I shall do what you urge . . .[14]

Although he admits at the end of his letter, in true Shakespearian fashion, that he finds comfort in believing 'that he cannot see by eyes alone', this desperate letter sits oddly beside the apparent submission to his fate in both the sonnet and the prose such as *Defensio Secunda*. Milton was clearly desperate to regain his sight.

> It is ten years, I think, more or less, since I noticed my sight becoming weak and growing dim, and at the same time my spleen and all my viscera burdened and shaken with flatulence. And even in the morning, if I began as usual to read, I noticed that my eyes felt immediate pain deep within and turned from reading, though later refreshed after moderate bodily exercise; as often as I looked at a lamp, a sort of rainbow seemed to obscure it. Soon a mist appearing in the left part of the left eye (for that eye became clouded several years before the other) removed from my sight everything on that side. Objects further forward too seemed smaller, if I chanced to close my right eye. The other eye also failing slowly and gradually over a period of almost three years, some months before my sight was completely destroyed, everything which I distinguished when I myself was still seemed to swim, now to the right, now to the left. Certain permanent vapours seem to have settled upon my entire forehead and temples, which press and oppress my eyes with a sort of sleepy heavyness, especially from dinner time to evening . . . But I must not omit that, while considerable sight still remained, when I would first go to bed and lie on one side or the other, abundant light would dart from my closed eyes; then, as sight daily diminished, colours proportionately darker would burst forth with violence and a sort of crash from within. But now, pure black, marked as if with extinguished or ashy light, and as if interwoven with it, pours forth. Yet the mist which always hovers before my eyes both night and day seems always to be approaching white rather than black; and upon the eyes turning, it admits a minute quantity of light as if through a crack.[15]

Why was the world denied a poem
"on His Flatulence?"

Can we, at this distance of time, diagnose these symptoms? Many attempts have been made to do so, but one of the most interesting was by Dr Lambert Rogers in the Proceedings of the Cardiff Medical Society in 1955. He suggested that Milton was suffering from chiasmal arachnodoiditis, started by a cyst or tumour of the pituitary gland. He lists a number of test cases with symptoms remarkably similar to Milton's, which even included the gastric disorders mentioned in the letter to Philaras. When the tumours were removed, Dr Rogers's patients recovered their sight; but if the cyst was not discovered until it was too late, then loss of sight inevitably followed. In 1933 he saw a bootmaker, aged forty-one, who had started to go blind three years before. His symptoms resembled Milton's exactly. Not only were his eyes clear 'to outward view of blemish or of spot', like Milton's, when he had gone blind; but he experienced the same sensation of seeing light through a crack: the bootmaker said it was like seeing light through a crack in the door. Like Milton, the bootmaker had intense pain behind his eyes, accompanied by headaches and nausea. His previously benign temperament became soured and angry. But, once his blindness was complete, the pain subsided. This appears, too, to have happened to Milton.

Dr Rogers's hypothesis is put forward modestly, but it has all the ring of truth about it. Though Milton's darker nature – his capacity to anger and scorn – continued for some while after his blindness and has more than purely physical causes, it is striking that the most vitriolic of his writing corresponds precisely to the period when he was likely to have been in the most acute physical pain.

If the theory of a cyst is accurate, it could very well have related to a general pituitary disfunction dating from Milton's earliest years which might have accounted for his very delicate and feminine appearance. In a hormonal, as well as merely visual sense, he might have been 'the Lady of Christ's Coll:'.

What is striking about the terrible treatment Milton received is that it seems so close to what Dr Rogers would have prescribed three hundred years later. He submitted to it first when his left eye went blind and we are told, 'the issues and setons, made use of to save or retrieve that, were thought by drawing away the spirits, which should have supplied the optic vessels, to have hastened the loss of the other'.[16]

Setoning was a treatment favoured by Thévenot, the French doctor whom Philaras consulted on Milton's behalf. It involved cauterizing the skin at the top of the brow and at the temples and passing threads underneath the skin of the forehead, dipped in white of egg.

There is a pathetic contrast between the 'content though blind' of his sonnets, and his preparedness to have this torture inflicted on him to preserve, or restore, his sight. All Milton's life at this date is a mass of contradictions. He was a blind man who had been punished unnecessarily by God. He was an independent republican, increasingly disenchanted by Cromwell, but devoting almost all his time and energy to his various appointments as Latin Secretary, translating letters, drafting treaties, and leading the life of a full-time civil servant. He was a man blighted by affliction, stung into elaborate self-defence on a disproportionately detailed scale. But at the same time he was a man who charmed his friends, and had plenty of them. If one surveys the *Life Records* for this period, and the evidence of how hard Milton worked in his official capacity, and if one remembers that he was also pursuing very elaborate theological researches throughout his career as a civil servant, his sonnets of friendship seem particularly delightful: a glimpse of an affable, private man.

One poem, to the son of the President of Cromwell's Council, Henry Lawrence – 'Lawrence of virtuous father virtuous son' – expounds, in a needlessly ambiguous conclusion, a doctrine of Horatian moderation. The weather has been bad and it has prevented the two men from seeing one another. Milton asks his young friend 'what may be won / From the hard season gaining?' The question is applicable not only to the poor weather of a particular season, but to the trough of misfortune in which Milton found himself at this date. 'Extreme pleasant in his conversation and at dinner, supper etc.', we are told.[17] This is a poem by that extremely pleasant conversationalist. The concluding lines mean that frequent, but moderately tempered occasions of social enjoyment – conversations with young friends, a glass of wine, a 'neat repast' are a necessary part of the good life.

> He who of those delights can judge, and spare
> To interpose them oft, is not unwise.

'Nothing in excess' is the saying of the ancients. But there are few pleasanter celebrations of the ordinary intercourse of friendship and conviviality than this poem.

Similarly, in his lines to the young Cyriack Skinner he seems to imply, with his use of the phrase 'deep thoughts' that there is no consolation for the major horrors of life except minor pleasures. Milton, it is so important to remember, was not always conceiving of means in which he could justify the ways of God to men. He was not always defending the republic, or blasting out assaults on his pamphleteering foes, or drafting letters to Cardinal Mazarin or the Dutch ambassador.

> Today deep thoughts resolve with me to drench
>   In mirth, that after no repenting draws;
>   Let Euclid rest and Archimedes pause,
>   And what the Swede intend, and what the French.
> To measure life, learn thou betimes, and know
>   Toward solid good what leads the nearest way;
>   For other things mild heaven a time ordains,
> And disapproves that care, though wise in show,
>   That with superfluous burden loads the day,
>   And when God sends a cheerful hour, refrains.

It is important to remember that God, too, sends cheerful hours. Milton's capacity for serenity, remarked upon by his early biographers, is deeply attractive; the ability to snatch happiness from trifles seems to have been what saved him from despair.

All was not lost, after all. He had friends about him. He was a much needed and much respected servant of the state. He was nicely housed, in 'a pretty garden-house in Petty-France in Westminster'. His neighbour was Lord Scudamore, who had been at the British embassy in Paris in 1638 and introduced him to Grotius.

Lord Scudamore's presence would remind him of one very striking fact. Whether in hard season or cheerful hour, his great poem, the 'one talent which is death to hide', was not being written. Grotius had written, how could Milton forget it, a great play on the theme of Adam expelled from Paradise – *Adamus Exul*. Milton, too, had contemplated a drama on the theme; he was toying with it in 1643, when the trained bands had marched out to Turnham Green. Nothing much had been done in the dramatic or epic line since then. Occasional verse, of Horatian brevity, had trickled from his pen. It should not be underestimated. Every poetic form which Milton touched he transformed. The sonnet became detachable from its place in sequence and in love-story – the form in which it had evolved from Petrarchan original during the Elizabethan period – and he used it as a vehicle of oblique and epigrammatic autobiography.

By the standards of the merely very good poet, he was not idle. But his output for the years after the outbreak of the war is scarcely what we should expect from the greatest poet since Virgil. The plan for the great work, however, was hatching in his now darkened brain. On every side, in his own life, and in politics, and in religion, this drama of Adam, this consequence of his first eating that forbidden fruit, was made daily more obvious. And yet, though Milton's foes appeared, in dark moments, to prosper, life could always be made bearable by the cheerfulness of human affection, by his young friends such as Skinner, Lawrence, or Andrew Marvell. The more consolation life offered, the more troubling seemed the theological implications of it. God had called for His Englishmen, and they had done what He had told them. They were, however, in just as bad a mess as they had ever been in the days of Charles I. Far from liberty having been established, Cromwell was gradually usurping more and more power into his hands. God's –and Cromwell's – most loyal servant had destroyed his own sight in their service, and retained his own personal virtue and dignity in a way which, far from depending on the richness of divine grace, put God slightly to shame. Where was the place in all this for the idea of God as an omnipotent lord of the universe? Or for the necessity of his grace, a cardinal doctrine for all Christians? Why, if we were all free under God, was Cromwell desirous to establish a state church once again, with a sort of theological lowest common denominator – a belief in the Trinity, in salvation through faith, in original sin? How did such doctrines come about? The Trinity seemed like a nonsense. Was it in the Bible? What of faith? Milton was manifestly a good man without the prop of divine grace. He had searched his soul and found no vice in it. What then of Adam? What of God? These questions were to occupy the next decade of his life.

CHAPTER 12

THE BEGINNINGS OF *PARADISE LOST*

> There is yet, after all the decrees of Councils and the
> niceties of the Schools, many things untouched,
> unimagined, wherein the liberty of an honest reason
> may play and expatiate with security, and far without
> the circle of an heresy.
>
> Sir Thomas Browne, *Religio Medici*

MILTON'S children were growing up without a mother. Deborah was now four, Mary eight, and Anne was ten. It is not known how they were provided for while their father toiled as Latin Secretary, endlessly drafting documents, interviewing diplomats or interpreting their conversations for the Lord Protector. It is not particularly surprising that, unlike the energy he expended on educating his sister's children, he took no particular pains to acquaint his daughters with foreign languages or ancient literature. John and Edward Phillips had, after all, been boys.

Nor, as it turned out, had the nephews been influenced by their frantic over-education. As far as one can tell, Milton had no influence upon them whatsoever. They both wrote about him perfectly affectionately after he had died, and there is no reason to suppose that they bore him any grudges for making them plough through Syriac grammars when they could have been playing hopscotch. But they certainly seemed to have picked up none of his political convictions.

The habit of scorn, on the other hand, was easily learnt. Clearly, for all his piety, Milton found the Protestant sectaries who flourished in their multitude swarms during the Protectorate quite as contemptible as, before that, he had found the Presbyterians and the Laudian Anglicans. Jonathan Richardson's *Life* records 'Milton had a servant, who was a very honest, silly fellow, and a zealous and constant follower of these teachers; when he came from the meeting, his master would frequently ask him what he had heard, and divert himself with ridiculing their fooleries, or (it may be) the poor fellow's understanding; both one and t'other probably; however, this was so grievous to the good creature, that he left his service upon it.'[1]

It was one thing to take delight in mocking the servants. This had always been a source of merriment to Milton, ever since he had laughed at Hobson the carrier, veering from one side of the road to the other as his cart made the tedious journey from London to Cambridge each week. But it was another thing altogether to be openly scornful of simple Protestant sentiment. A man in Milton's position could hardly afford to mock at gifts of divine utterance and inspiration, since it was only too common for Almighty God to speak directly with his employer, the Lord Protector.

John Phillips, Milton's elder nephew, had little time for Cromwell, as is apparent from his nickname, given him by friends in taverns, as the Anti-Oliverian. In 1655 his merry quips against the Presbyterians were allowed to pass uncensored in *The Satyr Against Hypocrites*. But when he published, the following year, a further satirical book against the government, *Sportive Wit: The Muse's Merriment. A New Spring of Lusty Drollery, Jovial Fancies, and à la Mode Lampoons on some Heroic Persons of These Late Times*, it was felt that he had gone too far. He was arrested and fined. Cromwell personally approved of the burning of this volume.

It was Milton's punishment. His scornful habits of mind had rubbed off on the young man far more than the political convictions, or his devotion, arrived at haphazard in middle age, to liberty. Indeed, it is very hard to imagine that the extreme satirical edge of Milton's mind was never directed towards his employer. In the First Protectorate, Cromwell had been inducted wearing merely a black velvet suit and with a gold band round his hat. But the ceremonies attached to the beginning of the Second Protectorate far outshone the wealth of Ormus and of Ind in the absurdity of their magnificence. Gone was the simple black suit. His Highness Oliver now appeared in thick purple robes, carrying not a mayoral sword, but a royal sceptre of massy gold. Mrs Cromwell, his wife, was now Her Highness the Lady Elizabeth; and even his mother, the Dowager Mrs Cromwell, was given much of the honour and dignity which would in the past have attached to the figure of a Queen Mother. Admirers and enemies of Cromwell alike noted how easily the new and gorgeous garment, Majesty, sat upon him.

Milton's very keen sense of the ridiculous must have made his job as Latin Secretary hard. The need for domestic consolations must have been acute, as the fourth year of his widowerhood passed into the autumn of 1656.

It is not known how Milton met Katherine Woodcock, the twenty-eight-year-old woman who became his second wife. It is generally supposed that he literally never *saw* her; his poetic memorial to her would suggest as much. Her father had been a Captain Woodcock of Hackney, but this mildly Dickensian-sounding figure had died by the time of her marriage. Her two sisters, however, were still alive, and so was her mother, Elizabeth Woodcock, who was more or less the same age as her new son-in-law. The wedding took place before a magistrate as the law under the Protectorate drearily required. It almost certainly happened at the Guildhall with Alderman John Dethicke – Sir John, as he had just become – presiding over the nuptials.

Since Milton at this date had come to believe in polygamy, it is not necessary to infer that he had especially strong feelings about Katherine Woodcock when he married her. But it would be perverse to suppose that the marriage was anything but harmonious. At last, he had found a domestic helpmate who could look after the little girls, supervise the running of the household, prepare the meals, and above all provide that dear companionship which, perhaps, he had never felt he got from Mary Powell.

It was an exceedingly busy year for him. He received, as well as diplomatic visits in his capacity as Latin Secretary, a large number of foreign visitors who had heard of his fame and wanted to meet the great Milton on their travels, just as he had met Grotius, Manso, and Galileo on his own tour. In spite of the fact that Andrew Marvell had now taken over the Secretaryship for Foreign Tongues, and Milton only worked on Latin papers and conversations, there was a huge amount of routine paperwork. And he was, as we shall see, heavily engaged at this stage of life on a major work of Christian theology. But it is very hard to resist the conclusion that in the course of the year he fell deeply in love with his kind young wife. The happiness of Adam and Eve in the fourth book of *Paradise Lost* is very strikingly unvisual. While they do not need

> the putting off
> These troublesome disguises which we wear
>   (IV. 739)

their nakedness is something *felt*, not seen.

> half her swelling breast
> Naked met his under the flowing gold
> Of her loose tresses hid . . .
>   (IV. 495–7)

in one passage; while in another, the virtuousness of their joy is extolled in a passage of great generalization:

> Hail wedded love, mysterious law, true source
> Of human offspring, sole propriety
> In Paradise of all things common else.
>
> (750–2)

There is a particular poignancy about their happy sleep together:

> These lulled by nightingales embracing slept,
> And on their naked limbs the flowery roof
> Showered roses, which the morn repaired. Sleep on
> Blest pair; and O yet happiest if ye seek
> No happier state, and know to know no more.
>
> (IV. 771–5)

For, as he conceived of their marital happiness, Milton conveys the cruel knowledge that the Paradise of Adam and Eve is about to be shattered. Even as they are 'Imparadised in one another's arms', Satan stands, enviously full of the gift of sight, and determined to bring about their ruin.

Katherine Milton gave birth to a daughter on 19 October 1657. They called the baby Katherine too, but neither mother nor child was strong. After the birth, neither Katherine quite recovered. The mother 'fell ill of a consumption'; and on 3 February 1658, Milton lost his second wife. He had been married to her for about fifteen months. The child lived until 17 March.

Milton arranged a most elaborate funeral for his second wife, at St Margaret's, Westminster. The parish register records that he spent £2. 13s. 4d. 'for right taffaty escouti', that is, escutcheons, and for a dozen buckram escutcheons he paid an additional one pound as well as a pound for the pall. Milton's coat of arms, with the spread eagle, was hung over the heavily draped coffin, and we can readily believe that the obsequies were conducted with full solemnity. They buried her in St Margaret's itself, in an elaborate coffin in which Milton had specified that there should be twelve locks with twelve different keys. He distributed these keys to twelve friends at the funeral 'and desired the coffin might not be opened till they all met together'.[2] We do not know who the twelve friends were, but almost certainly they would have included young men like Cyriack Skinner and Andrew Marvell. Milton always got on best with young men.

The locks in the coffin were a deliberately potent image. The wells of his emotional life were now locked up. What he had felt for Katherine Woodcock could never be felt again. And it was only in the company of younger men, who carried the keys of that lugubrious container, that his heart could be at ease.

At some stage after Katherine Woodcock's death Milton had the dream which was to prompt his most moving sonnet, and his last. The sonnet, as Milton almost certainly knew, had its origins in Italian literature in the epigram, and it was only in the hands of Petrarch that its narrative and discursive potential had been exploited. In England, the sonnet tradition, as understood in Milton's youth, had become a matter of sequences: 'Astrophel and Stella', 'Delia', 'Idea' or the sonnets of Shakespeare, if not actually *telling* a story, like a verse novel, at least imply a story: a story, which in the case of Shakespeare's sonnets, new generations of readers never tire of retelling and reinterpreting.

But for Milton the sonnet was a thing complete in itself. It needed no narrative background; it did not need to be appended to lots of other sonnets, and it nearly always related directly and personally to himself. In his hands it became a vehicle for the thoughts of reflective mood, as well as for combative and comic reactions to his political opponents: 'shallow Edwards and Scotch what d'ye call'. But in the final sonnet, it is not absurd to be reminded of the bleak confessional realism of Hardy's 1912–13 poems to the memory of his dead wife. Whether a real dream or not, it has all the inconsequential force of actual experience; the fact that, in the dream, he did have the gift of sight, but that his wife's face was, nevertheless, 'veiled'; the face which he had never seen in life was so unimaginable that even a dream could not supply its features, even though as her figure leant to embrace him, he had the illusion that he was about to *see* her, and then, with the shattering monosyllables of the final line, day, and truth, and dark come back to him:

> Methought I saw my late espoused saint
>   Brought to me like Alcestis from the grave,
>   Whom Jove's great son to her glad husband gave,
>   Rescued from death by force though pale and faint.
> Mine as whom washed from spot of childbed taint,
>   Purification in the old Law did save,
>   And such, as yet once more I trust to have
>   Full sight of her in heaven without restraint,
> Came vested all in white, pure as her mind:
>   Her face was veiled, yet to my fancied sight,
>   Love, sweetness, goodness in her person shined

> So clear, as in no face with more delight.
> But O as to embrace me she inclined
> I waked, she fled, and day brought back my night.

The twenty years in which poetry had been but an occasional exercise in a life too busy and too controversial for a thoroughgoing devotion to the arts, were now over. Milton had been more lyrical than this in the past: he was to be grander, larger, stranger in the future. But there is nothing he wrote which is, in its own terms, more perfect, than this sonnet to the memory of a woman who passed out of Hackney and into oblivion, and whom he knew for barely more than a year.

In a passage already quoted, we know that Milton's blindness was white. In Book III of *Paradise Lost* he describes himself

> from the cheerful ways of men
> Cut off, and for the book of knowledge fair
> Presented with a universal blanc . . .
>
> (III. 46–8)

It is in this milky haze that his dream had its origins, his wife in her purification robes, as he hopes to see her face to face, and for the first time in heaven.

But what sort of a heaven, what sort of a God, did Milton believe in? Opinions differ, ranging from Charles Symmons's view that Milton's opinions were 'orthodox and consistent with the creed of the Church of England' (1806)[3] to Hilaire Belloc's notion (1931) that the *De Doctrina Christiana* 'is a conclusion in the fullest sense; the ultimate result of his philosophy and the last testament of his pen. He died disbelieving the omnipotence of his Creator, the divinity of his Saviour and the native immortality of mankind'.[4] Neither point of view, alas, is inconsistent with the other, since orthodoxy, as Belloc would have understood it, is not something which one would look for in the 'creed of the Church of England'. Certainly, it has to be said that many members of the Church of England during Milton's lifetime would, if questioned, have seen nothing wrong with *most* of the opinions expressed in the *De Doctrina*; and, of course, by the heretical standards of later ages, it seems a model of orthodoxy. Scholars for whom Milton is a great firebrand, a secret supporter of the Devil, an arch-heretic, have concentrated on the few points in the *De Doctrina* where Milton's views are conspicuously heterodox. Scholars who are themselves Christian believers have perhaps erred further in the opposite direction and not wanted it to be thought that the author of *Paradise Lost* was anything but a believer in the straight sense of the word.

But more striking perhaps, than anything it contains is the fact that he wrote the *De Doctrina* at all. 'No man, no synod, no session of men, though called the church, can judge definitely the sense of scripture to another man's conscience.' This is his fundamental starting-point, not merely of his long-unheard-of theological work, but, much more importantly, of the poem which was taking shape on his lips.

Belloc was right, surely, to detect a tension between the inner life reflected in the *De Doctrina*, and Milton's surface reputation in the centuries since his death. He is thought of, according to Belloc, as 'the exponent of English orthodox Protestantism and its champion', whereas the *De Doctrina* reveals him to have been someone who 'had renounced the Creed'.

But in fact, the *De Doctrina* is *so* Protestant that Belloc entirely fails to grasp its ethos. He assumes that, just as (in his day at least) there was something which could be identified as orthodox Catholicism, from which a man may be said to deviate to this or that extent, so there was a rival orthodoxy, which he calls 'orthodox Protestantism'. But the whole starting-point of Milton's position is that orthodoxy is an anathema to Christian liberty. Each human mind, made in God's image, is free to pursue the truth for itself. Christian liberty means a liberation from the idea of the Mosaic law, and all which the idea of a religious law entails. 'Who can be at rest, who can enjoy any thing in this world with contentment, who hath not liberty to serve God and to save his own soul, according to the best light which God hath planted in him to that purpose by the reading of his revealed will and the guidance of his holy spirit?'[5] The question he asks in *The Ready and Easy Way to Establish a Free Commonwealth* (1660) is perpetually before his mind in the contemporaneous *De Doctrina*. The whole point of his attitude to doctrine is the fundamentally Protestant one that orthodoxy is itself an alien concept to the free Christian man.

Aelfric, a monk of the tenth century who was to become Abbot of Eynsham in Oxfordshire, saw the issue very clearly six centuries before Milton. He had been commissioned to translate the Book of Genesis, and he did so with some trepidation, 'lest some fool reads this book or hears it read, and thinks he can live now in the new dispensation as the patriarchs lived in the time before the old law was established'.[6] He even remembers his old schoolmaster at Winchester, a monk who knew very little Latin, saying that the Patriarch Jacob had four wives. 'Very truly he spoke, but he did not know (nor did I at that period) what a huge difference exists between the old law and the new.' Aelfric, as a Benedictine who was alive five hundred years before Luther, sees that the only logical objection to living by the Scriptures is that to do so bypasses the laws of Holy Mother Church. The Reformation leaders all saw the same truth, but from the other angle: if the Scriptures were at variance with the teachings of the Church, then the Church must be wrong. Yet, of course, as Milton had observed in pamphlet after pamphlet, none of the 'Churches' of the Reformation had had the courage of their convictions. They had all sought to establish mini-orthodoxies of their own, to become their own popes. They were all frightened of the Gospel liberty. Aelfric had been right (Milton had read him, though he does not mention him in this context). It took a man of Milton's clarity of mind to see that he had been right. The only objection to polygamy was that the Church forbade it. The reason, for instance, that bishops are told to be the husband of one wife in the New Testament is that it is assumed (so his casuistry affirms) that ordinary Christians will be polygamous. Just as the Old Testament allows divorce, so it allows polygamy. Only Catholicism, the notion of an earthly authority binding on men's consciences and interpreting the Scriptures for them in the Church's way, can deny a man's right to divorce or to a multiplicity of wives.

Yet, heterodox as this unquestionably is by Catholic standards, it is not altogether true to say with Belloc that Milton 'had renounced the Creed'. This is where Belloc misunderstands the Protestant mind. Milton had not renounced the Creed. He believed that he alone had found the correct interpretation of it. At the conclusion of his long chapter on Christ, 'De Filio', in the course of which he argues against the Trinitarian point of view, against Christ's divinity, against Christ's equal Godhead with the Father, he wrote 'the Apostle's Creed itself, the most ancient and the most widely accepted creed which the Church possesses, offers us this belief and no other'; and he meant, the belief which he had himself just propounded.

It is easy to suppose, having said that Milton did not believe in the divinity of Christ, that he had lost his faith or that he was not really a Christian. But, of course, his unbelief in Christ's divinity needs to be explained. He believed that the Carpenter of Galilee was a man in all things like us, but a man infused with the spirit of God, and chosen by God to act as mediator between the divine and the human. The priesthood of Christ is, therefore, an important doctrine to Milton. The heterodox Milton of Belloc would have been unlikely to write, as the real Milton of *De Doctrina* did, that 'to neglect the sacraments and to receive them in an unworthy way are both equally displeasing to the Deity . . . So the sacraments can and should be put off until one has a proper time and place, a pure mind, holiness of life, and a regular communion of believers'. Milton sees no reason for a human priesthood. There is no reason why anyone might not celebrate the Lord's supper and share in Christ's priesthood. 'Christ as the only priest offered himself . . . not at the holy supper but on the cross.' This last, as it happens, is 'orthodox' Christian doctrine.

It is a mistake, then, to read the *De Doctrina* as a covert expression of doubt about the Christian orthodoxies. It represents, on the contrary, an affirmation of Milton's constancy and faith. It is not known, precisely, how this enormous book, with its continual scriptural reference and cross-reference, came into being; but it probably represents the movement of Milton's mind over a long period. Edward Phillips records during the 1640s that

the Sunday's work was for the most part the reading each day a chapter of the Greek Testament, and hearing his learned exposition upon the same. The next work, after this, was the writing from his own dictation, some part, from time to time of a tractate which he thought fit to collect from the ablest divines who had written of that subject . . .

Probably by 1649 Milton did actually possess some form of scriptural digest of his own compilation.

I deemed it therefore safest and most advisable to compile for myself, by my own labour and study, some original treatise, which should always be at hand, derived solely from the word of God itself.

But there existed a third stage, after the endless perusal described by his nephew, and the writing of a digest described by Milton himself, and that was the compilation of the *De Doctrina* proper. This dated from about 1656 onwards, and the manuscript in the Public Record Office is written primarily in the hand of Jeremy Picard, who was Milton's secretary at this date. But, on top of Picard's fair copy, there is a great deal of revision in the hand of a further secretary, and it would seem likely that Milton went on tinkering with the *De Doctrina* for a number of years: some would say that the final revisions happened after the Restoration.

Following his total disillusionment with institutional Christianity, the *De Doctrina* became Milton's Church, and the book in which he both worked out and proclaimed his own beliefs. He fully intended it for publication. As things turned out, it did not see the light until Robert Lemon found the long-lost manuscript in 1823. The immediate reaction, among the pious nineteenth-century reviewers, was astonishment. Milton's 'heresies' were seized upon. The man who wrote 'Hail wedded love, mysterious law' was apparently thinking of something more like George IV's domestic arrangements than publications like the *British Critic* thought tolerable: divorce, concubines, and harems were to be accepted into the Christian scheme of things. As for when we die, Milton was a thnetopsychist: he thought the soul died with the body, and that both together would be reconstituted on Judgement Day. Here, the *British Critic* thought Milton's 'aberration of mind ... approaches almost to dotage'.[7] In addition, he denied the orthodox doctrine of Creation – that God created all things, visible and invisible out of nothing; he denied the Trinity; he denied the Calvinist notion of God's pure will: indeed, he appeared to deny God's omnipotence.

All this is perfectly true. But more needs to be said than that. Since the first Regency reactions to the *De Doctrina*, research into the seventeenth-century religious scene has blossomed and flourished to the point where scholars are far better equipped to see Milton's views in their contemporary context. Throughout this book, for instance, allusion has been made to his spiritual kinship with the so-called Cambridge Platonists. Arthur Sewell pointed out as long ago as 1939 how Milton's view of the will and the power of God overlapped markedly with that of Ralph Cudworth, 'the greatest of the Cambridge Platonists' who, in a sermon preached before the House of Commons in 1647, had said:

Now, I say, the very proper character, and essential tincture of God himself is nothing else but goodness. And it is another mistake which sometimes we have of God, by shaping him out according to the model of ourselves, when we make him nothing but a blind, dark, impetuous self-will, running through the world; such as we ourselves are ... that have not the ballast of absolute goodness to poise and settle us ...[8]

Milton's view of the modified power of God, in relation to man's free will, has much in common with Cudworth's. We are free to reject God: and this is one aspect of God's goodness; it necessarily involves a recognition that God's power, in this respect, is limited.

C. A. Patrides has amplified our sense that the *De Doctrina* is not all pure 'heresy', if by that we understand opinions which have no relation to what contemporary Christians believed.[9] His work has reminded us that Protestantism was not an alternative orthodoxy (however much Calvin, for instance, had wanted to make it that), so much as a ferment of contradictory ideas in which intellectual freedom was tempered by the knowledge that salvation was at stake.

In the years immediately preceding the compilation of *De Doctrina*, Milton suffered a series of great misfortunes and disillusionments. He lost two wives, he lost two children, he lost his sight. The Protectorate of Cromwell was not the embodiment of Christian liberty that Milton had hoped for, although he served it loyally enough. In all these respects it is natural to look to Milton's work for signs of uncertainty about divine providence, a tense puzzlement that the noble and puissant nation which in the *Areopagitica* was rousing herself like a strong man after sleep should appear to have dozed off again by the late 1650s. This is what we look for, but we find something much more characteristic. It was cardinal to Milton's view of things that he was never really wrong. In his more strident moods this habit of arrogance is unattractive; in defeat and disappointment, his constancy is magnificent and admirable. The cause of his whole life had been, from earliest years, to be a great poet. He had been distracted by the political developments of 1638 onwards, and devoted his energy and his sight to liberty's defence. But now, at fifty, his life took some shape in his mind, and he saw both avocations as the same. In both, he had been the servant of God. At twenty-three, all was, if he had grace to use it so, as ever in his great task-master's eye. Patiently, he abided the calling of the Lord; he read more and more in all the known tongues. After his blindness, he still had this sense, expressed in 'Sonnet XVI', that he was abiding: 'They also serve who only stand and wait'. The *De Doctrina* was part of this waiting, part of this self-preparation. The drama of *Adam Unparadised* had long ago been set aside. So had the great national epic which he had discussed with Manso. But now, the time of waiting and abiding was over, and poetry came to his lips. It was to be the same theme as the *Divine Weeks and Works* of Du Bartas which had beguiled his boyhood in Bread Street, but he brought to it all the reading and thinking of a patient life. Though intended for publication the *De Doctrina* remained, in effect, the record of a private, internalized debate with himself. The public, declamatory self of the pamphlets at last became one with the poet who had effectually slept for twenty years. Some time while he was actually in the process of revising the *De Doctrina*, the poem began. The anonymous biographer ('John Phillips')[10] tells us what the experience was like:

And he waking early (as is the use of temperate men) had commonly a good stock of verses ready against his amanuensis came; which if it happened to be later than ordinary, he would complain, saying he wanted to be milked.[11]

Milton's mind (as *De Doctrina* shows unequivocally) had moved very far from some of the traditional Christian ways of looking at God, and the world. Some of his quest had begun, as we have suggested, because he found his contemporary clergymen so inescapably absurd that he knew he could not believe as they did. Some of his views developed for less negative reasons, because he found himself in agreement with such serene intelligences as Cudworth. But at every stage it was his own, supremely independent vision of things which guided him. Even before his blindness he existed in his own world, belonged strictly to no sect, party, or group. To every issue he brought

> A mind not to be changed by place or time.
> The mind is its own place, and in itself
> Can make a heaven of hell, a hell of heaven.
>
> (I. 253–5)

This freedom did not breed humility, but it brought serenity. It was in serene mood that he began to dictate his great epic of *Paradise Lost*. The poem opens with a great invocation and prayer that he should be illumined by the spirit who inspired Moses, the shepherd who was inspired on the secret top 'Of Oreb, or of Sinai'; an interesting prayer for one who in the *De Doctrina* believed that the Mosaic law had been utterly overthrown by the Gospel liberty.

> . . . I thence
> Invoke thy aid to my adventurous song,
> That with no middle flight intends to soar
> Above the Aonian mount, while it pursues
> Things unattempted yet in prose or rhyme.
>
> (I. 12–16)

God had spoken to Moses; but he had spoken again and undone the work of Moses. He had spoken to Jesus, in a deeper way, and Jesus now called all men to his liberty. But now, in exactly the same way, God was speaking to Milton. It was indeed true that God called, as his manner was, for his Englishmen. The very language itself, what modern critics have called 'the grand style' makes it quite clear what is happening. *Paradise Lost* was dictated by God. It is written in the language of God. But it was dictated to a man who no longer believed (without

complication) in the things he was being called upon to prophesy. Like
the great prophets of the Old Testament, Milton was a mouthpiece
who was greatly at odds with the words he had to speak. Critics ever
since have disputed with one another whether or not the prayer of
humility with which the invocation ends was answered or not.

> . . . what in me is dark
> Illumine, what is low raise and support;
> That to the highth of this great argument
> I may assert eternal providence,
> And justify the ways of God to men.
>   (I. 22–6)

What is certain is that the prayer was meant most sincerely. Milton's
inner arguments, his public controversies, were over. He now felt called
merely to assert.

This constancy, this vocation to assertion rather than debate or
lampoon, is reflected in his political writings as the Protectorate came to
an end, and England prepared itself for the Restoration.

We have said a lot in this book about the scornful Milton, the
scabrous assailant of political opponents, the arguer *ad hominem*, the
unscrupulously personal pamphleteer. *The Ready and Easy Way to
Establish a Free Commonwealth* deserves consideration before Milton's
career as a prose-writer comes to an end.

Oliver Cromwell, whom Milton had gallantly served (without much
personal sympathy), had died on 3 September 1658. The Council
declared that 'the Lord Richard should succeed as Protector', and, after
a stunned period of silence, Richard Cromwell declared his allegiance
to

The liberty of the nation as we are men.
The liberty of conscience as we are Christians.
The keeping of the army in the hands of godly men.
The godly magistracy and godly ministry.[12]

'Godly' in each case means, of course, Independent Calvinists of the
kind elevated by the late Oliver. So, the Good Old Cause was, nominally
at least, to be kept ticking over. But everyone knew that it could not last.

Moments of great uneasiness in national history are often marked by
splendid funerals. The magnificence of Churchill's obsequies was a sign
that the British knew their Empire had finally gone down the sink; just as
the splendour of Queen Victoria's funeral sixty-odd years before was a
symptom that people half knew that the process had begun. Cromwell's

funeral put both these famous displays of national mourning in the shade. The common man, if popular song is anything to go by, felt as much indifference to Cromwell as he would feel for Churchill:

> Oliver Cromwell is buried and dead,
> Hey-ho buried and dead.
> There grew an old apple tree over his head,
> Hey-ho, buried and dead.
>
> The apples were ripe and ready to fall,
> Hey-ho etc.
> There came an old woman and gathered them all,
> Hey, ho, gathered them all.

This increased, rather than the reverse, the desire for a state funeral of stupendous proportions. After three weeks the corpse was removed from Whitehall to Somerset House. A superb effigy of His Highness was put on display. It reposed on a bed of state with a golden sceptre in his right hand, the orb in his left, on his head a regal cap of velvet, purple in colour and trimmed with ermine. Eight silver candle-holders, five feet high, stood round the bed, dripping with huge three-foot tapers, constantly alight. At the four corners of the bed stood four pillars surmounted by heraldic beasts.[13]

Not surprisingly, all this had the desired effect; crowds trooped to see this majestic doll, and the idea got about that Cromwell *père* had been a much-loved national institution. At length, on 23 November, the procession moved down to Westminster Abbey to deposit Cromwell's actual remains (ten weeks dead!) in the Henry VII chapel. In fact, they left it all too long, and the funeral itself was an anti-climax. Twelve gentlemen carried the canopy over the effigy. Cromwell's solitary horse, draped in scarlet, led off the procession; colonels and commanders followed, bearing eight pieces of armour. Colonel Fleetwood as the Chief Mourner walked between Lords Fauconberg and Lisle, preceded by the Garter King of Arms. His train was borne by five peers and fourteen earls or barons. But the ceremony was marred, partly because security arrangements were so tight that crowds (such as they were) could not get near enough the procession to have a good view; and because at the Abbey itself, the solemnity of the proceedings was made ridiculous by the open quarrels which developed among foreign ambassadors about who was to take precedence. Milton was in all probability in the Abbey while the Swedish envoys claimed equal status with the Dutch ambassadors and caused a rumpus in the choir-stalls during the singing of the

anthem.[14] Understandably Fauconberg wrote afterwards: 'Our solemnity is (God be praised) well over'.

But their difficulties were not. Richard Cromwell was quite manifestly unsuitable to succeed his father; he did not particularly want the office
and there were now strong moves afoot, even among former republicans, to come to terms with the exiled Charles II.

After Monck became commander-in-chief of the army in the spring
of 1660, there was not much hope left for godly men, either in the army
or the magistracy, to whom Richard Cromwell had sworn continued
attachment. Indeed, he began a purge 'till he had left not a zealot or a
preacher amongst them'.[15] It was at this juncture, with a Presbyterian
revival well under way, that Milton rushed through the presses the first
and second editions of *The Ready and Easy Way to Establish a Free
Commonwealth*. The need for the second edition was dictated by the
rapidity with which events were changing. Even as he wrote, as he says in
his opening paragraph, 'the face of things hath had some change'.[16] But,
in fundamental principle, Milton could not change. *The Ready and Easy
Way* is not his most exciting prose work but there are few documents
which illustrate more eloquently 'A mind not to be changed by place or
time'. Milton was not arguing for parliamentary democracy or anything
of that sort. He wanted 'a grand or central Council' and that chosen, it
should be perpetual. Characteristically, he defended his point of view by
saying that this was the system obtaining in the Israel of Our Lord's day,
with its Sanhedrin; in ancient Athens with its Areopagus; and in Rome
with its Senate. Such a body, he believed, could be most trusted to
guarantee the liberty of individuals. It is true that 'it is well and happy for
the people if their King be but a cypher', but there is no stopping
absolute monarchs abusing their authority. And 'kings to come, never
forgetting their former ejection, will be sure to fortify and arm themselves sufficiently for the future against all such attempts hereafter from
the people'.[17]

Milton, again characteristically, remembers Christ in scoffing mood,
and asks, 'What will they say of us and of the whole English nation but
scoffingly as of that foolish builder, mentioned by our Saviour, who
began to build a tower and was not able to finish it . . .' Far from having
established a new Roman republic, the English have so far merely
created a new Babel, but they should press forward to establish a
perpetual republicanism. Quietly, and with an unwonted dignity, he dug
in his heels. 'What I have spoken is the language of that which is not
called amiss the Good Old Cause'.

In the *De Doctrina*, Milton had set down, or was setting down, an attempt at a *summa* of his theological position. Doubtless, had it been finished, and had he had less devoted friends, he would have published it. In *Paradise Lost*, now begun, he was trying to assert with as much simplicity as he could muster, 'eternal providence'. It was his life's work. But he was prepared to put everything in jeopardy for a last-ditch defence of the Good Old Cause. He had written most scathingly of the royal martyr, he had debunked the *Eikon Basilike*, he had defended the idea of regicide and he had been a loyal servant of Oliver Cromwell. Only the most monstrous contortion could have made Milton salute the Restoration. His constancy, quietly self-confident, was perhaps inevitable. But it is the most impressive feature of his grandeur.

Dryden, who had written inconsolably for Oliver Cromwell's funeral, claimed that 'Peace was the prize of all his toils and care'. Yet mysteriously, only a few months later, he was able to celebrate 'the happy restoration and return of His Sacred Majesty Charles the Second'. It suddenly seemed that the Protectorate had not been such a happy time after all: 'For his long absence Church and State did groan', Dryden remembered; 'Madness the pulpit, faction seized the throne', which was odd, considering that of Cromwell he had written

> No borrowed bays his temples did adorn,
> But to our crown he did fresh jewels bring.

Milton remained a friend of his old colleague Dryden, but he could not have brought himself to this sort of absurdity. The Restoration happened, and like all the other disasters of the previous twenty years – marital, personal, and national – Milton greeted it stoically. But there could be no doubt that by his firm assertion in his belief in the Good Old Cause, he was endangering his life and, in so doing, he was endangering the possibility of finishing *Paradise Lost*.

CHAPTER 13

PARADISE LOST

He strives hard to say the finest things in the world,
and does say them.

William Hazlitt, *The English Poets*,
'On Shakespeare's Milton'

ON 30 January 1661, a little over two years after it had been buried with
such pathetic grandeur, the body of Oliver Cromwell was dug out of the
Henry VII chapel in Westminster Abbey and hoisted on the gallows at
Tyburn, alongside his son-in-law Ireton, and Milton's old attorney
Bradshaw. Evelyn, who had not been able to face seeing the royal
martyrdom, went along to look at the stinking corpses as they swung in
the air from nine in the morning till six at night, 'Thousands of people
(who had seen them in all their pride and pompous insults) being
spectators'. There was, as far as he was concerned, a clear moral: 'Fear
God and honour the King, but meddle not with them who are given to
change'.[1]

Some reprisals were inevitable against the Regicides. Of the forty-
one survivors of those who had signed the death warrant, fifteen fled to
America, Switzerland or the Low Countries. Some surrendered themselves to the new king's mercy, pleading that they had not wanted to be
involved in the King's trial, or that their hands had been forced. In the
end only nine of them suffered the ignominy of public disembowelling
and quartering. Colonel Harrison was the one who made the deepest
impression at his trial. He was completely unrepentant. 'I followed not
my own judgement', he said, 'I did what I did as out of conscience to the
Lord.' The crowd was hostile and as he made his way towards the
scaffold for his horrible fate they cried out, 'Where is your Good Old
Cause now?' 'Here in my bosom', he replied, 'and I shall seal it with my
blood.'[2] Followers of the Good Old Cause assumed that this was going
to be a cue for an angel to appear in the sky and for the rule of the saints
at last to begin. Unfortunately, this was not the case, and life, for some,
went on as usual.

Milton appears to have been in no immediate danger of any such ghastly fate as befell the actual perpetrators of the Regicide in January 1661. But that is not to say that he faced no danger at all of being brought to trial, or even of being sentenced to death, when Charles II returned in the summer of the previous year.

At the beginning of 1660 he had lost his position as Latin Secretary. It is said that he had saved £2,000 during the course of his employment, 'which being lodged in the excise, and that bank failing upon the Restoration, he utterly lost'.[3] The house, too, in Petty France, which had gone with the Secretaryship, and where Milton had lived for ten years, had to be left. Apart from his childhood home in Bread Street, it was the place where he had resided longest. He had got used to it since losing his sight. A hellish phase stretched ahead of unknown rooms and unfamiliar stairs and obtrusive furniture; a period of perpetual bruises and irritation and fear.

A friend – possibly a member of the Diodati family, but nobody knows for certain – took Milton into hiding in Bartholomew Close. We know that the Diodatis lived near Little St Bartholomew's during the 1640s[4] and there is a sort of pleasing appropriateness about these friends of childhood coming to his rescue as his public career cascaded to an unhappy end. There is even a story, known to Warton, that Milton's friends staged a mock-funeral for him to put the authorities off his scent, 'and that when matters were settled in his favour, and the affair was known, the king laughed heartily at the trick'.[5]

Certainly, it was too much to hope that the reversal in Milton's fortunes would be missed by those who had been infuriated by his controversial writings in the previous twenty years. G.S., the anonymous author of a bad poem called 'Britain's Triumph for her Imparalleled Deliverance' gloats mercilessly:

> But who appears here with the curtain drawn?
> What Milton! are you come to see the sight?
> Oh Image-Breaker! poor knave! had he sawn
> That which the fame of, made him cry outright.
>   He'd taken counsel of Achitophel
>   Swung himself weary, and so gone to Hell.[6]

Frequent gibes were made about his blindness, and it was assumed on all sides, in the enthusiasm of the moment, that Milton had been struck blind by God.[7]

Milton might have been taken into the protection of London friends, but he made no elaborate attempts at escape. He did not, like so many men closely associated with Cromwell's government, flee abroad; he did not even leave London.

In June, Parliament passed an order to the Attorney General that Milton should be arrested and that two of his books – the *Defence of the English People against Salmasius*,[8] and the *Eikonoklastes* – should be burnt. Mr John Milton, and Mr John Goodwin (author of an anti-royalist book called *The Obstructors of Justice*) were sent for, 'in custody, by the Serjeant-at-Arms attending this House'.[9] The royal proclamation calling for the suppression of these books was issued on 13 August. It is not hard to imagine how the author of *Areopagitica* felt. But clearly his friends insisted on his lying low, because the proclamation claims of Milton, and of Goodwin, that they 'are both fled, or so obscure themselves that no endeavours used for their apprehension can take effect whereby they might be brought to legal trial and deservedly receive condign punishment for their treasons and offences'.[10]

This does not mean, of course, that they had been out looking for Milton and unable to find him. It means that Charles II wanted, for the best practical and political reasons, to have as few reprisals as possible. The prospect of putting Milton on trial is not one which any government would have undertaken lightly. His replies from the dock would have been terrifying; besides which, God had already punished him by striking him blind; and probably more important than any of these things, his brother Christopher was an up-and-coming impeccably royalist barrister: he was called to the bench, indeed, on 25 November, and almost certainly had been working hard on his brother's behalf in the previous months.

After 29 August 1660, Milton knew that his life was not actually in danger. The Act of Free and General Pardon, Indemnity and Oblivion contained lists of persons who were *not* pardoned, and who were condemned to death. Milton's name was not on the list. It was shortly after this that Milton took a house in Holborn 'near Red Lion Fields', but he was not safe for in November he was arrested and imprisoned. The Journals of the House of Commons would suggest that he was in prison for about a month, since on 15 December they ordered 'that Mr Milton, now in the custody of the Serjeant-at-Arms attending this House, be forthwith released, paying his fees'. The fees were £150 and, true to form, he protested about them in a written complaint two days later. Andrew Marvell, MP for Hull, spoke up in Milton's defence, only to be answered by Sir Heneage Finch 'That Milton was Latin Secretary to Cromwell and deserved hanging'.[11] These were no idle words, of course. The death of Colonel Harrison on the scaffold happened only a week or two later.

But, in spite of the continued abuse which inevitably came in Milton's direction, he *was* now safe. Yet again, he moved house, this time to Jewin Street, and there, presumably, the epic continued to flow.

> Yet not the more
> Cease I to wander where the Muses haunt
> Clear spring, or shady Grove, or sunny hill,
> Smit with the love of sacred song; but chief
> Thee Sion and the flowery brooks beneath
> That wash thy hallowed feet, and warbling flow,
> Nightly I visit: nor sometimes forget
> Those other two equalled with me in fate,
> So were I equalled with them in renown,
> Blind Thamyris, and blind Maeonides,
> And Tiresias and Phineus prophets old.
>
> (III. 26–36)

His vocation to 'assert eternal providence' in verse drove him back to his old timeless desire for fame. The world, which he had so devotedly tried to change, now shrank from his consciousness; the earthly gave place to the celestial; the ephemeral to the eternal. Knowing that, even if death was not soon to overtake him, he had to live with the collapse of all his earthly hopes, Milton turned his inward eye heavenwards. There is a moving moment in Walton's description of the death of Hooker, before which the theologian was 'deep in contemplation, and not inclinable to discourse'. When he was asked his present thoughts, he replied, 'That he was meditating the number and nature of Angels, and their blessed obedience and order, without which, peace could not be in heaven: and Oh! that it might be so on earth!'[12] It is not fanciful to think that, as Milton submitted to the new and passive role of seer and epic poet, his mind, like Hooker's, turned towards the angels. Dr Johnson found it an 'inconvenience' that *Paradise Lost* 'comprises neither human actions nor human manners'. But if life is to be understood in Milton's terms, human actions have no meaning unless related to the number and nature of angels.

C. S. Lewis made an important point about *Paradise Lost* long ago when he pointed out that the corporeal nature of Milton's angels – the fact that they eat, have sexual intercourse and so on – derived directly from his Platonism. 'Milton's picture of the angels, though doubtless poetical in detail, is meant in principle as a literally true picture of what they probably were according to the up-to-date pneumatology of his century.'[13] Thomas Aquinas had taught that angels could not eat; if they appeared to be doing so it was 'not actual eating but a symbol of spiritual eating'. Milton's Archangel Raphael directly contradicts this point of view by actively enjoying the dinner prepared by Eve:

> So down they sat,
> And to their viands fell, nor seemingly
> The angel, nor in mist, the common gloss
> Of theologians, but with keen despatch
> Of real hunger, and concoctive heat
> To transubstantiate . . .
>
> (v. 433–8)

Lewis points out how Milton shares with the Cambridge Platonist Henry More (who was at Christ's shortly after him) the belief that angels have a physical reality. 'The appearance of armed men fighting and encountering one another in the sky is most notorious', More wrote in the *Antidote against Atheism*.[14]

Nowadays, antidotes against atheism have to take rather vague, spiritual forms, for fear of being contradicted by astronomers and physicists. Christian critics of the poem have been, if anything, more embarrassed than the atheists by Lewis's bluff fundamentalism. Dame Helen Gardner, for instance, while accepting that 'Milton's materialism runs very deep',[15] leaves the strong impression at the end of her first chapter that no reader of *Paradise Lost* was ever meant to take its heaven or its God quite literally. If you believe the Father of the poem to be 'God as He is', it is as naive as supposing that Michelangelo believed 'that God possessed a pair of powerful legs'.[16] But there is a danger in the analogy with painting which any Platonist would perceive. We know when we look at a ceiling or a canvas that the object before us is only an artefact; that the painted angels and the painted ancient of days have had human models as much as the painted Adam. But the effect of a poem is less obviously artificial, particularly when the poet is blind and prays

> So much the rather thou celestial Light
> Shine inward, and the mind through all her powers
> Irradiate, there plant eyes, all mist from thence
> Purge and disperse, that I may see and tell
> Of things invisible to mortal sight.
>
> (III. 51–5)

What Milton is vouchsafed by his Muse, and can promise to his reader, is a vision of reality. Of course, because the things of heaven are invisible to mortal sight, it is necessary to invest them with an appearance which Milton can only imagine. The majestic appearance of Raphael, for instance, has to be described with reference to the seraphim in the sixth chapter of Isaiah, and with Milton's own splendidly imagined sense of what an archangel looked like:

> Like Maia's son he stood,
> And shook his plumes, that heavenly fragrance filled
> The circuit wide.
>
> (v. 285–7)

And of course, as Raphael himself says, it is necessary when describing heavenly things to a creature of earth, to use a certain amount of analogy.

> . . . and what surmounts the reach
> Of human sense, I shall delineate so,
> By likening spiritual to corporal forms,
> As may express them best, though what if earth
> Be but the shadow of heaven, and things therein
> Each to other like, more than on earth is thought?
>
> (v. 571–6)

Raphael has been reading *The Republic* and probably Ficino's *Theologia Platonica*. But the idea of the angels, and the faculty which enables us to imagine them is as 'real'

> As when by night the glass
> Of Galileo, less assured, observes
> Imagined lands and regions in the moon . . .
>
> (v. 261–3)

Milton believed in the fundamental reality of what he was writing about in *Paradise Lost*. In the ninth book, when he describes the 'nightly visitation unimplored' of his Muse he contrasts the truth, the literal reality of what he is dictating, as opposed to the 'fabled knights in battles feigned' which he had for a long time imagined would be the subject of his epic.

The God, the angels, the Christ, the universe of *Paradise Lost* are as real, then, as those of *De Doctrina Christiana* and, as has often been pointed out, they were almost contemporaneously conceived. The Arian who wrote the prose work also conceived of a heavenly choir singing to the Son that

> . . . on thee
> Impressed the effulgence of his glory abides,
> Transfused on thee his ample Spirit rests.
>
> (III. 387–9)

The difference between the two works is that in the theological prose, Milton argues, speculates, amasses evidence from the Scriptures and from the Fathers; whereas in the poem, using the same evidence, he *asserts*. He does not assert analytically, like a bully who cannot really conduct an argument. He asserts imaginatively. He replaces the technique of debate by summoning up a vision of God and His creation in which, we can be quite certain, he firmly believed.

Strikingly, two of the most interesting books on *Paradise Lost*, of the hundreds published this century, have been of this fundamentalist standpoint: C. S. Lewis's *Preface to Paradise Lost* and William Empson's *Milton's God*. Lewis's assertion that 'many of those who say they dislike Milton's God only mean, that they dislike God' let in according to Empson, 'some needed fresh air'.[17] The punch of Empson's book, like all the atheism of that generation, seems a bit less daring than it once did; but it remains a most important work of Miltonic criticism – certainly most important to Milton's biographer – because it states more baldly than any other that the God of the poem is 'the traditional Christian God', and the God in which Milton believed. But he both elaborates and qualifies more boldly than any other critic the Romantic belief, first voiced by Blake, that Milton, like all true poets, was of the Devil's party without knowing it.

Much has been written, from a *critical* point of view, about this conceit; and no reader of the poem can ever have failed to sense Satan with his desperate courage, and his magnificent pride, getting quite out of control and throwing our response to the poem's theology off balance. 'Around this character [Milton] has thrown a singularity of daring, a grandeur of sufferance, and a ruined splendour, which constitute the very height of poetic sublimity', as Coleridge observed.[18] And the traditional biographical reading of this is explained in terms of Milton's attitude to the defeat of the Good Old Cause. 'Where is your Good Old Cause now?' asked the crowds, and Colonel Harrison could reply, 'Here in my bosom', before the hideous tortures were inflicted on him. So too, Satan, cast down to hell by a vindictive and smiling God, comes before us with all heroic magnificence, a conviction that 'Here at least/We shall be free' and 'Better to reign in hell, than serve in heaven'. How obviously like this is – so goes the argument – to Milton's own predicament at the time of the Restoration. Milton could scarcely write about *rebellion*, it is thought, without secretly being on the side of the rebels.

There is an absurdity about this way of reading the epic which hints that Milton would have had no imaginative ability – let alone desire – to distinguish between the rightful deposition of a tyrant and a crazy rebellion against God. But there is surely no absurdity in the romantic reading of the poem. Satan is not, of course, all that he makes himself out to be. Not without an angelic equivalent of malice, Gabriel recalls how in his old, unfallen days, Satan had really been rather a toady to God:

> . . . thou sly hypocrite, who now wouldst seem
> Patron of liberty, who more than thou
> Once fawned, and cringed, and servilely adored
> Heaven's awful monarch?
>
> (IV. 957–60)

Yet the heavenly party, true to Scripture, always have to fall back on thunderously bullying destruction of their enemies, or sneering at them when they are down. Against this, Satan's rhetoric, even if it is laced with falsehoods, seems more attractive.

But the biographer of Milton is bound to record that it would not necessarily have seemed so to the poet. Empson finds the sneering, 'the blood curdling jokes', the delight in endlessly tormenting their weaker foes deeply unpleasant in both the Father and the Son. Did Milton see how odiously cruel his God appeared? How could he not be on the side of the fallen angels? The only biographical answer to this is that if we are meant to hate his hectoring, bullying God we are also meant, presumably, to hate his bullying, hectoring pamphlets, his merciless assaults on Salmasius's sexual inadequacy, his badgeringly cruel gloatings over Charles I's last hours, and his contempt for almost every clergyman who ever crossed his path.

The 'dark' side of *Paradise Lost*, exaggerated and heightened by pedantic or hostile commentary, can be explained in terms of the 'dark' side of Milton's awareness and nature. His God, like the Psalmist's God, is a derisive figure, who laughs at the plight of the ungodly; he is a warlike God, who lets his enemies be scattered; he is a vengeful God, who loves righteousness and hates iniquity. But it is a complete distortion of *Paradise Lost* if we fail to recognize that the joyful and celebratory passages far outnumber the parts where close reading can unearth divine traits which do not coincide with the vacuities of agnostic hope. If He hates iniquity and punishes it, Milton's God is also

conceived in the strong Platonic terms of light and goodness. Satan, in
his encounter with the unfallen angels Ithuriel and Zephon, at first
blusters with the magnificently insulting, 'Not to know me argues
yourselves unknown' (IV. 830). But it is not long before he is 'abashed'
and before he 'felt how awful goodness is' (846–7). The *awfulness* of
goodness, its power, its brightness, its strength: this, in book after book
of his epic, Milton asserts. The reader who takes the Blakean view
seriously fails to sense, breathing as it were through the pores of the epic,
a sense of the abundant strength of goodness. 'Love virtue, she alone is
free' is the credo of *Paradise Lost*. We sense it in the delightfulness of
Paradise:

> . . . now gentle gales
> Fanning their odoriferous wings dispense
> Native perfumes, and whisper whence they stole
> Those balmy spoils. As when to them who sail
> Beyond the Cape of Hope, and now are past
> Mozambic, off at sea north-east winds blow
> Sabean odours from the spicy shore
> Of Arabie the blest, with such delay
> Well pleased they slack their course, and many a league
> Cheered with the grateful smell old Ocean smiles.
>
> (IV. 156–65)

Such lines breathe a delight in the good world, and the good God who
made it. Dr Johnson briefly deviated into sense in his reflections on the
poet of *Paradise Lost* in saying 'When he cannot raise wonder by the
sublimity of his mind, he gives delight by its fertility.' Food, sex, plants,
the animal kingdom – all alike seem to spring from God's goodness in
the Garden of Adonis which was Milton's mind. The most joyful book in
the epic, the seventh, is central, both in placing and in terms of the
poem's argument. Milton believed that

> on the watery calm
> His brooding wings the spirit of God outspread,
> And vital virtue infused, and vital warmth
> Throughout the fluid mass, but downward purged
> The black tartareous cold infernal dregs
> Adverse to life . . .
>
> (VII. 234–9)

He was faithful enough to his memories of the Scriptures not to attribute
to his Deity anything which could not be inferred from the canonical
books of the Bible. And in doing so, he returned, quite deliberately, to

the poet who had first delighted his childhood: Du Bartas. Nowhere is the influence of Du Bartas stronger in *Paradise Lost* than in its seventh book.[19] The close verbal parallels were long ago noted by the American scholar George Coffin Taylor. Although Du Bartas's influence is noticeable throughout the epic, it is in the eleventh book that one becomes aware of it again almost bubbling beneath the surface.

After the Fall Adam is appalled to realize that it will no longer be possible to read God clearly in the Book of his Works. Just as Milton in his blindness is

> Presented with a universal blanc
> Of nature's works to me expunged and razed
> (III. 48–9)

so Adam realizes that he is hopelessly cut off from 'the book of knowledge fair'.

In Paradise, God was close to him.

> On this mount he appeared; under this tree
> Stood visible, among these pines his voice
> I heard, here with him at this fountain talked . . .
> (XI. 320–2)

He is about to be thrown out into a world where God is no longer visible.

> In yonder nether world where shall I seek
> His bright appearances, or footstep trace?
> (XI. 328–9)

The Archangel Michael's reply is resoundingly important:

> surmise not then
> His presence to these narrow bounds confined
> Of Paradise or *Eden* . . .
> (XI.340–2)

And he continues

> Yet doubt not but in valley and in plain
> God is as here, and will be found alike
> Present, and of his presence many a sign
> Still following thee, still compassing thee round
> With goodness and paternal love, his face
> Express, and of his steps the track divine.
> (XI. 349–54)

We fail to understand what was happening to Milton personally, as he dictated *Paradise Lost* day by day in the early 1660s, if we fail to understand these lines. They relate directly to Du Bartas's

> For, yet his Fall, which way so e'er he rolled,
> His wondering eyes, God everywhere behold;
> In heaven, in earth, in ocean and in air,
> He sees, and feels, and finds him everywhere.

Throughout his blindness, but particularly in the months immediately following the Restoration, it was asserted that Milton had lost his sight because of God's wrath. He was the 'blind beetle that durst affront the Royal Eagle', and John Garfield declared in a fawning dedication of *Eikon Aklastos* that 'I shall leave him under the rod of correction, wherewith God hath evidenced His particular judgement by striking him blind'.[20]

If Milton allowed himself to believe these assertions, the previous twenty years of his life must inevitably seem quite pointless. Yet, like so many of the prophets and poets of the Old Testament, he was obliged to ask, 'Wherefore doth the way of the wicked prosper?'[21] The Bible told Milton repeatedly that God withheld himself from his people; He hid His face, and He appeared to allow the natural order to be overthrown, and the creation 'with vital virtue fused' to be wrecked by sinners and fools. In all this, the most worrying possibility for the believer was that God might be lost sight of. He had shown himself in England, 'as his manner is' with so many indisputable signs. Milton now returned to the heart of his beliefs. Like Hooker, he meditated the number and nature of the angels, and out of his meditation grew a great inner vision of man's place in the cosmos, and his relationship with God. *Paradise Lost* is really no more than one man's reading of the Bible; its size, its grandeur, its grotesquery, its ugliness, its beauty, are all reflections of Milton's mind.

For all that, it is the least egotistical of his works. Almost every poem he wrote before *Paradise Lost* turned on himself, or some theme immediately arising from his own life. In *Paradise Lost*, of course, there are the great passages about his blindness, and about the visitations of his Muse, but the self-references are less personal than Sylvester's in Du Bartas. It was the French poet who established the tradition of biblical poetry in which the poet made continual asides about himself: Sylvester, in his translations, merely imitates and paraphrases his original. There is a delightful parochialism about his desire to spend the rest of his days 'among the great unkenned' while introducing the Berkshire landscape of his home into *The Divine Weeks and Works*:

> Be Hadley Pond my sea: Lamsbourne my Thames;
> Lambourne my London: Kennet's silver streams,
> My fruitful Nile . . .
>
> (III. i. 1153–5)

London was Milton's London, but as he sat there in Jewin Street, inspired by *his* vision of the divine works, he did not feel inclined, as he almost invariably did in his prose writings, to focus the attention on himself. We are never, for one moment, away from Milton in *Paradise Lost*. It is overwhelmingly the product of his mind and genius. But the vocation to 'assert eternal providence' is faithfully pursued. His darkened eyes search out 'thrones, dominations, princedoms, virtues, powers'. And it is from the Archangel that Adam receives the reassurance that though He is now invisible, God's presence follows his people through the world. The vision must be *asserted* because it will never, in the realm of nature, be automatically *felt*. The epic begins with angels speaking among themselves – great and fallen angels, huge, ruined, but still with their old beauty hovering about them, still weeping tears such as angels weep, 'celestial spirits in bondage'. In those early books of *Paradise Lost*, the very existence of man is only mooted as an unhappy rumour. In their happy and innocent state, the only rational companions Adam and Eve have are the angels, and it is by the malice of an angel that they fall. By an angel Adam is instructed about the future of the human race, and its redemption by the all-powerful Son. And the last sight which Adam and Eve have of Paradise is as of ramparts, crowded with a heavenly militia:

> They looking back, all the eastern side beheld
> Of Paradise, so late their happy seat,
> Waved over by that flaming brand, the gate
> With dreadful faces thronged and fiery arms . . .
>
> (XII. 641–4)

It had been a large part of Milton's purpose and triumph in *Paradise Lost* to recreate the physical reality of the angel kingdoms. Like Hooker he contemplated 'their blessed obedience and order, without which peace could not be in heaven'. He did so, of course, with a fallen mind, and the need to have what was dark in him illumined. Inevitably, therefore, his unregenerate imagination could depict, and ours can respond to, the pathos and grandeur of Satan's rhetoric. Satan, of course, is the hero, at least of the first two books; and we are unable to respond with the rapturous innocence of Adam when he sees Raphael landing in Eden:

> what glorious shape
> Comes this way moving; seems another morn
> Risen on mid-noon . . .
>
> (v. 309–11)

Unbelievers, of course, do not share Milton's belief in angels. And Christians themselves are usually rather hazy in their minds about the existence of an angelic order. In October 1939 Rose Macaulay wrote to her sister:

I went in for 10 minutes yesterday to the R.C. church near here, where there was a sermon going on. It was all about how the Supreme Being had created various orders of Angels, good and bad. I *cannot* think why we have endured all these centuries of this lifeless nonsense. I thought as I sat there, what if the congregation all rose up and mobbed the preacher, and beat him up, and the women scratched his face, and the men kicked him, saying, 'We want something to the purpose, not angels & devils; give us bread not stones'.[22]

The point here is that, at a time of national emergency, preachers should be speaking of the emergency. The man should have been telling them to be brave during air raids, or how to respond when they got their call-up papers. It is hard to imagine Milton, at any age in history, stepping in for ten minutes to the Church of Our Lady of the Rosary in Marylebone Road. But had he done so in October 1939 he would have sympathized more with the priest than with Rose Macaulay. His own response to a national and personal emergency was to return to how 'the Supreme Being had created various orders of Angels'. He did not regard it as 'lifeless nonsense' but as the very heart of his faith. For, by asserting the reality of this physically true, but invisible order of creation, he was asserting too the everlasting, if invisible, presence of God in the hearts of believers.

Like all great works of art, *Paradise Lost* has been made susceptible to all manner of interpretations, and each reader brings to it his own religious obsessions and preoccupations. It has played a strange role in the national consciousness of the English. There is Layamon's *Brut* and there are Tennyson's *Idylls of the King*, but they have never occupied the place of *Paradise Lost* which takes the part which might be filled by a national epic. Each generation has endured 'this lifeless nonsense' and, whatever the dons may have told them, they have found new riches in it.

For the last three hundred years it has been as popular as the Bible.

Most great English writers have more or less known it by heart. And it has had more religious influence than most Christian readers would like to believe. But it is, on top of all these things, a tempestuous, but ultimately serene testimony to the brightness and sureness of Milton's own religious faith.

CHAPTER 14

THIRD MARRIAGE

Mistress Eliz: Minshull . . . a gent. person a peaceful and agreeable humour.

John Aubrey

WHILE the epic flowed, Milton's life became more private and domestic than it had been for twenty years or more. Foreigners, particularly from Italy, came to see him. Tourists even came to Bread Street to see 'the house and chamber where he was born'. But, as Aubrey says, he was still 'much more admired abroad than at home'.[1]

The foreigners who stood outside the Spread Eagle in Bread Street were remote from the central concerns of Milton's mind at this date. Predominant was the poem, the visitation of the Muse

> who deigns
> Her nightly visitation unimplored,
> And dictates to me slumbering, or inspires
> Easy my unpremeditated verse . . .
> *(PL, IX. 21–4)*

He would wake early, his mind brimming with the poem. By the time the amanuensis arrived he would find Milton waiting for him, a neatly made, impeccably dressed, slight figure, still with auburn hair and with a good complexion.

In the days when he could see, Milton had evidently spent most of the day reading, and the deprivation caused by his blindness must have been acute. He needed not only someone to copy as he dictated *Paradise Lost*; he also liked to have a passage of the Hebrew Bible read aloud to him before he had his sparse breakfast. The morning, too, would be spent reading – and not merely English books but Hebrew, Greek, Latin, Italian, Spanish, and French. When fine, his exercise was 'chiefly walking'; and once more a companion must be found to take his arm and walk around the streets of London; though, since he knew them so well, he could probably have managed to do so on his own.

Whenever possible, he met with his young friends. Andrew Marvell, Cyriack Skinner, and his doctor, Nathan Paget, were obviously habitual companions, who enjoyed his 'satirical wit' and who helped to drive away unwanted visitors, of whom, sometimes, there were 'more than he did desire'.[2] In the evenings, there would be music. Milton always had a chamber organ which moved about with him from house to house. It was the old instrument which had belonged to his father and on which he had first learnt to play. We are not told what he played; but probably the strains of Monteverdi pealed out into Jewin Street as Milton remembered the vast receptions and splendid liturgies which he had enjoyed in Venice. Doubtless, too, he played the airs of Harry Lawes, and perhaps sang songs from *Comus*, their strange mixture of baroque formality and freshness like a country folk-song, their thrilling notes recalling to his mind the youthful faces of Lord Bridgewater's children, or the aged eyes of the Countess of Derby that had gazed into the eyes of Spenser when young.

Such was the music played in the reign of Charles II by the blind poet. But life was not all delight. Idolized by the young men on whom he doted, Milton never really enjoyed the companionship of his daughters. Clearly, they had been brought up quite largely by their grandmother Powell, who had attempted, successfully, to turn them against their father. Even had Milton wanted to bestow on them the feminine equivalent of the education which he lavished on his nephews it would have been difficult, because, during the crucial years, they had moved to and fro between their grandmother's house and his own; he had been first heavily occupied in business of state (which he had never been in the boyhood of the Phillipses); then imprisoned or threatened. By the early 1660s the girls had already started to grow away from their father. In 1662 Anne was sixteen, Mary fourteen, and Deborah ten. It was ten years since their mother had died. Milton paid for them to have a governess in the Jewin Street house who instructed them as much as their capabilities would allow.[3] Anne Milton, as well as being lame, was slightly 'dippy' and must have been a great trial to live with. The other two sound irritatingly pert. But they were taught to read and write. Deborah, who looked extraordinarily like her father, was obviously the brightest of the three and, in later life, became a schoolmistress. Although she never went blind, she had to wear spectacles from the age of eighteen onwards.

No one ever emerges creditably from a family quarrel. Milton was to protest over the meal table that he had spent the greatest part of his

estate providing for these girls,[4] but it is doubtful, as he devoted his
evening to smoking with the young men,[5] or playing the organ, whether
they ever felt much loved. It is often said that he disliked them because
they reminded him of their mother. But life would be very simple if it
were possible to explain why parents fail to love their children.

Such bad blood existed between Milton and his daughters that it is
hard to accept any of their memories of their father without scepticism.
In such matters as Milton's eating habits, for instance, one sees the
distorting power of domestic irritation at work in Deborah's memories.
The accounts of friends recall a temperate man who did not eat or drink
much, but enjoyed what he ate.[6] Deborah remembers that, though
temperate, her father always insisted on the best of everything. The
outsiders who enjoyed Milton's conversation were merely struck by the
tiny helpings on Milton's plate; but for the family, this was written down
as faddishness.[7]

What is one to make, then, of the story that Mary and Deborah were
made to read aloud to their father in languages which they could not
understand?

> She informed me, that she and her sisters used to read to their father in eight
> languages, which by practice they were capable of doing with great readiness and
> accuracy, though they understood what they read in no other language but
> English; and their father used often to say in their hearing, 'one tongue was
> enough for a woman'.

As Edward Phillips remarks, all this 'must needs be a trial of patience'.[8]

W. R. Parker's biography makes out as good a case as possible for
Milton by saying

> If either Mary or Deborah Milton had evidenced the slightest aptitude for
> languages and the slightest desire to learn, their father would have taught them.
> The admirer of Queen Christina, the friend of Lady Ranelagh and Lady
> Margaret Ley, was no advocate of ignorance in women.[9]

It seems to the dispassionate mind, however, worse, not better that
Milton was not utterly misogynistic. If he seriously believed that 'one
tongue was enough for a woman', there would have been something
almost bearable about his treatment of the daughters. But the knowledge that he was all charm with his clever and aristocratic friends must
have made it hard to take the snub in a spirit of good humour.

Personally, I find it very hard to believe Deborah's claim that she read
to her father in eight languages which she could not understand. The
'trial of patience' on both sides would be excruciating. We know that

Milton was particularly fussy with those who read to him, and insisted that they pronounce Latin in the way that he found acceptable.[10] In 1662, Dr Paget introduced Milton to a young friend of a friend, a twenty-two year-old Quaker called Thomas Ellwood, and it was agreed that the poet would help him with his Latin if he came to read to him in the afternoons.

> I went therefore and took myself a lodging as near to his house (which was then in Jewin Street) as conveniently as I could, and from thenceforward went every day in the afternoon, except on the first days of the week, and sitting by him in his dining-room read to him in such books in the Latin tongue as he pleased to hear me read.

> At my first sitting to read to him, observing that I used the English pronunciation, he told me, if I would have the benefit of the Latin tongue, not only to read and understand Latin authors, but to converse with foreigners, either abroad or at home, I must learn the foreign pronunciation. To this I consenting, he instructed me how to sound the vowels; so different from the common pronunciation used by the English, who speak Anglice their Latin, that – with some few other variations in sounding some consonants in particular cases, as *c* before *e* or *i* like *ch*, *sc* before *i* like *sh* etc. – the Latin thus spoken seemed as different from that which was delivered, as the English generally speak it, as if it were another language.[11]

This was obviously the way that Milton began to teach a language to his pupils and protégés after he went blind. It began with their learning to read the language aloud. Perhaps he *did* intend to teach Mary and Deborah, but their sessions ended fretfully, either because he corrected their pronunciation too harshly, or because they were stupid or because of the natural antipathy which existed between father and daughters. Some such session, with the girls puzzling out the words of a Latin text, probably took place and gave rise to the story of their reading to him in eight languages which they did not understand. Since Milton had Ellwood and others to read to him, it is difficult to see why, with his 'excellent ear',[12] he should have chosen to hear the girls mangling his favourite passages of Greek poetry or Hebrew Scripture.

Milton liked Ellwood, whose studies had been neglected, partly by ill health, and partly because of his membership of the Society of Friends, which made it impossible for him to pursue a conventional education at an Inn of Court or a university. When he was not recovering from respiratory illnesses or contracting them in Bridewell (where he suffered for his religion) he made a happy addition to the band of Miltonic disciples and hangers-on.

Perhaps during one of Ellwood's absences Nathan Paget introduced
Milton to a cousin of his called Elizabeth Minshull. She was a Cheshire
woman of twenty-four years of age. She had golden hair. They were
married on the feast of St Matthias, 24 February 1663 in the beautiful
church of St Mary Aldermary, she being described as a spinster of the
parish of St Andrew's, Holborn. The apostle St Matthias was chosen
late, and for the rather arbitrary purpose of making up the number of the
twelve after the suicide of Judas. But Scripture tells us nothing about
him; we only know that 'they gave forth their lots and the lot fell upon
Matthias'. Elizabeth Minshull might well have felt that there was an
appropriateness about the date of her wedding. No one ever pretended
that this new marriage was a romance. She had been chosen, in effect, to
do a job; to be a sanctified housekeeper and concubine. It was the third
time that Milton had gone through a marriage ceremony, but he had not
had the words of the Prayer Book rite read over him since 1642. On this
occasion they were married by Dr Robert Gell, who had been a Fellow
of Christ's in Milton's time.[13]

Milton did not think to tell his daughters that he was getting married.
They heard it from the servant girl, Elizabeth Fisher. Mary replied
laconically 'that that was no news to hear of his wedding but if she could
hear of his death that was something'.[14]

Marriage gave him the chance yet again to move house, and the carts
were loaded up once more with books, pictures, and the old chamber
organ and trundled off to 'a house in the artillery-walk leading to Bunhill
Fields'. A good deal, one imagines, got 'lost' in the course of this
removal, particularly since the girls were not altogether honest. They
persuaded poor Elizabeth Fisher to cheat their father out of housekeep-
ing money, and they sold a large portion of his library.[15]

From the start there was open war between Elizabeth Milton – 'Betty'
as her husband called her – and her unfortunate stepchildren. Legend
from the girls' point of view depicts their stepmother as a 'termagant';[16]
but perhaps she had to be. If Anne, Mary, and Deborah were really
stealing from their father, and hating him so much that they longed for
his death, it is understandable that a hot-tempered young bride, not
much older than they were, would take a firm line. It is alleged that she
apprenticed Anne and Mary to gold-lacemakers 'without his knowledge', but it is all too painfully likely that Milton, feeling his daughters
to be impossible, threw up his hands and allowed Betty to take control.

Obviously, she was a good household manager. The marriage has
been encapsulated, rather unfairly, in many minds by a single anecdote;

the story of Milton at table saying, 'God have mercy Betty, I see thou wilt perform according to thy promise in providing me such dishes as I think fit while I live, and when I die thou knowest that I have left thee all'.[17]

This certainly suggests a rather less exalted view of marriage than the dizzier passages on Christian liberty to be met with in the divorce pamphlets. But even there Milton was quite clear in his traditional belief that 'as God is the head of Christ, and Christ the head of man, so man is the head of woman': almost traditional, at least, save for its Arian flavouring.[18] Just as, in his political writings, Milton never pretended to a general egalitarianism, which he dismissed as licence, not liberty, so, in his views of marriage, he never wavered from his belief that women played a subordinate marital role. 'Nevertheless man is not to hold her as a servant, but receives her into a part of that empire which God proclaims him to, though not equally, yet largely, as his own image and glory: for it is no small glory to him, that a creature so like him, should be made subject to him.'[19] Modern readers of both sexes must find it hard to accept that 'this makes marriage not a bondage, a blessing not a curse, a gift of God not a snare'.[20] Milton acknowledges, of course, that in some cases the wife might be superior to the husband, but these are 'particular exceptions' if 'she exceed her husband in prudence and dexterity, and he contentedly yield, for then a superior and more natural law comes in, that the wiser should govern the less wise, whether male or female'.[21] But he makes it fairly obvious that this would be an exception to the general rule that God has crowned man with 'an indelible character of priority'.[22]

This is simply orthodox Christian teaching, and only crackpots in Milton's lifetime would have found anything offensive in it. One must not conclude that Milton was wildly misogynistic as a result. Nor should we imagine, merely because he saw it as Betty's function to provide him with dishes as he thought fit, that Elizabeth Minshull was only a housekeeper. Doubtless she married Milton with the most prosaic of expectations. But she remained with him for twelve years, and there is every reason to suppose that they were suited to one another, and were reasonably happy together.

Music was a bond. Even though he thought she had 'no ear', he liked Betty's voice and would often accompany her on the organ after dinner (that is to say, in the late afternoon) while she sang.[23] Probably, she read aloud to him – not the foreign tongues that she would not have known, but his favourite English poets. It is to her that we owe our knowledge that he liked best Spenser, Shakespeare, and Cowley. 'And being asked what he thought of Dryden, she said Dryden used sometimes to visit him, but he thought him no poet but a good rhymist.'[24] These are not remarks which suggest the domestic illiterate that she is often made out to be.

And she it was who was closer than anyone to the author of *Paradise Lost* while it was in its final stages of composition. The previous chapter of this book, in which I reiterated that the epic contains a genuine expression of Milton's religious convictions, will have struck some readers as naïve. But it is from Betty Milton that we learn that the celestial inspiration was no figure of speech:

> ... and being asked whether he did not often read Homer and Virgil, she understood it as an imputation upon him for stealing from those authors, and answered with eagerness that he stole from nobody but the Muse who inspired him; and being asked by a lady present who the Muse was, replied that it was God's grace, and the Holy Spirit that visited him nightly.[25]

The attitude to 'borrowing' from the great epics of classical antiquity is perhaps rather simple-minded, and shows that Betty slightly missed her questioner's tone. But there can be no doubt that the religious conviction about the celestial origins of *Paradise Lost* came from her husband.

It is from Betty Milton, too, that we learn the really extraordinary story that Milton at this date 'was applied to by message from the King, and invited to write for the Court, but his answer was, that such behaviour would be very inconsistent with his former conduct, for he had never yet employed his pen against his conscience'.[26]

This is not as improbable as it sounds. The body, and the speed, of Milton's writing as a civil servant had been considerable. 'Whatever he undertook was despatched as soon as possible', we are told.[27] His retirement as Latin Secretary must inevitably have meant that affairs ran less smoothly. The offer is characteristic of Charles II's magnanimity and political cunning in choosing men on merit, his capricious desire to ignore old scores, when it suited his purposes to do so. It is equally characteristic of Milton to have pleaded, not ill health, which he could perfectly well have done, but political scruple.

If he was applied to by a message from the King, it would seem less likely that he was actually visited by the Duke of York, the future King James II. The story goes that the Duke had heard so much about Milton that he had a great desire to see him; Charles II said that he had no objection to his brother satisfying his curiosity. This was at a time when visits to see Milton were part of the ordinary tourist route through

London, and travellers from abroad were being shown round the birthplace in Bread Street by the proud local inhabitants.

Milton clearly got used to turning away the visitors, but when he heard that it was the Duke of York at the door, he asked for him to be admitted. It is at this point that the anecdote becomes too perfect to be credible:

In the course of their conversation, the Duke asked Milton, whether he did not think the loss of his sight was a judgement upon him for what he had written against the late King his father? Milton's reply was to this effect: 'If your Highness thinks that the calamities which befall us here are indications of the wrath of Heaven, in what manner are we to account for the fate of the King your father? The displeasure of Heaven, must, upon this supposition, have been much greater against him, than against me: for I have lost only my eyes, but he lost his head'.[28]

Like so many apocryphal stories, the tale arose because, spiritually speaking, it was true. This was what Milton believed. He minded his afflictions, and they tested his faith; but his belief that God had inspired and guided the Good Old Cause remained perfectly unshaken.

CHAPTER 15

SAMSON AGONISTES

> He knew, and the others did not know – not even his wife, least of all his medical adviser – that he had endured a great ordeal, and unaided, had emerged the victor.
>
> Evelyn Waugh, *The Ordeal of Gilbert Pinfold*

CHALFONT St Giles is a leafy outpost of Metroland. Nowadays, it is only a little over half an hour from Baker Street on the electric train. Coming up from the station, you pass the low-leaded windows of mock-Tudor houses, built for City clerks of rustic inclination in about 1932. Further back from the road, the slightly grander mock-Georgian front doors bespeak the successful lives of doctors and stockbrokers. Poetry certainly comes to mind there, but not, immediately, Milton's. This is Betjeman's terrain:

> Think of what our Nation stands for,
> Books from Boots' and country lanes,
> Free speech, free passes, class distinction,
> Democracy and proper drains . . .[1]

The lines came into my head as I strolled up to Milton's cottage. Perhaps, after all, they were not as inappropriate as all that. *Mutatis mutandis*, they are not a bad paraphrase of *Areopagitica*. It is a tribute to the valiance of the Good Old Cause and its supporters that we can now regard its achievements lightly. The squires and merchants who rallied behind Cromwell would have found nothing funny in the sentiments of Betjeman's woman at prayer in Westminster Abbey. We have been taught to emend R. H. Tawney's view of seventeenth-century Protestantism, but it is hard to read the life of Milton without realizing that *Paradise Lost* could not have been written if he had not been a capitalist.

> So, Lord, reserve for me a crown
> And do not let my shares go down.

The cottage itself nestles on the edge of this commuters' haven. It was bought by public subscription in 1887, and it remains in excellent hands. The present custodians are a retired colonel and his wife. They mow the lawns, plant the little flower-beds with lobelia and French marigolds, sell postcards, and give a friendly and well-informed talk to their visitors.

Only one room is kept in the seventeenth-century style, adorned with copies of the Janssen and the Onslow portraits, but with very few Miltonic remains – Milton's third wife having distributed most of his possessions about Cheshire at the beginning of the eighteenth century. There is a signature displayed in the glass-fronted bookcase, but when one peers at it, one sees that it is not Milton's, but that of Her Majesty Queen Elizabeth the Queen Mother, who smiles tolerantly from the photograph across the little room at the icons of that staunch republican. Again, this is less inappropriate than it might seem at first. True, he had dreaded the Restoration on the grounds that 'a king must be adored like a demigod, with a dissolute and haughty court about him, of vast expense and luxury . . . There will be a queen also of no less charge; in most likely outlandish and a papist; besides a queen mother such already . . .'[2] But the reason for his pessimism was that he was unable to conceive of a monarchy neutered of its power: 'It is well and happy for the people if their king be but a cypher . . .'[3]

The English monarchy has only survived because of the Good Old Cause, confirmed by the events of 1688–9. It is hard to imagine Milton as an ardent monarchist, but the benign face which stares across the cottage parlour at his own is an emblem of monarchy with a purely spiritual function. Milton's conviction that a free people should have the right to dismiss their leader has been more or less operative in England since the eighteenth century; and although Cabinet, and not the Grand Council of Milton's imaginings, is responsible for the government of the country, Milton would probably feel, if he were alive today, that his ideals had been vindicated. A far-sighted person could have felt so even within Milton's lifetime. Belloc, in his life of the poet, imagines such a person saying to Milton, at the end of his life, ' "Kingship is broken. Bishops mean less and less. The Papist cannot much longer endure. Ireland has been murdered: she shows no signs of life. While as for your cherished doctrine of divorce, it has already become the law of England" '.[4] But it is unlikely that these thoughts (if remotely accurate) were ever voiced in Chalfont St Giles when Milton was there.

Milton came out to the Buckinghamshire village in 1665 to escape the plague. The cottage was on the estate of Colonel Fleetwood, one of the

Regicides who had fled to America, and it was found for the poet by young Thomas Ellwood between his periods in gaol for Quaker activity:

Some little time before I went to Aylesbury prison I was desired by my quondam master, Milton, to take a house for him in the neighbourhood where I dwelt, that he might go out of the city for the safety of himself and his family, the pestilence then growing hot in London. I took a pretty box in Giles Chalfont, a mile from me, of which I gave him notice, and intended to have waited upon him, and seen him well settled in it, but was prevented by that imprisonment.[5]

Doubtless to the austere young bachelor it seemed a 'pretty box'. It is not recorded whether Betty Milton was pleased with it when she alighted. With Milton's three daughters, all adolescent girls on the edge of womanhood, and Elizabeth Fisher the maidservant, it must have been a tight squeeze for them all. There cannot have been above five rooms in the entire cottage. Milton probably slept downstairs, for fear of stumbling on the ladder which served as a staircase. In that way he could pursue his usual morning routines without having to clamber through a daughter's bedroom on to the precarious little landing. He rose at sunrise during winter (at 4 a.m. during the summer months) and meditated upon his own life and upon the Scriptures. That was the only hour of day when he got any peace or quiet.

It was the phase of life when a man starts to review the past. More years lay behind than stretched ahead. The sightseers who pressed around the house in Bunhill Fields had come to see the man who was the great Iconoclast: who had smashed the image of the divinely-appointed king, and who had attempted to destroy the traditional views of marriage; the staunch republican and defender of liberty; Oliver's Secretary, the brilliant Latinist, the famous controversialist. His celebrity in the Restoration had something of a ghoulish quality. He was being gazed upon as a spectacle: the man who had defied the divine order and been stricken blind. Now, for their sport, they visited him, English and foreign, high and low; the government had even asked him back to put him through his paces, and make him flex his rhetorical muscles for the amusement and service of the new Philistian lords.

These gazers knew nothing of Milton's inner life. They did not know that from his earliest years his father had set him apart as a man of God; trained him in music, and all known tongues, for the mighty service of God. It was as a man of God that he went to Cambridge, and as a man of God that he retired with his father to Horton. But his father could not at first understand or sympathize with the direction in which the young man's life seemed to be moving. He appeared to hold the Church and its ministers in scorn; he seemed to have abandoned all ambition for preferment in the Church (after such a promising beginning, as the elegist of Lancelot Andrewes). Yet he did so neither because he had attached himself to some sectarian group like the Anabaptists or the Brownists, nor for the more wholesome reason that he had developed worldly ambitions or sensual weaknesses which would have been incompatible with a priestly life. No, he was to be a poet. This desire had not stopped John Donne making a way in the world; it had not stopped Herbert or Herrick taking orders. Most of the poets of the age were either parsons or diplomats or courtiers or soldiers. But for John Milton, this was no idle whim, to be a poet. It was a divine vocation, a calling from God that he should himself become a true poem.

Encouraged to go abroad by his friend Sir Henry Wotton (one of the first to see his genius as a poet), Milton had, in spite of the adulation he received for his Latin verses, resolved to write a great poem in his native language: 'That what the greatest and choicest wits of Athens, Rome, or modern Italy, and those Hebrews of old did for their country, I in my proportion with this over and above of being a Christian, might do for mine.'[6] But political events had caught up with him. He had seen Galileo, the prisoner of the Inquisition, in the very weeks that news had come from home about the Bishops' War. The corruption, cruelty, and stupidity of the Laudian clergy now appeared in a more harsh, alarming light. Milton had seen at first hand the consequences of Catholic absolutism, and he met in Italy fellow-countrymen who were prepared to murder him rather than let him go home and denounce what was happening.

The voice of prophecy came from his lips, to save and to stir his nation to free themselves from the prelates and from the absolutism of Charles I. Like one of the great judges of Israel, he had been guided by God. He would deliver the new Israel from the Philistian yoke. And yet, at the very moment of crisis, as the puissant nation roused itself to arms, Milton had fallen in love with the daughter of a royalist squire. Poor Mary. Milton could see that none of it was her fault. She was not the prime cause of all that he suffered in those years. It was his own weakness for feminine charm, held at bay for so long, and collapsing so utterly and so inappropriately in that hot summer month before the outbreak of war.

Throughout his life he had been a man of divided loyalties: at first, an ecclesiastic who hated the Church. Then, an ardent campaigner for the parliamentary cause who was not only married to a royalist, but was the brother and the uncle of ardent royalists and (who knows?) the son of a royalist. Yet, once roped in as the great defender and propagandist for Cromwellian government, he became weary with its pseudo-monarchical trappings, of a man who could 'pageant himself up and down in progress among the perpetual bowings and cringings of an abject people'.[7] And although loyalty forbade him to say anything against the Protector in his lifetime, he could speak, when Cromwell died, of the restored Long Parliament, as the 'recoverers of our liberty after a short but scandalous night of interruption'.

Yet the cause to which God had called him was still true. And God was still true. Though his health was broken, his sight gone and, after the Restoration, his enemies triumphant, God was still true. Milton suffered all the fear of a political prisoner. In the dark autumn months of 1660 he was ensnared, assaulted, overcome, led bound; a figure of derision to his foes; thrust into a dungeon, captive, poor, and blind.

Throughout this period Milton doggedly refused to doubt the eternal providence of God. He continued to assert it as the Holy Ghost, night after night, came to his bedroom and dictated it to him. And yet Milton was no cypher, no neutral mouthpiece. It was not only his vast reading, his contemplation of the geographical magnitude of the world or his Platonic reading of angelology which coloured the poem dictated by the Holy Ghost. It was the Old Testament fear that God, whose goodness and providence and power he asserted, might actually be absent, or capable of deserting His servants.

The epic was now complete, and this troubling thought, through all his imaginings, had been stilled. His own life, which, with uncharacteristic reticence he had put to the borders of *Paradise Lost*, now came to preoccupy him.

When Thomas Ellwood came out of prison he visited Milton at Chalfont St Giles, 'to welcome him into the country'.

After some common discourses had passed between us, he called for a manuscript of his; which being brought he delivered to me, bidding me take it home with me, and read it at my leisure; and when I had done so, return it to him with my judgement thereupon.

When I came home, and set myself to read it, I found it was that excellent poem which he entitled, 'Paradise Lost'. After I had, with the best attention read it through, I made him another visit, and returned him his book, with due acknowledgement of the favour he had done me in communicating it to me. He asked me how I liked it and what I thought of it, which I modestly but freely told him, and after some discourse about it, I pleasantly said to him, 'Thou hast said much here of "Paradise Lost", but what hast thou to say of "Paradise Found"?' He made no answer, but sat some time in a muse; then brake off that discourse and fell upon another subject.[8]

It is a touching story. 'He asked me how I liked it and what I thought of it' will ring true in the ear of anyone who has written anything designed for a public readership. And there is something sad, but also magnificent, in the fact that he who had been lionized by Barberini and Manso, should, on the completion of his greatest work, shyly show it to a young pupil in his early twenties and ask anxiously for an opinion.

It is also a helpful story, because it tells us that *Paradise Lost* was finished by the time Milton went to Chalfont St Giles. But one should not imagine that Milton immediately sat down and began to dictate *Paradise Regained* on Ellwood's helpful suggestion. Milton's silence, and changing of the subject, might very likely reflect a slightly wounded fear that Ellwood had not read the ending of *Paradise Lost* very carefully, in which the story of 'Paradise Found' is all expounded to Adam by the Archangel. So thoroughly grounded in all this is Adam that he can exclaim that his loss of paradise was a *felix culpa*:

> O goodness infinite, goodness immense!
> That all this good of evil shall produce,
> And evil turn to good; more wonderful
> Than that by which creation first brought forth
> Light out of darkness! Full of doubt I stand,
> Whether I should repent me now of sin
> By me done and occasioned, or rejoice
> Much more, that much more good thereof shall spring,
> To God more glory, more good will to men
> From God, and over wrath grace shall abound.
>
> (XII. 469–78)

It was only several years later that he was to conceive of his poem of 'Paradise Found'. His nephew Edward Phillips says that it was 'begun and finished and printed after the other was published, and that in a wonderful short space considering the sublimeness of it'.[9] *Paradise Lost* was published in 1667. *Paradise Regained* was begun after 'the other was published'. There is therefore a two-year gap, during the years of plague and fire, in which we do not know what Milton was working on. Quite possibly, he was continuing with his historical writings – the *History of Britain* or the *Brief History of Moscovia*. But such enterprises surely required, for all Milton's prodigious memory, the presence of ready helpers, amanuenses and secretaries to get books down from shelves and, in cases where the daughters had stolen the books and sold them to buy clothes or sweetmeats for themselves, to look out replacements in the libraries of other men.

All this equipment could not possibly have been carted out to Chalfont St Giles. Some books no doubt were taken, but no major scholarly activity can have gone on in the tiny confines of the cottage. The late rector of Chalfont St Giles, in a helpful monograph, *Milton in Buckinghamshire*, asks the question, 'Who came to see him?' Anxious to oblige, he provides two paragraphs of quite plausible suggestions: 'We don't know but we can speculate'. And, having dismissed the possibility that Judge Jeffreys or Richard Baxter would have been likely to call, he proceeds:

Edmund Waller is a much more likely visitor: he had only to come from Beaconsfield, and for some time the Wallers owned property in Chalfont St Giles. We know that he visited Milton later on in London. John Dryden is also a possibility; he used to stay sometimes with his friend William Bowyer at Denham. He and John got on well together: he admired Milton's poetry and John liked Dryden, although he had reservations about his poetic gifts.

But we can be more sure of local friends. One of the best traditions is that Mrs Penington's daughter Gulielma Springett (who later married William Penn) came over from the Grange to sing to him, and play upon her lute. The Peningtons would surely come when they could: but Isaac, alas, was soon in Aylesbury prison again, this time at the instance of the Earl of Bridgewater, and whilst he was there his wife and children were turned out of the Grange and took lodgings at Bottrells Farm. I feel sure John walked up the hill to Bottrells sometimes to comfort them . . .[10]

Nothing could be more likely, but it is only speculation. One could, if necessary, map out a busy social programme for Milton while he was at Chalfont. If we assume that he was there between six and nine months, he could have been visited by everyone in the neighbourhood. But that does not really answer the question of what he did with himself in the mornings.

Milton was not a countryman. Apart from the brief spells when he lived with his parents in Horton and Hammersmith, his English life was a purely London life. For a blind man, used to city life, the seclusion of Chalfont St Giles must have been irksome, and the reasons for his uprooting painful. Thousands were dying of the plague; so much for the idea of God rejoicing with his people because the King enjoyed his own again. Through all the streets that Milton had known and loved since

childhood the dreaded carts were trundling their stinking load. It was
not the first plague that Milton had lived through, of course. There had
been a very bad one in 1647, and lesser outbreaks on and off throughout
his lifetime – one bad one during his undergraduate career. But it was
worse than an inconvenience.

Time, then, must have hung heavy as he sat in the garden in Chalfont
St Giles wondering what to do. Perhaps to this period belongs his
ill-fated attempt to get the girls to read to him in the books and languages
which he loved best. Perhaps the quarrels which inevitably developed as
a result of these tortuous sessions reminded him of the worst days with
their mother or grandmother. Perhaps, too, it was at this stage of life that
Milton revived the old idea he had of himself as a dramatist.

As Edward Phillips himself averred, 'it cannot certainly be concluded
when he wrote his excellent tragedy entitled *Samson Agonistes*',[11] but this
very fact suggests a time when Milton was living in obscurity, cut off
from his friends. We can date the first origins of *Paradise Lost*, its revival
as a piece of regular composition, and the poem's completion, from the
remarks of Milton's friends. He showed the epic to them at various
junctures, and obviously talked about it when they called. We further
know that *Paradise Regained* was composed quite fast after 1667. Since
these circumstantial details exist about the two major works of Milton's
later life, it is strange that no memory exists of the composition of his
'excellent tragedy'.

This has prompted some scholars to imagine *Samson Agonistes* as a
much earlier work than was ever traditionally supposed.[12] I find it
impossible to assign the drama to a period before Milton's blindness.
Yet, even while attacking the idea of *Samson* as 'a thinly veiled spiritual
autobiography', Parker finds himself wanting to point out that 'In 1647
John Milton had much in common with the mighty hero of Judges'.[13]
The idea of an early dating depends on Milton's severe remarks about
rhyme in his preface to *Paradise Lost* – 'rhyme being no necessary
adjunct or true ornament of poem or good verse, in longer works
especially, but the invention of a barbarous age, to set off wretched
matter and lame metre'. But that is not to say that the very measured use
of rhyme in some passages of *Samson Agonistes* is what Milton was
thinking of. He plainly had in mind the endless purling rhythms of the
heroic couplet, the sort of thing which made him consider Dryden 'no
poet but a good rhymist'. It is not strictly consistent with employing some
rhyme in *Samson* to attack it in *Paradise Lost*; but if one tried to rearrange
Milton's work so as to make it consistent with itself there is much that

would have to go altogether. Why did the great advocate of divorce
bravely endure an unsatisfactory first marriage? Why did the admirer of
Sidney's *Arcadia* attack the King for his alleged use of Pamela's prayer?
Why did the great assailant of censorship take a job which involved
(among other duties) those of a censor? Milton was always an honest
man, but he was very far from being consistent.

There is no evidence which proves conclusively that he dictated
Samson Agonistes during the plague year of his sojourn in Chalfont St
Giles, but there have been more absurd suggestions than this.

The poem certainly belongs to a period after his blindness; and, as
surely as one can be in these matters, it belongs to a period after the
Restoration. It is simply impossible to read the poem except as 'a thinly
veiled spiritual autobiography'. This is not to say that Samson 'is'
Milton; or Manoa 'is' the old scrivener, or that Dalila 'is' Mary Powell.
But it is impossible, simply impossible, to read the drama, and not to feel
that it reflects the tossings and tempests of Milton's own secret and
inner journey. There is the frustrated sense, which he never allowed
himself to voice in *Paradise Lost*, that his life has been a waste:

> Why was my breeding ordered and prescribed
> As of a person separate to God,
> Designed for great exploits; if I must die
> Betrayed, captived, and both my eyes put out,
> Made of my enemies the scorn and gaze . . .
>   Promise was that I
> Should Israel from Philistian yoke deliver;
> Ask for this great deliverer now, and find him
> Eyeless in Gaza at the mill with slaves . . .
>   (30–4, 39–41)

Gaza and *gazer* were, of course, for Milton homophones; there is an
intense bitterness about being eyeless in a place which sounds so full of
visionary possibilities. The appalling horror of Samson's blindness
reflects all the frustration and bitterness and sorrow of Milton himself:

> O loss of sight, of thee I most complain!
> Blind among enemies, O worse than chains,
> Dungeon, or beggary, or decrepit age!
> Light the prime work of God to me is extinct,
> And all her various objects of delight
> Annulled, which might in part my grief have eased,
> Inferior to the vilest now become
> Of man or worm; the vilest here excel me,

They creep, yet see, I dark in light exposed
To daily fraud, contempt, abuse and wrong,
Within doors, or without, still as a fool,
In power of others, never in my own . . .

(67–78)

The drama of *Samson*, unlike the scriptural narrative, is a purely inner conflict. In the Book of Judges the blindness of Samson is mentioned only in passing: 'But the Philistines took him, and put out his eyes, and brought him down to Gaza'. Nor is it made much of in the conventional Christian allegorical readings of the story, which see Samson, who destroys himself in order to bring about the salvation of Israel, as a type of Christ. The judge of Israel is a vast, brutal, superhuman figure, more savage and primitive than a *berserkr* in an Icelandic saga. He is a sensualist, and a fighter, who enjoys women and battles. He is not a man of feeling. It is only the imagination of Milton, playing on this story, which can make the particular torment of blindness the fact that it leaves him 'as a fool in power of others, never in my own'. The Chorus, in verse which can hardly be thought Milton's happiest, picks up the threads of the biblical narrative:

Then with what trivial weapon came to hand,
The jaw of a dead ass, his sword of bone,
A thousand foreskins fell, the flower of Palestine
In Ramath-lechi famous to this day . . .

(142–5)

How very much less good this is than the eloquence of the Authorized Version:

And Samson said, With the jaw-bone of an ass, heaps upon heaps, with the jaw of an ass have I slain a thousand men.

In Milton's version it sounds as though Samson has conducted not a slaughter but a mass circumcision. And the lame line-filler, 'famous to this day', besides being untrue has a schoolmistressy air.

In Judges there is an eloquence about the final phase of Samson's life. Delilah cuts off his hair. But when he wakes up, 'he wist not that the Lord was departed from him'. Samson does not speak after this until the moment when his hair has grown again and he asks, 'Suffer me that I may feel the pillars whereupon the house standeth, that I may lean upon them'. The agonies of paranoia felt in the drama, however, are all added by Milton:

> . . . tell me friends,
> Am I not sung and proverbed for a fool
> In every street, do they not say, how well
> Are come upon him his deserts?
>
> (202–5)

If it were not to compare a sublimely great writer with a merely brilliant craftsman, one would be able to say that *Samson Agonistes* was Milton's *Ordeal of Gilbert Pinfold*. The appearance of Manoa, while not being an actual representation of Milton's father, is the internal voice of guilt reminding Milton of the extraordinary conflicts of loyalty which had been raging in his inner life for the previous twenty-five years:

> I cannot praise thy marriage-choices, son,
> Rather approved them not; but thou didst plead
> Divine impulsion prompting how thou might'st
> Find some occasion to infest our foes.
> I state not that; this I am sure; our foes
> Found soon occasion thereby to make thee
> Their captive, and their triumph . . .
>
> (420–6)

Samson Agonistes does not reflect the straight feelings of guilt about the sexual impulse which non-Christian writers might expect to find there. In *Paradise Lost*, on the contrary, Milton was able to write in an uncomplicated way about the delights of sex.

> . . . nor turned I ween
> Adam from his fair spouse, nor Eve the rites
> Mysterious of connubial love refused:
> Whatever hypocrites austerely talk
> Of purity and place and innocence,
> Defaming as impure what God declares
> Pure, and commands to some, leaves free to all.
>
> (IV. 741–7)

Samson Agonistes is tormented not by sexual guilt, but by the much more tortuous sense that sex makes fools of us; or rather, that it has made a fool of Milton. The Book of Judges gives Milton no prompting here. It is entirely his own insight which makes it seem that the snare 'Of fair fallacious looks, venereal trains' has 'turned me out ridiculous'.

In the Bible, Samson's hair appears to grow remarkably fast, and it is no time at all, in the narrative, after his blinding, before he is led out to provide sport and destruction for the Philistian lords. But Milton's

Samson has to endure all the ignominy, having had a good government appointment, of sitting about at home unemployed, lifting up his feet while his irritating daughters sweep and dust underneath them; a prisoner in his own parlour, unable to escape unwanted visits from sightseers, most of whom are far from amiable or friendly:

> Now blind, disheartened, shamed, dishonoured, quelled,
> To what can I be useful, wherein serve
> My nation, and the work from heaven imposed,
> But to sit idle on the household hearth,
> A burdenous drone; to visitants a gaze,
> Or pitied object, these redundant locks
> Robustious to no purpose clustering down,
> Vain monument of strength; till length of years
> And sedentary numbness craze my limbs
> To a contemptible old age obscure.
>
> (563–72)

Again, such an existence of quiet domesticity only seems painful in the light of Milton's own personal circumstances. He had known his father deep into the old man's eighties; he had lived 'wholly retired to his rest and devotion, without the least trouble imaginable'.[14] The idea of old age being 'contemptible' simply reflects a passing mood of intense self-pity in Milton's own mind.

He realizes this, of course, and the drama is really an inner dialogue. The other voices speak to reassure the nagging self-pity and persecution mania:

> Believe not these suggestions, which proceed
> From anguish of the mind and humours black,
> That mingle with thy fancy.
>
> (599–601)

Milton, in his greatest spiritual crisis to date, must learn anew the

> better fortitude
> Of patience and heroic martyrdom
> Unsung . . .
>
> (PL, IX. 31–3)

This is the theme of the great central chorus in *Samson* –

> Many are the sayings of the wise
> In ancient and in modern books enrolled;
> Extolling patience as the truest fortitude . . .
>
> (652–4)

There then follows the terrible, and unforgiving encounter between Samson and Dalila. In *Paradise Lost*, the awful marital quarrels are resolved in tender forgiveness and reconciliation. Adam reviles Eve in the cruellest terms – 'Out of my sight, thou serpent' – but he is reconciled by her tender plea, 'Between us two let there be peace' (x. 867, 924). And, in perhaps the most moving lines in the whole poem, he as it were re-proposes marriage to her in her new fallen state:

> But rise, let us no more contend, nor blame
> Each other, blamed enough elsewhere, but strive
> In offices of love, how we may lighten
> Each other's burden in our share of woe.
>
> (x. 958–61)

No such optimistic or plucky spirit inhabits *Samson Agonistes* when the hero yells at his wife, 'Out, out, hyena' – the equivalent of Adam's 'out of my sight, thou serpent'. Samson refuses her hypocritical offer of reconciliation; he says that he cannot forgive himself for the folly of marrying her, so much less can he forgive her for betraying him, and they end in mutual cursing, egged on by the Chorus: 'She's gone, a manifest serpent . . .'

If Dalila is a nightmare-projection of Milton's unhappy experience of marriage (a projection which deliberately excludes all happy memories of peace and reconciliation), his encounter with Harapha is related, in the same kind of way, to Milton's career as a controversialist, a pamphleteering prize-fighter. Harapha is not to be identified with Salmasius, any more than Dalila is to be thought of as a portrait of Mary Powell. But Milton's mind, playing on this figure, naturally draws on the rough and tumble of the propagandist and political lampoonist. Then comes Samson's defiant speech:

> All these indignities, for such they are
> From thine, these evils I deserve and more,
> Acknowledge them from God inflicted on me
> Justly, yet despair not of his final pardon
> Whose ear is ever open; and his eye
> Gracious to readmit the suppliant;
> In confidence whereof I once again
> Defy thee to the trial of mortal fight,
> By combat to decide whose god is God,
> Thine or whom I with Israel's sons adore.
>
> (1168–77)

Samson is in exactly the position of Milton at the time of the Restoration;
but it was a position which Milton was unable to confess to himself as he
went on asserting eternal providence against all odds. God *has* visited
him with affliction. The crucial sentence of Judges which Milton omits
from his drama is 'he wist not that the Lord was departed from him'.
But, as the play proceeds, this fact is superbly dramatized. Milton
recognizes that he has been deserted and punished by God. But he is
going to remain sternly at his post, as in the implicitly reproachful sonnet
(reproachful to God) which sees that 'They also serve who only stand
and wait'. Milton risked everything in 1660 by defending, in a pamphlet
which he reissued only months before the King's return, his belief in
republicanism. He did so because he was confident that he was right.
Similarly, to Cyriack Skinner he said that he was able to bear his
blindness, which is the mark of 'heaven's hand', because he knew that he
had gone blind in the Good Old Cause

> In liberty's defence, my noble task,
> Of which all Europe talks from side to side.

The glory of the play is that Samson regains, in spite of self-hatred, a
spirit of his old self-confidence. He is asked to come to the solemn feast
of Dagon, just as Milton had been asked to play his rhetorical tricks in
the service of Charles II. And when he turns the honour down, his last
tormentor, the officer, warns him, 'Regard thy self, this will offend them
highly'. Samson picks up this colloquialism and pedantically turns it
back to its literal meaning. Self-regard has been the beginning and end
of his character; self-regard has been his salvation, for it is from
self-regard and self-respect that his virtue and his strength have
derived.

> Myself? my conscience and internal peace.
> Can they think me so broken, so debased
> With corporal servitude, that my mind ever
> Will condescend to such absurd commands?
>
> (1334–7)

From this loftiness springs the revival of his moral courage. He is now
above God's law:

> . . . the Philistian lords command.
> Commands are no constraints. If I obey them,
> I do it freely; venturing to displease
> God for the fear of man, and man prefer,

> Set God behind: which in his jealousy
> Shall never, unrepented, find forgiveness.
> Yet that he may dispense with me or thee
> Present in temples at idolatrous rites
> For some important cause, thou need'st not doubt.
>
> (1371–9)

His great moment approaches. Like Satan, he is divorced from immediate consideration of whether what he does is, or is not, accordant with the will of God. In *Paradise Lost* the thrill of such moral heroism is illicit. But here, it is overtly laudable. Samson, in the end, relies on his own power and virtue and strength. He will settle matters with his God, if at all, at some later juncture.

> Be of good courage, I begin to feel
> Some rousing motions in me which dispose
> To something extraordinary my thoughts . . .
> If there be aught of presage in the mind,
> This day will be remarkable in my life . . .
>
> (1381–3; 1387–8)

The action, as in so much great classical drama, happens off the stage. It is left to the messenger to describe the last, magnificent scene of Samson's triumph. The tumbling masonry, the destruction of the 'Lords, ladies, captains, counsellors, or priests' corresponds to no particular event in Milton's life of course. *Samson Agonistes* is not 'autobiography' in that way. But at the end, there is a great sense of cleansing. The demons of self-hatred and uncertainty have been purged. Milton, destitute of all worldly hope, hemmed in as the domestic captive of daughters who remind him of a woman he disliked (their grandmother Powell), was a pathetic creature. But, as he sat, internally dramatizing his life in this way, he felt again the reassurance which the nightly visitation of the Holy Spirit of God had brought; he reminded himself that he was the author of *Paradise Lost*. His power was not in question.

> But he though blind of sight,
> Despised and thought extinguished quite,
> With inward eyes illuminated
> His fiery virtue roused
> From under ashes into sudden flame . . .
>
> (1687–91)

These are odd images to use of the hero in Judges, who is little more
than a mysterious Strong Man, a sort of divinely-inspired Desperate
Dan. What would he have used his 'inward eyes' for? And where was
discernible 'his fiery virtue'? These are both qualities cultivated and kept
alight from earliest years by Milton himself. The flame which appeared
to have gone out and which blazed up once more, in his life, was the
flame of poetry, and with its divine return, all is peace. As has been said
more than once, *Samson Agonistes* is not purely a tragedy, if it can be said
that

> Nothing is here for tears, nothing to wail
> Or knock the breast . . .

> (1721–2)

But we have been caught up in a huge tempest, the images of storm and
sea with which the play is filled reflecting a great personal and internal
tornado. The final chorus reassures the audience that this storm is now
over. There is a deep and divine peace about it, a reconciliation to 'the
unsearchable dispose/Of highest wisdom'. No great poet wrote better
final lines to his poems. All Milton's endings are superb. The ending of
Samson infects the audience or the reader with its cleansing submission.
We, with the author feel 'calm of mind all passion spent'.

CHAPTER 16

PARADISE REGAINED

Blessedness lies only in progress towards perfection, and a halt at any stage is a cessation of this blessedness.

Leo Tolstoy, *The Kingdom of God is Within You*

WHEN the plague abated, Milton was happy to return to London, and did so as soon as possible. His personal crisis was over. Tranquillity and serenity of mind, such as he had not known since the days of his early manhood, returned. His last years were years of calm.

Yet the calamities which had been oppressing him for the previous two decades were not over. He had not been long returned to London, walking again its familiar streets, hearing its old sounds and breathing its old smells before the most physically disruptive event of his life took place.

Evelyn wrote thus in his diary for 2 September 1666:

The conflagration was so universal, and the people so astonished, that from the beginning (I know not by what desponding or fate), they hardly stirred to quench it, so as there was nothing heard or seen but crying out and lamentation, and running about like distracted creatures, without at all attempting to save even their goods; such a strange consternation there was upon them, so as it burned both in breadth and length, the churches, public halls, exchange, hospitals, monuments, and ornaments, leaping after a prodigious manner from house to house and street to street, at great distance one from the other, for the heat (with a long set of fair and warm weather) had even ignited the air, and prepared the materials to conceive the fire, which devoured after an incredible manner, houses, furniture and everything.

Not to see the Fire must have been more terrifying than to see it. Milton would have only heard 'the noise and crackling and thunder of the impetuous flames, the shrieking of women and children, the hurry of people, the fall of towers houses and churches . . . like an hideous storm'.[1] The fire continued to burn for days, and when it was over, London, the city of Milton's boyhood, was no more than a

smoking and sultry heap which mounted up in dismal clouds night and day, the poor inhabitants dispersed all about St. Georges, Moorfields, as far as Highgate, and several miles in Circle, some under tents, others under miserable huts and hovels, without a rag, or any necessary utensils, bed or board, who from delicateness, riches and easy accommodations in stately and well furnished houses, were now reduced to extremest misery and poverty . . .[2]

There were no insurance companies, to speak of, who could pay for the losses of these people. The house where Milton lodged in Bunhill Fields with Betty and the girls was not burnt, else we should almost certainly have not been able to read *Paradise Lost* and *Samson Agonistes*. They would have gone up in smoke. But Milton's last piece of real estate, in Bread Street, was destroyed, and with it the remnant of his fortune. Having been born in prosperity, and risen to a modest position of wealth under the Protectorate, Milton in his latter years lived in considerable poverty.

Probably it was poverty which made him set about trying to find a publisher for *Paradise Lost*. First, it had to be read by the Licenser, the government censor, who objected, on political grounds,[3] to the lines in Book I

> . . . as when the sun new risen
> Looks through the horizontal misty air
> Shorn of his beams, or from behind the moon
> In dim eclipse disastrous twilight sheds
> On half the nations, and with fear of change
> Perplexes monarchs.
>
> (594–9)

Eclipses of the sun and moon are well known to perplex monarchs and everyone else, as in Shakespeare's declaration that 'The mortal moon hath her eclipse endured'. But the Licenser knew Mr Milton had a shady political record and he found this line objectionable. Had he the time he would doubtless have read on in the epic and found other lines objectionable. But public employees have better things to do with their time than to read epics, and, after this token objection, the poem was handed back to the poet.

Taking no notice of the censor's remarks, Milton then looked about for a bookseller or publisher. Most of the publishing offices in London, together with everything else, had been burnt to the ground the previous year. He turned to the widow of his old friend Matthew Simmons, who still kept his printing business going, spared by the fire, next door to the Golden Lion in Aldersgate Street where Milton had lived at the beginning of the Civil War. Her nephew Samuel Simmons helped to run the shop, and it was with him that Milton drew up his contract. It was signed on 27 April 1667. If Voltaire is right that Milton found some difficulty in placing this book,[4] there is no evidence to substantiate his view. Simmons drove quite a hard bargain, but he paid about the same amount that a modern London publisher would have paid for the book. Milton got £5, as we would say nowadays, 'on signature' – that is, on 27 April itself. He was offered a further £5 when 1,300 copies had been sold. Should a second and further edition be called for, he was offered a further sum of £5 on each reprinting. No literary agent nowadays would allow an author to sign such a contract, of course, since, were the book to have been a best-seller, all the monies after 3,900 copies had been sold would revert to the publisher. As it happened Milton only managed to collect one more payment of £5 when, nearly two years later, on 26 April 1669, Simmons had presumably sold out the first edition. But although he in fact received only £10, Milton's contract is the seventeenth-century equivalent of an advance of £20 – a tenth of his top salary as a senior civil servant in Cromwell's time. Most poets would be pleased today if they were offered the tenth of a top civil servant's salary for an epic: or, indeed, if they found themselves able to sell an epic at all. The fact that it sold out in two years must have pleased Milton. His previous attempt to sell poems had been less successful, the first volume of 1645 still being on sale fifteen years later.

If 1,300 copies were bought in those two years, it must have meant that almost every bookish or literary person in England had read or looked into *Paradise Lost* before 1669. Milton's reputation, of which he was so jealous, was thereby completely changed. For the first time in his life he was generally thought of as a poet. At last, after nearly sixty years, his true vocation had received public recognition. His *Masque* had delighted the *cognoscenti* like Sir Henry Wotton. The Italians were in awe of his genius in the Latin tongue. But even English poets who doted on Milton, such as Marvell, had hitherto admired him for his prose. It was *Defensio Secunda* which Marvell attempted to get by heart, not 'Lycidas'. To the general public, Milton was a sort of professional Diogenes, a man whose opinions, expressed in grotesquely colourful prose, were eagerly lapped up by a disapproving readership; his mixture of piety and scorn being at once repulsive and 'selling'.

Now, at last, Milton was seen in his true colours. Marvell confessed that he had not liked the sound of *Paradise Lost*; that he feared

> That he would ruin (for I saw him strong)
> The sacred truths to fable and old song
> (So Sampson groped the Temple's post in spite)
> The world o'erwhelming to revenge his sight.

This might suggest that Marvell read *Samson Agonistes* fresh from Milton's pen (or rather the pen of his secretary) before he read *Paradise Lost*. Or it might merely mean that, as an intimate of Milton's, he was privy to the intimate identification between the figure of Samson and Milton's own dark demon. Whatever the case, all fears were dispelled when he actually came to read *Paradise Lost*. Aware that Thomas Ellwood had not responded as articulately as he should have done, Marvell makes his tribute to the poem a tribute to Milton himself and his powers of mind; and that is right, for the two are inseparable:

> Pardon me, mighty poet, nor despise
> My causeless, yet not impious, surmise.
> But I am now convinced, and none will dare
> Within thy labours to pretend a share.
> Thou hast not missed one thought that could be fit,
> And all that was improper dost omit:
> So that no room is here for writers left,
> But to detect their ignorance or theft.
>
> ('On *Paradise Lost*')

It is striking, when one considers how much reverence and love Marvell felt for Milton, that his ode reflects such a very frank acknowledgement, also, of Milton's faults. The spiteful genius of the pamphlets would have wrecked a sacred epic; it is, Marvell says, the side of Milton's nature which comes out in his Samson fantasies. But even in saying how much he admires *Paradise Lost* he fears that Milton's lofty mood might 'despise' him for saying it. And it is an odd tribute (though, as it happens a very appropriate one) to a friend's poem to say that the wonderful thing about it is that it will show up everyone else's ignorance.

Nevertheless, the book caught on. Sir John Denham praised it in the House of Commons. The Earl of Dorset 'was in Little-Britain, beating about for books to his taste' when he came upon it. 'He was surprised with some passages he struck upon by dipping here and there and bought it.'[5] Dryden amazed his friends by speaking highly of the epic and by saying that if he could write his Virgil over again it would be in blank verse rather than in rhyme.

No world could have been ready for *Paradise Lost*. It descended on the bookseller like a dragon from the sky, and readers only began to absorb it slowly. But it was a decade peculiarly suited to a grand theological epic. Not all that was going on in the late 1660s would have pleased Milton, but it was a time when there was intense interest, of the most various kind, in religion. Bunyan had started to pour forth his disturbing prose fantasies. It was a period of very frequent church-going (Evelyn never seems happy unless he has been to church at least three times on a Sunday, and heard at least two sermons); and, of course, after the Great Fire, it was a great period of church-building. Wren's fifty-two city churches are not the only ones which were put up, and the repeated legislation – the Test Act, the Five Mile Act, and so on – throughout the reign of King Charles II, suggest a Parliament and a country more obsessed by religion, if that is possible, than the generation of their fathers in the 1640s. An epic which sought to 'justify the ways of God to men' caught the 6th Earl of Dorset's fancy as he rummaged about in the bookshop. Of how many later earls or dukes of Dorset could this be said? The seventh earl (created the first Duke of Dorset in 1720) 'believed a certain Sir Matthew Germaine to be the author of St. Matthew's Gospel'.[6]

Milton, meanwhile, had started work on his next – and his last – poem. It was, as I have already quoted, written 'in a wonderful short space considering the sublimeness of it';[7] which makes me want to assign it to the closing years of the decade.

Milton had not written a poem with Christ as its central theme or character or concern since he abandoned his poem on the Passion nearly forty years before:

> He sovran priest, stooping his regal head
> That dropped with odorous oil down his fair eyes,
> Poor fleshly tabernacle entered,
> His starry front low-roofed beneath the skies;
> O what a mask was there, what a disguise!

'This subject the author finding to be above the years he had when he wrote it, and nothing satisfied with what was begun, left it unfinished.'

The Christ of Milton's Nativity ode was a 'dreaded infant' who scattered abroad the old devils and pagan Gods like the God in Psalm 68. It was a poem less about the person of Christ than about the

Incarnation, the coming of the New Dispensation into the world. It is one of the most gloriously imagined, or mythologized pieces of theology in any language.

In *Paradise Regained*, however, it is in the person of Christ that the interest of the poem resides. Because God became Man, and because we know almost nothing about the person of that Man, everyone responds to a different Christ; their Christ reflects their idea of human perfection. The gods whom he banished, who never took human form, remain fixed and frozen within their old stereotypes: the Delphic Apollo, mooned Ashtaroth and sullen Moloch are always and everywhere the same. Every statue of Bacchus is recognizable as Bacchus; every Mercury as Mercury. But Christ, though in theology the same, yesterday, today, and forever, is iconographically most astonishingly various. He is the stern, all-powerful figure of Byzantine mosaics; he is the wretched, enfeebled young man of high medieval crucifixes. He is the gentle, beautiful Son of Michelangelo's 'Pietà'; he is the all-conquering hero of 'The Dream of the Rood'. He is the ruddy-cheeked Italian countryman of Caravaggio. He is the austere Dominican of Fra Angelico. To Stanley Spencer, he is an early twentieth-century Englishman of the lower-middle class. He has been depicted as African, Japanese, Eskimo, and Indian. Knowing that God made them in His image and likeness, Christians have been shameless in making Christ in *their own* image and likeness because, as the Victorian poet believed

> Christ plays in ten thousand places
> Lovely in limbs, and lovely in eyes not his.

So, in Milton's Christ we see an embodiment of all that he believed to be good. He was a precocious, learned child, noted by all for his cleverness:

> When I was yet a child, no childish play
> To me was pleasing, all my mind was set
> Serious to learn and know, and thence to do
> What might be public good . . .
>
> (*PR*, I. 201–4)

He was brought up as a devout, orthodox Jew – 'The Law of God I read, and found it sweet' – and the cleverness, which stands him in such good stead when catching out the Doctors of the Law as a child is equally useful when meeting his adversary the Devil. Unlike Eve, who had been tricked and flattered into eating the apple, Christ is at every stage too clever for Satan.

What are his temptations in the wilderness? Belial is rebuked by Satan for suggesting to lure Christ to sin with a woman.

> For beauty stands
> In the admiration only of weak minds
> Led captive . . .
>
> (*PR*, II. 220–2)

and the Devil realizes that what he is up against is a mind. Yet although Christ is as chaste as Milton had been during his Continental travels, when the feast is spread before him,

> A table richly spread, in regal mode,
> With dishes piled, and meats of noblest sort
> And savour, beasts of chase, or fowl of game,
> In pastry built, or from the spit, or boiled,
> Grisamber-steamed . . .
>
> (*PR*, II. 340–5)

one is struck by the extreme beauty of the servers, both the handsome waiters –

> Tall stripling youths rich-clad, of fairer hue
> Then Ganymede or Hylas . . .
>
> (*PR*, II. 352–3)

– and various female attendants who were 'fairer than feigned of old or fabled since'. This is a temptation (that of eating elaborate pastry in the company of the *jeunesse dorée*) which is not recorded in the Scriptures and appears to have been Milton's invention. One can see without much difficulty that it corresponds directly to a feature of Milton's own personality: the courtier who wrote the masque at Ludlow. We have already had the more traditional evangelical temptation to make the stones bread in the first book. This is a temptation, this second, to luxury. He is being given the advantages of a comfortable upbringing: he could, as it were, squander his capital on riotous living. But, as Christ replies, virtue, valour, and wisdom are more important than riches, as is shown by the lives of innumerable great men:

> . . . canst thou not remember
> Quintius, Fabricius, Curius, Regulus?
>
> (*PR*, II. 445–6)

It is a good, schoolmasterly riposte, and it temporarily silences Satan, for evidently he had read Livy (if at all) less recently than the Saviour.

The next important temptation – and all this is Milton's ingenious elaboration of the temptation to have 'the kingdoms of the world and the glory thereof' – is the suggestion made by Satan that Christ owes it to his country to be a great national liberator. He appeals to his 'duty to free/Thy country from her heathen servitude' (*PR*, III. 175) and assist the Jews to throw off their heathen yoke, rather as Milton had assisted England to throw off the monarchist, and episcopalian yoke. Christ rejects any attempt to ally himself to a first-century equivalent of the Good Old Cause. He preaches a doctrine of submission.

> Who best
> Can suffer, best can do; best reign, who first
> Well hath obeyed . . .
>
> (*PR*, III. 194–6)

In the splendid catalogue that follows, he surveys the kingdoms of the world, and the Tempter explains the world situation to the Saviour:

> . . . for now the Parthian king
> In Ctesiphon hath gathered all his host
> Against the Scythian, whose incursions wild
> Have wasted Sogdiana . . .
>
> (*PR*, III. 299–302)

And after this tongue-twisting exposition there is the splendid military vision which has the slightly Nazi excitement of a great parade:

> He looked and saw what numbers numberless
> The city gates outpoured, light-armed troops
> In coats of mail and military pride;
> In mail their horses clad, yet fleet and strong,
> Prancing their riders bore, the flower and choice
> Of many provinces from bound to bound . . .
>
> (*PR*, III.310–15)

These, it takes little imagination to see, were the aspects of Cromwell's extraordinary rise to power which had so immediately impressed Milton: the troops riding out of city gates, the prancing horsemen, the marvellous size and order of a military parade. But Christ is unmoved by them.

Satan presents as good all the things which, in his previous years, Milton had hoped were good: courtly success in hall and high table; political dedication to the cause of liberty; military excellence. Christ stoically stands firm. Stoically? Perhaps not. For the last, and most surprising series of temptations comes in the final book of *Paradise*

Regained. Two cities are there presented to Christ. Rome is the first, and, since Tiberius is at that moment

> Old, and lascivious, and from Rome retired
> To Capreae an island small but strong
> On the Campanian shore, with purpose there
> His horrid lusts in private to enjoy,
>
> *(PR*, IV. 91–4)

it would seem a good moment for a *coup d'état*. Christ rejects the offer. He is then offered a much more beguiling series of temptations in Athens. There he finds a city 'native to famous wits'.

> See there the olive grove of Academe,
> Plato's retirement, where the Attic bird
> Trills her thick-warbled notes the summer long . . .
>
> *(PR*, IV. 244–6)

But Christ's objection to both cities is primarily the same. To the temptation of political power offered by Rome, he proclaims the everlasting power of the throne of David. Satan, in turning to Athens, provides the much more insidious suggestions that

> All knowledge is not couched in Moses' law,
> The Pentateuch or what the prophets wrote,
> The Gentiles also know, and write, and teach
> To admiration, led by nature's light . . .
>
> *(PR*, IV. 225–8)

But Christ has not time for the intellectual allurements which had delighted Milton's early manhood. The Peripatetics and the Epicureans we might expect him to censure. But he has especially hard words for

> The Stoic last in philosophic pride,
> By him called virtue; and his virtuous man,
> Wise, perfect in himself, and all possessing,
> Equal to God, oft shames not to prefer,
> As fearing God nor man, contemning all
> Wealth, pleasure, pain or torment, death and life,
> Which when he lists, he leaves, or boasts he can,
> For all his tedious talk is but vain boast,
> Or subtle shifts conviction to evade.
> Alas what can they teach, and not mislead;
> Ignorant of themselves, of God much more,
> And how the world began, and how man fell
> Degraded by himself, on grace depending?
>
> *(PR*, IV. 300–10)

There can be no doubt that, for Milton's Christ, this is the most crucial and difficult of temptations. As has often been observed, he has many of the Stoic qualities himself. Moreover, the soteriology of the whole poem would seem, at first thought, more Stoic than Christian. Christ appears to have regained Paradise – for those who can follow in his austere paths of self-discipline – by the mastery of self, and the overcoming of temptation. Many people must have picked up *Paradise Regained* for the first time and expected it to be about the Crucifixion or the Harrowing of Hell, the traditional parts of Christ's ministry to be regarded as saving the world from sin. But this Christ seems to be saying, like that musical voice forty years before,

> Mortals that would follow me,
> Love virtue, she alone is free,
> She can teach ye how to climb
> Higher than the sphery chime . . .

Paradoxically, the moral excellence of Stoicism is what makes it such a snare.

Milton's Christ rejects it as he has rejected the lure of Roman glory. Just as David's throne will live for ever and ever, so it is the Jewish sages, and not the Greeks, who provide the most excellent rule of life. Greek poetry? It does not compare with the Psalms:

> Remove their swelling epithets thick-laid
> As varnish on a harlot's cheek, the rest,
> Thin-sown with aught of profit or delight,
> Will far be found unworthy to compare
> With Sion's songs, to all true tastes excelling . . .
>
> (*PR*, IV. 343–7)

As for political writings of the Greek orators they are

> herein to our prophets far beneath,
> As men divinely taught, and better teaching
> The solid rules of civil government
> In their majestic unaffected style
> Than all the oratory of Greece and Rome.
>
> (*PR*, IV. 356–60)

One feels that the Milton of *Paradise Regained* would not have been all that interested in being considered the new Areopagite; nor the dramatist who was 'sad Electra's poet'. A deeper simplicity, a deeper Hebraism, has entered in. Milton, we are told, read the Hebrew Bible every morning of his adult life. He had moved, for his only years of professional life, among those who believed, as Christ proclaims, that in the Hebrew Scriptures

> is plainest taught, and easiest learnt,
> What makes a nation happy, and keeps it so,
> What ruins kingdoms, and lays cities flat;
> These only with our Law best form a king.
>
> (*PR*, IV. 361–4)

It was an important part of Milton's understanding of Christian liberty in the *De Doctrina*, to believe that Christ had superseded the Mosaic law and that through Christ, having made us free from the law, we were redeemed not by our own works, but by grace. To this idea in *Paradise Regained*, Milton again pays lip-service. But in Christ, of course, he cannot depict fallen nature dependent on grace. Nor does he choose to depict a man who is disillusioned with the Law, the Torah. It seems to contain all that we need to lead a virtuous life.

So, from the speculative Stoicism of his earlier life, Milton turns as a substitute to the rigours of Mosaic law, and the dignified simplicities of the Old Testament. Since Protestantism derived so much of its distinctive colouring from an endless perusal of the Old Testament, we should not be surprised by the extreme Hebraism of the later Milton. From the earliest years of the century a Hebraizing movement was apparent in the Church, ranging from the complaints of the Bishop of Exeter that there was so much 'jewism' in his diocese, to the extreme case of the followers of John Traske, who were imprisoned in 1618 for 'Judaizing'. On their release, they went to Amsterdam and actually joined the synagogue.

Milton never went as far as this, but his increasing devotion to the Torah and the moral purity of the Jewish codes must have been increased by his actual dealings with the Jews. As Cromwell's Latin Secretary, it must have been he who negotiated with the famed Rabbi Menasseh ben Israel for the readmission of the Jews to London. Cromwell was largely interested in this incursion because it would spite the Dutch, since Menasseh ben Israel and his companions all came from Amsterdam, with promise of rich trade to the city. But there were religious reasons for their coming, too. The Diaspora, or the scattering of the Jews across the face of the earth needed to be complete before the final Redemption would begin. This was clear from the Book of Daniel (12: 7), and from the Book of Deuteronomy which stated that the dispersal would be 'from one end of the earth even to the other' (28: 64). The classical Hebrew translation of *Angleterre* was 'the end of the earth', so it followed that the Scriptures could not be fulfilled until Menasseh ben Israel had established his synagogue in London.

He was an arresting preacher, and a great scholar. While he was in Amsterdam in 1643, Henrietta Maria had come to hear his oratory. Milton, passionately addicted not only to the Hebrew Scriptures, but also to their Midrash and Talmud, would have had much to talk about with this fascinating stranger. He appealed, successfully, for the freedom to worship in the tradition of his fathers and, in spite of the inevitable protests, a synagogue was established in Cree Church Lane, and was allowed to continue after the Restoration. It became one of the sights of London, and people came in such hordes to hear the ancient chants that it was eventually necessary to close the synagogue to all but bona fide Jewish worshippers. Pepys went more than once. It is hard not to think that Milton got himself taken along, if only for the musical fascination of hearing a language with which he was so familiar in the privacy of his study sung collectively by those for whom it was a liturgically natural tongue.[8]

It was the traditional view of medieval Catholicism that the Jews rejected Christ because they were so wicked. But Christ himself, and St Paul, both knew that the opposite was the case. They rejected him because they were so good. The Pharisee thanked God that he was not as other men are (Luke 18: 11) and St Paul, before his conversion, was entirely self-sufficient, spiritually speaking; he 'profited in the Jews' religion above many my equals in mine own nation, being more exceedingly zealous of the traditions of my fathers' (Gal. 1: 14). The Christ of *Paradise Regained*, unlike the author of *De Doctrina Christiana*, is able to achieve virtue simply by being good. He disdains the self-sufficiency of the Stoics, but as much because of their ignorance of the Book of Genesis as because they are fundamentatlly wrong in their attitudes to life.

> Ignorant of themselves, of God much more.

Milton, who loved virtue because 'she alone is free', must have felt strongly the attraction of the Jewish position. For the Christian who believes that he can only be saved by divine grace, the religion of the Psalms must often seem disturbing. In so many of them, the speaker is not fearing the judgement of God, but actively asking for it: 'Judge me O Lord; for I have walked in mine integrity . . . Examine me, O Lord and prove me' (Ps. 26: 1, 2); 'Judge me, O God, and plead my cause against an ungodly nation' (43: 1). 'Search me, O God, and know my heart: try me, and know my thoughts: And see if there be any wicked way in me, and lead me in the way everlasting' (139: 23, 24). The speaker is confident, like the Pharisee in the parable, of his own virtue. He begs God to judge him and take note of the fact. He reassures God that he hates his enemies and has contempt for them. 'Do not I hate them, O Lord that hate thee? . . . I hate them with a perfect hatred' (139: 21, 22).

These are the prayers, traditionally and historically, on which Christ's spirituality was nurtured. It is not unreasonable of Milton to have made his Saviour so self-confidently lofty. Hardly a word of *Paradise Regained* could not be inferred from Scripture. And yet its ethos, as we have already said, is surprising. The angels singing at the end of the poem appear to think that Paradise is already regained, three years before Calvary:

> A fairer Paradise is founded now
> For Adam and his chosen sons, whom thou
> A Saviour art come down to reinstall
> (*PR*, IV. 613–15)

But all that he has achieved is a dogged resistance to evil.

The unattractive things about Judaism are obvious: its legalistic dietary fuss, its vengeful attitude towards adulteresses, its cult of racial superiority. But its attractions, too, are strong, and Milton felt them. 'My dear,' Sir Walter Scott might or might not have said to Lockhart on his deathbed, 'be a good man – be virtuous – be religious – be a good man. Nothing else will give you any comfort when you come to lie here.'[9] Such simple trust in natural virtue is more possible to the mind which has discarded the demoralizing notion of grace. There is not much in Milton's Christ of that humility which, in sinners, is the beginning of repentance. But there is a great simplicity; a virtuous and in conclusion a domestic simplicity:

> Home to his mother's house private returned.

This private cultivation of domestic virtue was to mark Milton's serene last years.

CHAPTER 17

DEATH

He has outsoared the shadow of our night;
Envy and calumny and hate and pain,
And that unrest which men miscall delight,
Can touch him not and torture not again . . .

Shelley, 'Adonais'

BUNHILL FIELDS are still an oasis of green on the edge of the City of London. If you stand in the City Road, only the tops of stately beech trees would tell you that they were there: a happy garden. There is a fine extent of lawn, a rich planting of trees, and, nowadays, a Nonconformist burial ground. Richard and Henry Cromwell are buried here; so is Bunyan. Here lie Defoe, and Isaac Watts and Susanna Wesley; George Fox is here, and Lieutenant-General Fleetwood, Cromwell's chief-of-staff at Worcester. William Blake is buried here, but not the author of *Paradise Lost*.

In his day, Bunhill Fields were much bigger. The little burial ground was only a small part of a large, open, well-planted common. He was often seen here, walking with a friend. Millington, the bookseller from Little Britain, would take him out on his arm, a slight, neat figure. In cold weather he would wear a grey camlet coat. His bands were broader than was common, a sartorial eccentricity which suggests that, even in his blindness, he took care to give particular instructions to his tailor.

The house in Artillery Row was not a large one. There was only one room on each floor. Betty and he were alone there now, with one maid, the same old Elizabeth Fisher. Anne and Mary, both in their early twenties, were lacemakers. Deborah became a lady's companion to a woman called Merian, who took her to Ireland. A month or two before her father's death she married a weaver called Abraham Clarke. Once away from her father, Deborah was able to see his excellences. She was always the one who resembled him most, in appearance and temperament, and she began to remember, a little wistfully, the Milton his friends knew, his charm when Marvell or Paget or Millington or Ellwood stayed for a meal. She thought, somewhat nostalgically, of his handsome face; his good hair, still auburn, though flecked with grey, parted neatly in the middle, as often as not by her own hands. But she could not live with him. At the time, it was all anger and rivalry. Only when she was away from home could she recall with such clarity his handsome features; his sweetness and affability; the pleasantness of his conversation.[1]

Millington the bookseller enjoys it instead, and well he might, for the great library Milton had built up over the previous forty years was dispersed at this time. There was simply no room in the house for so many books and papers; none of the children would have appreciated either the contents of the books, or their financial value. It was as well to get rid of them via bookselling friends.[2] Presumably, the trunksful of Italian music disappeared, or were dispersed, in this way.

What of the manuscripts of his own work? There was much work for a secretary here, reading things aloud and sorting into packages and boxes. Two versions, at least, survived of the old masque he had written for Ludlow Castle. Skinner had asked for that: it must be put to one side for him. Then there were the old undergraduate writings, the prolusions. Were they of any interest to anyone? Perhaps they could be sold. Much more important, there were letters of state, including important documents from foreign dignitaries. These must be kept for posterity, for when the true history of the Protectorate came to be written. What was this? Old correspondence of his own? A little bundle of letters beginning 'Dearest Marie'? No. They were for the bonfire; posterity was not interested in those. But the Latin letters to Thomas Young and others were worth keeping. Future generations would be glad of those. What was that? A billet-doux signed 'Emilia'? He does not understand how it came to be there. Something more for the bonfire. And there was a letter here from Somebody Dawes; the handwriting was bad. Dawes? Dares? Davis? Oh, *Davis*. That, too, had better not be kept. But the *Artis Logicae*, that was a different matter. Again people would be interested. It was publishable.

The *De Doctrina*, tinkered with so frequently, was to go to Brabazon Aylmer, who probably helped sort through some of the papers. He undertook to publish it. A hundred and forty years were to pass before Lord Macaulay's generation were the first to see it in print.

Aylmer also took the *Brief History of Moscovia*. That *was* published eventually in 1685. There was *The History of Britain*, on which Milton had been working for years. That appeared in 1670. A volume containing *Paradise Regained* and *Samson Agonistes* was also licensed that year, but, again because of some delay in a publisher's office, it did not appear until the following year. There were, moreover, a number of poems which had never been published before: some of the metrical psalms he had done in the early Fifties just after losing his sight; the sonnets – to Lawrence, 'On the late Massacre in Piedmont'; and the one to the memory of Katherine Woodcock – 'Methought I saw my late espoused saint'. These were printed in a new collection of poems, an expanded version of the 1645 collection, in 1673. There were, too, as far as he could gather from the detailed readings he had been given, a number of corrections to be made in *Paradise Lost*. A revised version appeared in 1674.

So, neatly and methodically, Milton put his literary remains in order, with the result that he published more in the last few years of his life than he had done in all the previous sixty. His days were spent quietly. Some of the old friends came less often than they used to. Marvell, for instance, had not been up to Bunhill Fields for over two years when he got involved in the controversies of which the *Rehearsal Transprosed* (1672) was the result. Ten years before, Marvell and Samuel Parker had been quite close in their religious and political opinions. But Parker had soon enough reconciled his conscience to the Established Church and he was now the Archdeacon of Canterbury, writing in strong terms against the Nonconformists. When Marvell replied, Parker claimed that it was clear that the *Rehearsal Transprosed* had been strongly influenced by Marvell's 'fellow-journeyman' the 'blind schoolmaster J.M.':

> O marvellous fate, O fate full of marvel,
> That Nol's Latin pay two clerks should deserve ill!
> Hiring a gelding and Milton the stallion,
> His Latin was gelt, and turned pure Italian.

The remarks about Milton in Parker's diatribe were most offensive, the more painful since Marvell's friendship with him had slightly cooled. The opening lines of Book III of *Paradise Lost* were ridiculed by this charitable Archdeacon who said that 'No doubt but the thoughts of this "vital lamp" lighted a Christmas candle in his brain'.

Marvell replied, in the second part of the *Rehearsal Transprosed*, and tried to give a kindly public reason why he had allowed his friendship with Milton to fall into disrepair. 'For by chance I had not seen him of two years before; but after I undertook writing, I did more carefully avoid either visiting or sending to him, lest I should any way involve him in my consequences'.[3] This was not enough for Milton, who was furious about the attack from Parker. He remembered him as a hesitant young man who had suffered agonies of conscience, and sought his advice, about the legitimacy of the Church of England. Furiously, he dictated his own reply. But, Phillips says, 'whether by the dissuasion of friends, as thinking him a fellow not worth his notice, or for what other cause I know not, this answer was never published'.

Clearing the boxes and desk drawers was an occupation which did not satisfy either Milton's creative instincts or his lust for controversy. He must have been sorry when they talked him out of replying publicly to Archdeacon Parker. Whoever took his arm at this period, walking him round Bunhill Fields for three or four hours at a stretch, would have heard endlessly satirical references to the Archdeacon. But, though angered, Milton was not cast down. Gradually, as his limp got worse, the walks had to be curtailed. He was much troubled by gout. His knuckles were swollen now, and he did not play the organ as easily as he had done. But 'he would be cheerful even in his gout-fits and sing'.[4]

When the weather was fine, he liked to sit in 'a grey coarse cloth coat at the door of his house near Bunhill Fields . . . to enjoy the fresh air, and so, as well as in his room, received the visits of people of distinguished parts, as well as quality'.[5]

A clergyman called Wright remembered calling and being surprised by how tiny the house was. He was shown up a narrow staircase, 'hung with a rusty green' and found Milton sitting in an elbow chair. He was 'pale but not cadaverous, his hands and fingers gouty, and with chalk stones. Among other discourse he expressed himself to this purpose; that was he free from the pain this gave him, his blindness would be tolerable'.[6]

Parson Wright got him on a bad day. Others – particularly foreigners and noblemen – remarked on his cheerful welcome. The Earl of Anglesey enjoyed his conversation in these days, 'as likewise others of the nobility'.[7] Sir Robert Howard, too, was a constant visitor. Once he asked Milton what made him side with the republicans. He answered 'among other reasons, because theirs was the most frugal government; for that the trappings of a monarchy might be set up an ordinary commonwealth'.[8] *Trrrrappings*. ('He pronounced the letter R very hard.')

It was a very characteristic reply. Religion was presumably discussed by many of the visitors. One of the major issues of the day was the question of toleration. In 1671 the Royal Declaration of Indulgence to Dissenters had pleased the Nonconformists until it became clear that it was part of an undercover agreement between Charles II and Louis XIV to protect, if not actively to encourage, the Roman Catholic interest. Feelings reached crisis point by the time, two years later, Parliament insisted on repealing the toleration measure. Milton felt impelled to contribute to the flood of pamphlets which poured from the presses on the subject. He produced a dull little work called *Of True Religion, Heresy, Schism, Toleration, and what best means may be used against the growth of Popery*. True religion he equates with what can be deduced from the Scriptures. The only true heresy was popery. Other forms of Christianity were at least trying to follow the truth according to their lights. He even has some kind words to say about the Thirty-nine Articles – or about four of them: VI, XIX, XX, and XXI. He mounts an old hobby-horse on the subject of the Trinity which, as he rightly points out, is not a strictly scriptural doctrine. But he had little to add to the general cry of 'no popery'; and his genius really only shone forth in controversy when he could be scathingly rude. Now, little as he approved of the papists, he was unable to summon up any very personalized attacks:

Are we to punish them by corporal punishment or fines in their estates, upon account of their religion? I suppose it stands not with the clemency of the Gospel more than what appertains to the security of the State.[9]

Had he been writing in the 1640s, he would have been less interested in the clemency of the Gospel. In spite of his urgent desire to 'remove their idolatry and all the furniture thereof whether idols, or the mass wherein they adore their God under bread and wine', he plainly saw the papists chiefly as a political rather than a spiritual threat to the health of the nations. The Good Old Cause had already, in so many ways, been triumphant. No one could mistake the Restoration Anglican bishops for prelates in the tyrannical, Laudian mould. The King, for all his political genius, was firmly a constitutional monarch, his power much determined by Parliament. Old habits of thought do not die, but, if he searched his heart, Milton had to realize that he no longer hated the papists.

This was probably just as well, since many of his intimates adhered to that faith. It was even said of him that he was a 'frequenter of a club of papists'.[10] This was nonsense. Dryden, who was eventually to embrace Roman Catholicism, was a regular visitor, however. Milton was much amused by his former colleague's desire to make *Paradise Lost* into an

opera with rhyming couplets. 'Mr Milton received him civilly, and told
him he would give him leave to tag his verses.'[11]

An equally regular visitor and, at this date, a wholly convinced papist,
was his brother Christopher. He was now living in Ipswich, but he
always made a point of calling on his blind brother, after term at the
Inner Temple, before he left London.

On 20 July 1674, when he arrived at the house in Bunhill Fields,
Christopher found his brother unwell. He was talking of death, and
saying that he wanted to draw up a will.

'Brother, the portion due to me from Mr Powell, my former wife's father, I leave
to the unkind children I had by her; but I received no part of it, and my will and
meaning is they shall have no other benefit of my estate than the said portion and
what I have beside done for them. And all the residue of my estate I leave to the
disposal of Elizabeth my loving wife.'[12]

Christopher Milton, in recalling the conversation, does not say what had
given rise to this revival of fury against the daughters. Perhaps his
brother was hurt to have heard that Deborah had just married Abraham
Clarke in Dublin without telling her father.

Oddly, for two such orderly men, the sons of a scrivener, they did not
think to commit the will to paper. Elizabeth Fisher remembers the
conversation between the two brothers, as she remembered Milton's
later remarks to his wife as they sat in the kitchen having their dinner:
'Make much of me as long as I live for thou knowest I have given thee all
when I die at thy disposal'.[13]

We do not know whether Betty realized how soon his death was to
come. The summer turned into autumn, a phase he always associated in
his memory with his golden months in Tuscany, and his expedition,
while staying in Florence, to the wooded hillside of Vallombrosa. The
autumnal leaves rustled thickly beneath the feet of passers-by in Bunhill
Fields. For Milton, seized with gout and arthritis, walking was yet
another pleasure of the memory. Rather fast, and rather surprisingly,
and (the first time this could be said of him) rather prematurely, he had
become an old man. He pottered about. He ate less than he had done.
He would nibble a few olives, of which he was fond, at his supper, and
then feel about for his pipe. Smoking was one of the few pleasures left. It
helped to numb the pain in his hands and feet. But, like his great poems,
he had a quiet ending. There were no dramatic last scenes, no great last
words. Could he, like Hazlitt, have said, 'Well, I have had a happy life'?
The banality would not have been quite meaningless. In controversy he

had given as good as he got. In family life, there had been tempestuous ups and downs; and, like many people, he failed to get on with his children. But he spent his last days in the company of a wife and friends who loved him. In November, the gout got even worse. He was not alone, but his death was so peaceful 'that the time of his expiring was not perceived by those in the room'.[14]

It was Thursday, 9 November. Had he lived a month longer, he would have been sixty-six years old.

The funeral was on Sunday the 12th. It was a big affair. Presumably his wife followed the coffin, with his brother Christopher and the Phillips brothers. 'All his learned and great friends' came: Marvell, Nathaniel Paget, John Dryden, the Earl of Anglesey, 'not without a friendly concourse of the vulgar'.[15] For all his heterodox religious opinions, they did not bury him in the Nonconformist plot which was to contain Richard Cromwell, and Bunyan and Blake. They wove their way down to the parish church, St Giles, Cripplegate, nestling in those days amid narrow streets, with shops built against its walls. The parson read the burial service of the Established Church, and they buried him, a little to the north of the chancel steps, next to his father.

Time has obliterated Milton's London. What was left of it after the Blitz was ploughed away by builders and bulldozers. The Barbican is now an immense plate-glass fantasy, enormous gleaming towers soaring upwards into the sky. But, doggedly, in the middle of it all, St Giles, Cripplegate, bombed and repaired, stands as the last imaginable little memory there of that vanished City which Shakespeare knew.

It is a bleak church, with little atmosphere. A small square stone marks where they buried Milton. In the eighteenth century, drunk after a party, some 'gay young blades' dug up the body and pulled it to bits. Hair, teeth, fingers, ribs, and leg-bones were said to have been peddled by relic-mongers. So, the last remains of that spoiled priest suffered the fate of a Catholic saint. Such behaviour would not have surprised Milton, who had, in general, a low opinion of the human race. Nor would it have troubled him unduly. In his own belief, body and soul, dispersed and deadened, wait in oblivion until they are woken by the task-master.

NOTES AND REFERENCES

QUOTATIONS from Milton's poetry in this book, and translations from Milton's Latin, Italian, and Greek poetry come, with some emendations, from *The Poems of John Milton*, ed. John Carey and Alastair Fowler (Longmans, 1968). Prose quotations are taken from *The Complete Prose Works of John Milton* (Yale University Press, 1953–). Even in his blindness Milton minded about the spelling and punctuation of his publications; but to make them more accessible to the modern reader, and for the sake of consistency, seventeenth-century quotations have, throughout the book, been modernized.

The following abbreviations have been used in the notes that follow:

Darbishire   Helen Darbishire (ed.), *The Early Lives of John Milton* (Constable, 1932)

LR   *The Life Records of John Milton*, compiled by J. Milton French (Rutgers University Press, 1949–58), 5 vols.

Parker   W. R. Parker, *Milton. A Biography* (Clarendon Press, 1968), 2 vols.

Yale   *The Complete Prose Works of John Milton* (Yale University Press, 1953)

PROLOGUE

1. John Stow, *Survey of London*, ed. C. L. Kingsford (OUP, 1908), I. 263
2. Ibid., II. 49
3. Quoted John E. N. Hearsey, *London and the Great Fire* (John Murray, 1965), p. 61
4. Valerie Pearl, *London and the Outbreak of the Puritan Revolution* (Clarendon Press, 1961), p. 163
5. Parker, I. 9
6. S. Schoenbaum, *Shakespeare's Lives* (Clarendon Press, 1970), p. 326

CHAPTER 1: THE PIGEON OF PAUL'S

1. Anthony à Wood, quoted in Darbishire, p. 35
2. John Aubrey, quoted Darbishire, p. 1
3. 'Best of fathers, when the eloquence of the Roman tongue had been made accessible to me, at your expense, the beauties of Latin and the high-sounding words of the sublime Greeks, words which graced the mighty lips of Jove himself, then you persuaded me to add to my stock those flowers which are the boast of France, and that language which the modern Italian pours from his degenerate mouth (his speech makes him a living proof of

the barbarian invasions), and also those mysteries which the prophet of Palestine utters.' ('Ad Patrem', 78–85)

4. John Stow, quoted Donald Lemen Clark, *John Milton at St Paul's School* (Columbia University Press, 1948), pp. 34–5
5. E. J. Dobson, *English Pronunciation 1500–1700* (Clarendon Press, 2nd edn. 1968), p. 131
6. Ibid., p. 149
7. Yale, II. 510
8. *Areopagitica*, Yale, II. 508
9. Ibid.
10. *LR*, VI, 123
11. J. B. Leishman, *Milton's Minor Poems* (Routledge & Kegan Paul, 1969)
12. *The Divine Weeks and Works of Guillaume de Saluste, Sieur du Bartas*, trans. Josuah Sylvester, ed. Susan Snyder (Clarendon Press, 1979): 'The First Day of the First Week', 159–62
13. Ibid., pp. 33–41
14. Ibid., p. 316
15. Ibid., p. 324
16. Sir Philip Sidney, *Selected Poems*, ed. Katherine Duncan-Jones (Clarendon Press, 1973), p. xv
17. Geoffrey Chaucer, 'The Parson's Tale' (*The Canterbury Tales*)
18. *Of Reformation*, Yale, I. 542
19. *Hierurgia Anglicana* (The De La More Press, 1904), II. 73
20. 'Philip Sparrow'
21. *Paradise Regained*, IV. 426–7
22. 'Epitaphium Damonis', ll. 55–6
23. 'Psalm 136'
24. 'A Paraphrase on Psalm 114'

CHAPTER 2: THE LADY OF CHRIST'S COLL:

1. Darbishire, p. 10
2. Ibid.
3. Ibid.
4. Ibid.
5. Samuel Johnson, *Lives of the English Poets* (1779–81), 'Milton'
6. e.g. Parker, p. 29: 'John was evidently sent home, in "rustication", for a failure to conform . . . It is not easy to distinguish between foolish boys and future bards at seventeen.'
7. *LR*, II. 54–5
8. *The Poetical Works of William Cowper*, ed. H. S. Milford (OUP, 1967 reprint), p. 584
9. Harris F. Fletcher, *The Intellectual Development of John Milton* (University of Illinois Press, 1961), II. 398
10. Ibid., 64
11. Ibid., 67
12. I give, of course, not the view now held by scholars but the view of European intellectual history entertained in Milton's day, and by Milton himself.
13. C. A. Patrides, *Milton and the Christian Tradition* (OUP, 1966)

14. Frederick J. Powicke, *The Cambridge Platonists: A Study* (Dent, 1926)
15. C. A. Patrides, *The Cambridge Platonists* (CUP, 1980), p. 7
16. Quoted F. J. Powicke, op. cit., p. 81
17. See C. A. Patrides, op. cit., *The Cambridge Platonists*
18. Quoted in John Buxton, *Sir Philip Sidney and the English Renaissance* (Macmillan, 1962), p. 26
19. *The Reason of Church Government*, Yale, I. 768
20. Quoted Christopher Hill, *Milton and the English Revolution* (Faber, 1979) p. 28
21. Counting its inception from the 'Elizabethan settlement'. The Thirty-nine Articles were the result of a convocation in 1563.
22. Geoffrey Soden, *Geoffrey Goodman* (Collins, 1953) refutes *DNB*'s 'shown by his will to have been a Roman Catholic'.
23. Valerie Pearl, *London and the Outbreak of the Puritan Revolution*, p. 163
24. *The Sermons of John Donne*, ed. Evelyn Simpson & George R. Potter (University of California Press, 1948), V. 51
25. The Book of Common Prayer, 'The Preface'
26. *Hierurgia Anglicana*, I. i. 126
27. C. V. Wedgwood, *The King's Peace* (Collins, 1955), p. 101
28. *An Apology, LR*, I. 97
29. Samuel Johnson in Boswell's *Life of Johnson* (OUP, 3rd edn. 1976), p. 1125

CHAPTER 3: THE COURTIER

1. Katherine A. Esdaile, *English Church Monuments 1510–1840* (Batsford, 1946), p. 18
2. J. B. Leishman, *Milton's Minor Poems*, p. 160
3. *Ben Jonson* (Complete Critical Edition), ed. C. H. Herford and P. and E. Simpson (Clarendon Press, 1925–51), 11 vols., VII. 124
4. Leishman, op. cit., 168
5. Ibid., p. 107
6. Barbara Breasted, *Comus and the Castlehaven Scandal* (*Milton Studies*, III. 201). For further details of the trial I have used the account in MS. Rawlinsoniani D 924, ff. 100–18
7. MS Ashmole 824, ff. 21–5; MS Rawlinsoniani D 924, ff. 100–18; MS Harleian 738, ff. 25–31; MS Harleian 2194, ff. 73–84
8. It all happened at Fonthill in Dorset, the scene a century and a half later of William Beckford's absurd erotic fantasies. There must be some lecherous Genius of the wood on that beautiful hillside.
9. MS Rawlinson D 924
10. *Calender of State Papers, Domestic Series*, vol. cxcviii
11. John Wain, *Professing Poetry* (Macmillan, 1977), p. 202
12. *Histriomastix* (1st edn., 1631), p. 214
13. Ibid., p. 202
14. Ibid., p. 190
15. Ibid., p. 202
16. Ibid., p. 295
17. Ibid., p. 294
18. Leishman, op. cit., pp. 178–82

19. Philip Sidney, *The Arcadia* (1590), III. 10
20. Robert Burton, *The Anatomy of Melancholy* (1621), III. ii. 3
21. Herford and Simpson, op. cit., VII. 486
22. Ibid., X. 574
23. Ibid., X. 585
24. Ibid., VII. 491
25. John Wain, op cit., p. 196
26. John Collinges, *Par Nobile: Two Treatises* (1669), quoted Parker, p. 792
27. John Buxton, op. cit., p. 253

CHAPTER 4: 'LYCIDAS'

1. Yale, VI. 172
2. Yale, I. 319
3. Yale, I. 398
4. Quoted E. M. W. Tillyard, *Milton* (Cambridge, 1930), p. 376
5. Saurat, quoted Tillyard, op. cit., p. 374
6. *LR*, I. 277
7. *LR*, I. 291
8. Now in the Pforzheimer Library in New York.
9. *LR*, I. 304
10. *LR*, I. 320
11. 'After "Lycidas" no more: no more song'. Hilaire Belloc, *Milton* (Cassell, 1935), p. 120
12. *The Poems of John Milton*, ed. Carey and Fowler, p. 242

CHAPTER 5: CONTINENTAL

1. *LR*, I. 363
2. The Italian may be translated: 'My Lord Harry, thoughts concealed and an open face'
3. *Areopagitica*, Yale, II. 528
4. Thomas Carlyle, *Oliver Cromwell's Letters and Speeches* (1845), I. 96
5. *Areopagitica*, Yale, II. 537
6. Victor L. Tapie, *France in the Age of Louis XIII and Richelieu* (Athlone Press, 1974)
7. *LR*, I. 368
8. John Buxton, op. cit., p. 86
9. Christopher Hill, *Milton and the English Revolution*, p. 69
10. Yale, IV. 592
11. *Modern Language Notes*, lxxii (Nov. 1957), pp. 486–8
12. J. H. Hanford, *John Milton, Poet and Humanist* (Western Reserve UP, 1966), p. 91
13. Yale, VI. 10
14. *The Diary of John Evelyn* (OUP, 1959), p. 97
15. *LR*, I. 372
16. *LR*, I. 373
17. Quoted F. T. Prince, *The Italian Element in Milton's Verse* (CUP, 1954)
18. John Arthos, *Milton and the Italian Cities* (John Murray, 1962), p. 42
19. *LR*, I. 372

20. John Arthos, op. cit., p. 12
21. Ibid., p. 18
22. Yale, I. 809
23. *LR*, I. 389
24. Ibid., 375
25. Ibid., 378–9
26. Anthony à Wood, *Athenae Oxonienses* (1691–2), ed. P. Bliss (OUP 1813–20, 4 vols.), IV. 130
27. *LR*, I. 420
28. *LR*, I. 375
29. Carey and Fowler, op. cit., p. 255
30. John Arthos, op. cit., p. 19
31. *LR*, II. 413
32. Quoted Arthos, p. 41
33. *LR*, I. 414
34. *LR*, I. 415
35. Ibid.
36. Ibid.

CHAPTER 6: ANTI-EPISCOPAL

1. Darbishire, p. 60
2. Samuel Johnson, op. cit.
3. Darbishire, p. 60
4. Genesis 12: 11–13
5. Rose Macaulay, *Milton* (Duckworth, 1934), p. 68
6. *Edinburgh Review*, Aug. 1825
7. *The Works of John Milton* (Columbia University Press, 1931–8), 18 vols, XIV. 15
8. Yale, I. 525
9. Ibid., 521
10. Ibid., 597
11. Ibid., 625
12. Ibid., 653
13. E. M. W. Tillyard, op. cit., p. 130
14. Yale, I. 729
15. Ibid.
16. Ibid., 812
17. Yale, II. 429
18. Ibid., 431
19. Yale, I. 568
20. Ibid., 572
21. Yale, I. 886
22. Yale, I. 890
23. Ibid., 893
24. Darbishire, p. 72

CHAPTER 7: MARY POWELL

1. C. V. Wedgwood, *The King's War* (Collins, 1958), p. 126
2. Valerie Pearl, *London and the Outbreak of the Puritan Revolution*, pp. 152–3
3. *LR*, I. 436
4. Darbishire, p. 63
5. 'Ad Joannem Rousiam' is best explained by this prosaic possibility.
6. Darbishire, p. 63
7. Yale, II. 597
8. Darbishire, p. 74
9. Darbishire, p. 63
10. Ibid., p. 64
11. Ibid., p. 40
12. Anthony à Wood, quoted Darbishire, p. 7
13. *Ludovico Ariosto's 'Orlando Furioso'*, trans. into English Heroical Verse by Sir John Harington (Clarendon Press, 1972), 'The Forty-Second Book', stanza 62
14. 'Sonnet X'
15. Darbishire, p. 74
16. *The Memoirs of Lucy Hutchinson* (Everyman, 1965), p. 76
17. Ibid., p. 91
18. Lord Clarendon, *History of the Rebellion*, ed. W. D. Macray (OUP, 1888), 6 vols. Vol. I, p. 218
19. *The Memoirs of Lucy Hutchinson*, op. cit., p. 75
20. Lord Macaulay, *Essays and Lays of Ancient Rome* (Longmans, 1905), p. 27

CHAPTER 8: MISS DAVIS AND THE LIBERTIES OF ENGLAND

1. Commons Journals, iii. 960
2. *Mercurius Aulicus*, p. 236 (Bodleian Library). It is only fair to state that political pamphlets on both sides during the Civil War were not always truthful about atrocities committed by their enemies.
3. Ibid., p. 321
4. Yale, II. 222
5. *Plaine Scottish or Newes from Scotland* (anonymous pamphplet, 1643)
6. Yale, IV. 624–5
7. Darbishire, p. 64
8. Ibid., p. 66
9. Parker, p. 266
10. C. V. Wedgwood, *The King's War*, p. 321
11. Ibid., p. 347
12. Yale, I. 540
13. Ibid., 521
14. Ibid., 603
15. Yale, II. 213
16. Ibid., 258
17. Christopher Hill, *Milton and the English Revolution*, p. 123
18. Yale, II. 246
19. Ibid., 247

20. Ibid., 235
21. Ibid., 277
22. Ibid., 356
23. Ibid., 351
24. Ibid., 351
25. *LR*, II. 76
26. John Aubrey, quoted Darbishire, p. 13
27. Thomas Carlyle, *Oliver Cromwell's Letters and Speeches* (1845), p. 27
28. Sir Charles Firth, *Oliver Cromwell and the Rule of the Puritans in England* (OUP, 1953), p. 106
29. *LR*, II. 152
30. Yale, II. 57
31. Ibid.
32. Yale, II. 489
33. Ibid., 515–17
34. John Phillips, quoted Darbishire, p. 72
35. Edward Phillips, quoted Darbishire, p. 112
36. Yale, II. 392
37. Ibid., 400
38. Ibid., 401
39. Ibid., 379
40. Ibid., 411
41. Ibid., 366
42. Ibid., 376
43. Ibid., 415
44. Ibid., 405
45. Ibid., 737
46. Ibid., 601
47. Sir Charles Firth, *Oliver Cromwell and the Rule of the Puritans in England* (OUP, 1953), p. 111
48. Sir Charles Firth, op. cit., p. 123

CHAPTER 9: BARBICAN

1. Darbishire, p. 67
2. For a full treatment see J. Milton French, *Milton in Chancery* (New York, 1939)
3. *LR*, II. 409
4. Darbishire, p. 68

CHAPTER 10: PROPAGANDIST

1. *The Diary of John Evelyn* (OUP, 1959), p. 275
2. C. V. Wedgwood, *The Trial of Charles I* (Collins, 1964), p. 224
3. Christopher Hill, *Milton and the English Revolution*, p. 168
4. Thomas Carlyle, Introduction to *Oliver Cromwell's Letters and Speeches*, I
5. Yale, II. 566
6. *Paradise Lost*, II. 751
7. Ibid., I. 660
8. Yale, III. 202

9. Ibid., 198
10. Ibid., 230
11. Ibid., 236
12. Ibid., 241
13. C. V. Wedgwood, *The Trial of Charles I*, p. 154
14. Reproduced Yale, III. 150
15. *Eikonoklastes*, Yale, VI. 187
16. Yale, III. 335
17. Ibid., 337
18. Ibid., 344
19. Ibid., 366
20. C. V. Wedgwood, *The Trial of Charles I*, p. 208
21. Yale, III. 601
22. Quoted Wedgwood, op. cit., p. 214
23. *LR*, IV. 46
24. Darbishire, p. 70
25. *Mercurius Politicus*, No. 37, February 1651
26. Matthew 25:24, Luke 19:22
27. *LR*, IV. 93

CHAPTER 11: HARD SEASON

1. E. M. W. Tillyard, *Milton*, quoted Yale, IV. 538
2. Ibid., 543
3. Yale, IV. 1050
4. Ibid., 582–3
5. Ibid., 583
6. John Henry Newman, *Apologia Pro Vita Sua* (1864), Chapter One (Clarendon Press, 1967, p. 18)
7. Yale IV. 558
8. Ibid., 590
9. Ibid., 587
10. Ibid., 619
11. Ibid., 670
12. Ibid., 666
13. Ibid., 668
14. Ibid., 869
15. Ibid., 869
16. Darbishire, p. 28
17. Ibid., p. 6

CHAPTER 12: THE BEGINNINGS OF *PARADISE LOST*

1. Darbishire, p. 238
2. *LR*, IV. 218 describes this story as 'fantastic', which it is, but there is no very strong reason for doubting it; it comes directly from a next-door-neighbour of Milton's in Petty France, and it seems too circumstantial to have been worth inventing.
3. Charles Symmons, quoted Arthur Sewell, *A Study in Milton's Christian Doctrine* (OUP, 1934), p. 76

4. Hilaire Belloc, *Milton*, p. 125
5. *The Ready and Easy Way*, Yale, VII. 456
6. Sweet's *Anglo-Saxon Primer* (Clarendon Press, revised N. Davis 1961), p. 73
7. *British Critic*, II. 301–2 (1826).
8. Arthur Sewell, *A Study in Milton's Christian Doctrine* (OUP, 1939), p. 192
9. C. A. Patrides, *Milton and the Christian Tradition* (OUP, 1966)
10. See Darbishire, p. xv for her reasons for identifying the author of this anonymous early life of Milton as his nephew John Phillips. W. R. Parker believed this anonymous life to be by Cyriack Skinner (*TLS*, 13 Sept. 1957, p. 547). In referring to the author as 'John Phillips', I do not mean to dispute Parker's reasons; I simply use the words to indicate pp. 17–34 in Darbishire, an indispensable volume for any Milton-lover, even if she was wrong in her identification. *LR* also transcribes substantial passages of this 'anonymous' life, where it is so-called. Where the readings of *LR* differ from Darbishire, they are to be preferred.
11. Darbishire, p. 33
12. Robert Ramsey, *Richard Cromwell, Protector of England* (1935), p. 54
13. Ramsey, op. cit., p. 65
14. Ibid., p. 67
15. Yale, VII. 398
16. Ibid., 353
17. Ibid.

CHAPTER 13: *PARADISE LOST*

1. *The Diary of John Evelyn* (OUP, 1959), p. 416
2. C. V. Wedgwood, *The Trial of Charles I*, p. 224
3. Darbishire, p. 32
4. *LR*, IV. 316
5. Ibid., 317
6. Ibid., 318. The Author was probably George Starkey.
7. Ibid., 315ff.
8. *Johannis Miltoni, Angli, pro Populo Anglicano Defensio contra Claudii Anonymi, alias Salmasii, Defensioniem Regiam*
9. *LR*, IV. 322
10. Ibid., 329
11. Ibid., 353
12. Isaak Walton, *The Life of Hooker* (Macmillan, 1901), p. 349
13. C. S. Lewis, *A Preface to Paradise Lost* (OUP, 1960), p. 108
14. Ibid., p. 111
15. Helen Gardner, *A Reading of Paradise Lost* (OUP, 1967), p. 42
16. Ibid., p. 28
17. William Empson, *Milton's God* (CUP, 1981), p. 9
18. Samuel Taylor Coleridge, *Miscellaneous Criticism*, ed. Thomas M. Raysor (OUP, 1936), p. 163
19. George Coffin Taylor, *Milton's Use of Du Bartas* (Harvard University Press, 1934), p. 85
20. Quoted Parker, I. 571

21. Jeremiah 12:1
22. Rose Macaulay, *Letters to a Sister* (Collins, 1964), p. 95

CHAPTER 14: THIRD MARRIAGE

1. Darbishire, p. 7
2. Ibid.
3. *LR*, V. 109
4. Ibid., 220
5. Ibid., 113
6. Ibid., 107
7. The point was first made by Dr Johnson
8. *LR*, V. 109
9. Parker, I. 586
10. *The History of the Life of Thomas Ellwood*, ed. C. G. Crump (Macmillan, 1900), p. 90
11. Ibid.
12. Darbishire, p. 32
13. *LR*, IV. 381–3
14. Ibid., 375
15. Ibid.
16. Darbishire, p. 108
17. *LR*, V. 220
18. *Tetrachordon*, Yale, II. 591
19. Ibid., 589
20. Ibid., 613
21. Ibid., 589
22. Yale, II. 590
23. *LR*, V. 113
24. Ibid., 123
25. Ibid.
26. *LR*, IV. 392
27. Darbishire, p. 110
28. *LR*, V. 211

CHAPTER 15: *SAMSON AGONISTES*

1. Sir John Betjeman, 'In Westminster Abbey', *Collected Poems* (John Murray, 1979), p. 85
2. Yale, VII. 425
3. Ibid., 426
4. Hilaire Belloc, op. cit., p. 18
5. *The History of the Life of Thomas Ellwood*, p. 145
6. Yale, I. 812
7. Ibid., VII. 361
8. *Ellwood*, op. cit., p. 145
9. Darbishire, p. 75
10. G. C. Edmonds, *Milton in Buckinghamshire* (privately printed, 1969), p. 26
11. Darbishire, p. 75

12. W. R. Parker is the most notable exponent of an early dating, some time between 1647 and 1653. This view is accepted by John Carey in his edition of the poem (Longmans, 1968), but has since been recanted.
13. Parker, I. 313
14. Darbishire, p. 64

CHAPTER 16: *PARADISE REGAINED*

1. *The Diary of John Evelyn* (OUP, 1959), p. 495
2. Ibid., 497
3. Darbishire, p. 180
4. *LR*, IV. 429
5. Ibid., 447
6. V. Sackville-West, *Knole and the Sackvilles* (Lindsay Drummond Ltd., 1947), p. 170
7. Darbishire, p. 75
8. See Cecil Roth, *A History of the Jews in England* (Clarendon Press, 3rd edn. 1964), Ch. VIII
9. J. G. Lockhart, *The Life of Scott* (1838), VII. 393

CHAPTER 17: DEATH

1. Darbishire, pp. 6, 9, 32
2. Ibid., p. 192
3. *The Rehearsal Transpros'd and the Rehearsal Transpros'd; The Second Part*, ed. D. I. B. Smith (Clarendon Press, 1971), p. 311
4. *LR*, IV. 448
5. Ibid.
6. Ibid.
7. Ibid., 450
8. Ibid.
9. Yale, VII. 29
10. *LR*, IV. 452
11. Ibid., 460
12. Ibid., 411
13. Ibid., 412
14. Ibid.
15. Ibid.

INDEX

JM = John Milton

Act of Free and General Pardon (1660), 204

Aelfric, 192–3

Agar, Anne (née Milton, then Phillips; JM's sister), 4, 19, 69, 95

Agar, Thomas, 95

Andreini, Giovanni Battista, 83

Andrew, Father, SDC, quoted, 157

Andrewes, Lancelot, Bishop of Winchester, 24–5, 28, 61, 69, 102, 227

Anglesey, Arthur Annesley, 1st Earl of, 256, 259

Anne of Austria, Queen of France, 74

Apatisti (society), 81–2, 90, 129

Aquinas, St Thomas, 206

Ariosto, Lodovico, 80, 103, 117

Aristotle, 22, 23–4, 89, 140–1

Arne, Thomas, 52

Arnold, Matthew, 143

Ascham, Anthony, 167

Assembly of Divines, 130, 137

Astley, Sir Jacob, 88

Attaway, Mrs, 134–5

Aubrey, John, 5, 10, 17–18, 95, 114–15, 136, 216

Auden, W. H., 78

Audley, Lady Elizabeth, see Castlehaven, Elizabeth Touchet, Countess of

Augustine, St, 11

Augustus Caesar, 32

Baillie, Robert, 130

Barnerini family, 84

Barberini, Francesco, Cardinal, 89–90, 152, 229

Baroni, Leonora, 89

Barrymore, Richard Barry, 2nd Earl of, 141

Barrymore, Lady, 129

Bastwicke, John, 73

Baxter, Richard, 176, 230

Behn, Aphra, 6

Belloc, Hilaire, 191–4, 225

Berwick, Pacification of (1639), 94

Betjeman, Sir John, 224

Bishops' War, 78, 88, 99, 176

Blackborough family, 148, 149

Blake, William, 99, 208, 210

Bodleian Library, Oxford, 110, 112, 147, 152–3

Bogislav XIV, Duke of Pomerania, 74

Bonmatthei, Benedetto, 81–3, 157

Bowyer, William, 230

Bradshaw, John, 155, 156, 158, 161, 164, 171, 177, 202

Branthwait, Michael, 71

Bridgewater, Frances Egerton, Countess of, 39

Bridgewater, John Egerton, 1st Earl of, 40, 46–7, 49, 53, 56, 60, 139, 217

Briggs, Sampson, 62

British Critic (journal), 195

Brooke, Robert Greville, 2nd Baron, 121

Browne, Sir Thomas, 27, 176; quoted, 186

Browning, Robert, 170

Bucer, Martin, 141

Buckingham, George Villiers, 1st Duke of, 26

Buckingham, George Villiers, 2nd Duke of, 6

Bunyan, John, 244

Burton, Henry, 73

Burton, Robert, 47

Byron, George Gordon, Lord, 79

Calamy, Edward, 100

Calvin, John, 196

Cambridge University, 16, 17–25, 29–31, 72, 104–6

Camden, William, 15

Campion, Thomas, 53

Cardiff Medical Society, 182

Carlyle, Thomas, 73, 136, 159–60

Castlehaven, Lady Anne, Countess of, 39, 42–4

Castlehaven, Elizabeth Touchet, Countess of (Lady Audley), 43, 44, 49

Castlehaven, James Touchet, 3rd Earl of (Lord Audley), 43–4

Castlehaven, Mervyn Touchet, 2nd Earl of, 39, 42–5, 47, 50

Chalfont St Giles, 224–6, 228–31
Chappell, William, 17–19, 21, 64, 104
Charles I, King of England: succession, 19; early opposition to, 26; and religious controversy, 28; in Jonson masque, 48; JM presents *Comus* to, 60; and impending Civil War, 73–4, 77, 88, 108; Catholic leanings, 86; and Bishops' War, 88, 94; sends family to safety abroad, 109; refused book from Bodleian Library, 112; in Oxford, 119, 127; and conduct of War, 120–4, 147; censorship, 131; trial and execution, 156–67, 209; reaction abroad to death, 167, 173; weakness, 180; absolutism, 227
Charles II, King of England, 162, 200–1, 203–4, 222, 237, 244, 257
Chaucer, Geoffrey, 11–12, 170
Chestlin, Robert, 30
Christ's College, Cambridge, *see* Cambridge University
Christina, Queen of Sweden, 218
Church of England, 27–9, 67–8, 76, 130
Churchill, Sir Winston S., 198
Cicero, 22, 24, 136, 145
Civil War: and Charles I's rule, 73–4; preparations, 109–10; conduct and campaigns, 120–1, 146–7; end, 156
Clarendon, Edward Hyde, 1st Earl of, 109, 121
Clarke, Abraham, 253, 258
Clement of Alexandria, 23, 58
Coleridge, Samuel Taylor, 208
Colet, John, Dean, 9, 69
Collins, Edward, 18
Colt, Maximilian, 39
Coltellini, Agostino, 81, 90–1
Cook, John, 167
Cotton, John, 61
Cowley, Abraham, 221
Cowper, William, 21
Crashaw, Richard, 37
Cromwell, Oliver: government and power, 6, 161, 167–8, 177–80, 185, 196, 201; abuses Wilson, 125; achievements, 126; military successes, 137, 146–7, 168; and Hartlib, 142; severity, 143; political ambitions, 146, 158; and death of Charles, 159, 164; and *Clamor*, JM on, 177–80, 228; growing ostentation, 187; death, 198–9, 228; disinterred, 202
Cromwell, Richard, 198, 200
Cudworth, Ralph, 23–4, 52, 195, 197

Cyprian, 56

Dante Alighieri, 34, 40, 54, 80
Dati, Carlo, 81–2, 91, 156, 157
Davies, Sir John, 53
Davis, Dr, 129, 144
Davis, Miss, 129, 144–5, 148
Denham, Sir John, 243
Derby, Alice Spence, Countess of, 36, 38–41, 44, 52, 54, 58, 61, 217
Dethicke, Sir John, 188
Diodati family, 203
Diodati, Charles: friendship with JM, 15–16, 19, 21, 34, 60–1, 72, 91, 93; at Oxford, 16, 19; and Gil, 26; and JM's 'Nativity Ode', 32; death, 76–8, 91–3, 94, 169, 176; Italian origins, 81
Diodati, Giovanni, 92–3
divorce, 127–8, 131–5, 138, 141, 144, 232
Donne, John, 3, 13–14, 28, 30, 53, 227
Dorchester, Henry Pierrepont, 1st Marquis of, 44
Dorislaus, Isaac, 167
Dorset, Charles Sackville, 6th Earl of, 243–4
Dorset, Lionel Cranfield Sackville, 7th Earl & 1st Duke of, 244
Downes, Andrew, 18
Dryden, John: on Spenser's influence on JM, 11, 32; on JM and Homer and Virgil, 72; on Cromwell, 201; on Restoration, 201; JM on, 222, 231; visits JM, 222, 230; and *Paradise Lost*, 243, 257; becomes Roman Catholic, 257; at JM's funeral, 259
Du Bartas, Guillaume de Saluste, Seigneur, 11–12, 33, 72, 196, 211–12
Du Moulin, Peter, 173
Du Plessis-Mornay, Philip, 75

Ecoppe, George, 30
Edgehill, Battle of, 120
Edmonds, G. C., Rector of Chalfont, 230
education, 141–4
Egerton, Lady Alice, 48–51, 217
Egerton, Lady Frances, 50, 52, 217
Eikon Basilike, 164–6, 173, 201
Eliot, George, quoted, 109, 114
Ellwood, Thomas, 219, 226, 228–9, 243, 254
Ely, Bishop of, *see* Felton, Nicholas
'Emilia', 35, 36, 47, 56, 254
Empson, Sir William, 208–9

Essex, Robert Devereux, 3rd Earl of, 120–1, 124, 128, 146
Eton College, 70
Eunomius, 104
Euripides, 122–3
Evelyn, John, 80, 158–9, 202, 240, 244
Exeter, Bishop of, *see* Hall, Joseph

Faber, Father Frederick William, 80
Fairfax, Thomas, 3rd Baron, 142, 146
Fairfax, Lady, 164
Falkland, Lucius Cary, 2nd Viscount, 85
Fauconberg, Thomas Belasyse, Earl, 199–200
Fell, Dr John, 112
Felton, John, 26
Felton, Nicholas, Bishop of Ely, 25
Ferdinand III, Emperor, 74
Ficino, Marsilio, 207
Finch, Sir Heneage, 204
Fisher, Elizabeth, 220, 226, 253, 258
Florence, 80–4, 89–91
Fleetwood, Colonel George, 199, 225
Forest Hill, 154–5, 171; *see also* Powell family
Fortescue, Sir Nicholas, 85

Gaddi, Jacopo, 81, 157
Galileo Galilei, 90–1, 152, 158, 176, 188, 227
Gardiner, Sir Thomas, 141, 155
Gardner, Dame Helen, 206
Garfield, John, 212
Gawen, Thomas, 85–6, 89, 157–8
Geddes, Jenny, 73
Gell, Robert, 220
Genoa, 80
Gerard, Sir Gilbert, 129
Germaine, Sir Matthew, 244
Gil, Alexander (the elder), 10–11, 14, 16, 18, 142
Gil, Alexander (the younger), 10, 26–7, 29, 129
Goodman, Godfrey, Bishop of Gloucester, 27
Goodwin, John, 204
Gratian, 133
Graves, Robert, 114
Great Fire of London (1666), 240–1
Gregory of Nyssa, 56, 104
Grotius, Hugo, 74–5, 96, 121, 184, 188

Hall, Joseph, Bishop of Exeter and Norwich, 100–1, 103, 250

Hallam, Arthur, 93
Hampden, John, 73, 121
Hardy, Thomas, 190
Harefield (Middlesex), 38–40, 44, 54
Harington, Sir John, 117
Harrison, Colonel Thomas, 202, 208
Hartlib, Samuel, 129, 142
Harvey, Gabriel, 23
Hazlitt, William: quoted, 202; death, 258
Henrietta Maria, Queen of Charles I, 26, 71, 73, 109, 128, 251
Herbert, George, 28, 136, 227
Herrick, Robert, 227
Hill, Christopher, 159–60
Hobson, John, 118, 187
Hobson, Lady Margaret (*formerly* Ley), 36, 73, 118, 129, 218
Hobson, Thomas, 35–6
Holding, Dr, 85
Hollis, Colonel, 121
Holstenius, Lucas, 89
Homer, 33
Hooker, Richard, 68, 205, 212–13
Horace, 33, 56, 169, 183
Horton (Buckinghamshire), 54, 60–1
Howard, Sir Robert, 256
Huntingdon, Elizabeth, Countess of, 39
Hutchinson, Lucy, 122

Independents, 137, 139–40, 158, 198
Ireton, Henry, 202
Islip, Battle of, 147
Isocrates, 139
Italy, 76–92, 176

James I, King of England, 19
James II, King of England (Duke of York), 222–3
James, Henry, 114
Jeffrey, Sara, *see* Milton, Sara
Jenny, William, 134
Jerome, St, 11
Jews, Judaism, 249–52
Johnson, Samuel: writes prologue to *Comus*, 52; on 'Lycidas', 66; and JM in Italy, 78, 95; on JM and Italian poets, 81; on JM in Geneva, 92; on JM's academy, 95, 129; as JM's biographer, 95; and Scots, 130; on *Paradise Lost*, 205, 210
Johnson, William, 2, 6
Jones, Inigo, 2, 29, 46, 48
Jonson, Ben: London life, 2–3; and Countess of Derby, 40; masques, 40–1,

Jonson, Ben (*cont.*):
  46, 48; death, 61–2; influence on JM,
  72; *Jonsonus Virbius* (tribute), 62;
  Pleasure Reconciled to Virtue, 48, 50–1;
  'The Satyr', 40–1
Juxon, William, Bishop of London (*later*
  Archbishop of Canterbury), 166

Keats, John, 35
Killigrew, Lady Mary, 162
King, Edward, 30, 60–6, 83, 88, 169
Knox, John, 162

Lamb, Charles, quoted, 38
Landor, Walter Savage, 83
Languet, Hubert, 75
Laud, William, Archbishop of
  Canterbury: and Gil, 27; and religious
  controversy, 28–9, 68, 100, 137, 158;
  career, 28, 30; and Prynne, 73;
  unpopularity, 73; severity, 90, 176; in
  Tower, 126; censorship, 131, 138
Lawes, Henry, 39–40; and JM's
  'Arcades', 40–1; and Ludlow Castle
  masque, 46, 48–9, 51; and Countess of
  Derby, 58; relations with JM, 60, 72, 83,
  123, 129, 170; JM's poem to, 88; music,
  217
Lawrence, Henry, 183, 185, 255
Layamon, 214
Lee, John, 162
Lemon, Robert, 195
Lewis, C. S., 205–6, 208
Ley, Lady Margaret, *see* Hobson, Lady
  Margaret
Lisle, Lord (Philip Sidney, 3rd Earl of
  Leicester), 161, 199
Lockhart, John Gibson, 252
Louis XIII, King of France, 74–5
Louis XIV, King of France, 257
Lovelace, Richard, 88
Ludlow Castle, 46–50, 52

Macaulay, Rose, 97, 99, 214
Macaulay, Thomas Babington, Lord, 94,
  97–8, 123
Malatesta, Antonio, 83
Manchester, Edward Montagu, 2nd Earl
  of, 146, 163
Manning, Anne: *Mary Powell*, 114
Manso, Giovanni Battista, 86–7, 89–90,
  95, 152, 157, 188, 196, 229
Marini, Giambattista, 86

Marlborough, James Ley, 1st Earl of,
  118
Marshal, Stephen, 100
Marshall, William, 150–1, 164
Marston Moor, Battle of, 127, 137–9, 146
Marvell, Andrew: friendship with JM, 185,
  189, 217, 254–5; as Secretary for Foreign
  Tongues, 188; pleads for JM, 204;
  admires JM's writing, 242; on *Paradise
  Lost*, 243; at JM's funeral, 259; 'Horatian
  Ode', 165–6; *Rehearsal Transprosed*, 255
Mary, Queen of Scots, 162
masques, 40–1
Masson, David, 95
Mazarin, Jules, Cardinal, 184
Mead, Joseph, 18
Menasseh ben Israel, Rabbi, 250–1
Mercurius Politicus, 168
Middleton, Thomas, 53
Millington (bookseller), 253–4
Milton, Anne, *see* Agar, Anne
Milton, Anne (JM's daughter), 161, 186,
  217–18, 220, 231, 253
Milton, Christopher (JM's brother):
  childhood, 4; career, 6; on JM at
  Cambridge, 17–18; as lawyer, 59, 69,
  204; and father's illness, 61; marriage,
  69; family, 95; in Civil War, 109, 111, 123,
  128, 149; lives with father, 111; and
  Phillips boys, 112; papism, 258; relations
  with JM, 258; at JM's funeral, 259
Milton, Deborah (*later* Clarke; JM's
  daughter): birth, 172, 179; childhood,
  186; education, 217–19; relations with
  father, 217–20, 231, 253–4; marriage, 253,
  258
Milton, Elizabeth (*née* Minshull; JM's 3rd
  wife), 220–2, 225–6, 253, 258
Milton, John (JM's father): background
  and work, 4, 5–7, 16; children, 4, 6; and
  Oxford, 16, 29; provides for JM, 29–30,
  111; and Lawes, 40; musical interests,
  40, 94, 111, 128; retirement, 54, 58, 155,
  235; JM's poem to, 58–9; ill health, 61;
  as widower, 61, 69; and JM's return
  from Italy, 94; and Civil War, 111, 128;
  and JM's destiny, 226; in *Samson
  Agonistes*, 232, 234–5
MILTON, JOHN: birth, 4; education, 7–10,
  14, 21–2; portraits and appearance, 9, 31,
  150–1, 174, 182; friendships, 15–16, 82,
  93, 184–5, 217; knowledge of Italian
  language and literature, 15, 34, 80–2, 117;

at Cambridge, 16, 17–25, 29–31, 104–6;
question of 'rustication', 18–20;
character, 19, 31–2, 82, 183; poetic
ambitions, 20–1, 24–5, 36, 60, 196, 227;
classical learning, 21–2, 24, 31, 54, 82,
136, 142–4; career prospects, 29–32, 38,
53, 55–6; private income, 30, 111; love for
women, 34–5; views on marriage, 35, 56,
112, 188, 221; snobbishness, 36, 129;
graduation, 38; and Ludlow Castle
masque, 46–52; Christian beliefs and
theology, 52, 67–8, 106–7, 160, 191–7,
201, 257; and music, 40, 54, 217, 221;
egotism, 59–60, 67, 103, 134; travels
abroad, 71–2, 74–93, 176; wide reading,
72; development of radicalism, 76–9,
88; genius unrecognized in England,
83, 169; and Phillips nephews, 95,
111–12, 115–17; runs private academy,
95–6, 129, 141–2; biographers, 95–6;
projected works, 96; as pamphleteer,
97, 99–105; prose style, 97, 99; attacks
bishops, 97–105, 130, 158;
autobiographical accounts, 105; in Civil
War, 110, 120–3, 154; 1st marriage (to
Mary Powell), 113–19, 127, 129, 133–4,
139, 145, 172, 227; supports parliamentary
cause, 124–7, 159–61, 227–8; on divorce,
127–8, 131–5, 138, 141, 144; and
Presbyterians, 130, 158, 162–3;
pre-Christian sympathies, 136, 139; on
censorship, 138–41, 162, 232; on
education, 141–4; eye trouble, 144, 150,
168; reconciliation with Mary, 148–50;
takes in Powell family, 155–6; children,
154–6, 161, 172, 189, 217; Secretaryship
(of Foreign Tongues, later Latin), 157,
160–2, 186–8, 203; and death of Charles
I, 158–60, 162–6; dispute with
Salmasius, 168–9, 173–5, 177; total
blindness, 168, 170, 174, 181, 203, 212, 216,
232–3, 237; low poetic output, 169–70,
184; Mrs Powell sues, 171–2; and Mary's
death, 172, 181; vanity, 174–5; blindness
diagnosed, 182; serenity, 183–4; 2nd
marriage (to Katherine Woodcock),
188; favours polygamy, 188; and
Restoration of Charles II, 201, 203–4,
225; loses money, 203; arrested, 204;
relations with daughters, 217–19, 231,
238, 253–4, 258–9; 3rd marriage (to
Elizabeth Minshull), 220–1; celebrity,
222, 226, 242; sense of destiny, 226–8;

library and papers dispersed, 254–5;
death, 258–9
WORKS:
Abram in Paradise, 96
'Ad Joannem Rousium', 152–3
'Ad Patrem', 58–60, 143, 152
Adam Unparadised, 96, 107, 121, 196
'L'Allegro', 34, 46, 60
Animadversions . . . Smectymnuus, 100,
103, 130
An Apology against a Pamphlet, 104
'Arcades', 38, 41–2, 45
Areopagitica, 51, 102, 126–7, 138–41,
144–5, 148, 152, 196
Arthuriad, 96
'At a Solemn Music', 60, 152
Brief History of Moscovia, 229, 254
Colasterion, 144
Comus (*Masque Presented at Ludlow
Castle*), 7, 47, 48–51, 53, 56–7, 60, 71,
135, 254
De Doctrina Christiana, 77, 98–9, 161,
191–7, 201, 207, 250, 254
Defensio Secunda, 77–9, 110, 127, 173,
175–8, 181
The Doctrine and Discipline of Divorce,
115, 131, 133–4, 144–5, 148
Eikonoklastes, 159, 166–7, 204
'Elegia prima', 15, 19–21, 31, 57, 104
'Elegia quarta', 8, 25–6
'Elegia tertia', 24–5
'Epitaphium Damonis', 93, 169
History of Britain, 229, 254
'Italian Sonnets', 34, 57
'Letter to a Friend' (MS), 55–7
'Lycidas', 63–9, 83, 85, 93, 169–7
Masque Presented at Ludlow Castle, see
Comus
'Ode on the Morning of Christ's
Nativity', 32–3, 152, 244
Of Education, 141–3
Of Practical Episcopacy, 100
Of Reformation, 69, 97–9
Of True Religion, 257
'On His Blindness', 171
On Time, 152
Paradise Lost, 67; ambivalence, 84;
genesis of, 87, 157, 196; reconciliation
in, 149, 236; and JM's second
marriage, 188–9; on blindness, 191,
211–12; writing, 197–8, 205, 212, 216,
231; and Restoration, 201;
summarized and described, 205–15,

Paradise Lost (cont.):
    222, 238; influence and importance, 214–15; Ellwood on, 228–9; and sex, 234; publication and reception, 241–4, 255; Dryden and, 257–8
Paradise Regained, 51, 229, 231, 245–52, 255
'Il Penseroso', 13, 34, 57, 60
Poems (1645), 150–2, 242
Pro Populo Anglicano Defensio, 159, 168–9, 171, 204
Psalms (translations), 180
Ready and Easy Way to Establish a Free Commonwealth, 192, 198, 200
Reason of Church Government, 101–3
Samson Agonistes, 92, 231–9, 241
Sonnets, 36, 40, 55, 118, 121, 122–3, 152, 168–9, 179, 181, 190, 196, 255
The Tenure of Kings and Magistrates, 159, 162–4, 167
Tetrachordon, 144–5
Virgidemiarum, 101
Milton, John (JM's son), 172
Milton, Katherine (*née* Woodcock; JM's 2nd wife), 188–91, 255
Milton, Katherine (JM's daughter), 189
Milton, Mary (*née* Powell; JM's 1st wife): marriage and desertion, 113–19, 123, 127, 129, 133–4, 139, 145, 178, 227; reconciliation, 148, 149–50; children, 154–6, 172; and mother's litigation, 172; death, 172, 179; in *Samson Agonistes*, 232, 236
Milton, Mary (JM's daughter), 161, 217–20, 231, 253
Milton, Richard (JM's grandfather), 5–6, 111
Milton, Sara (*née* Jeffrey; JM's mother), 4–6; death, 55, 61
Milton, Thomasine (*née* Webber; Christopher's wife), 69, 95, 109, 111–12, 128, 149
Minshull, Elizabeth, *see* Milton, Elizabeth
Monck, General George (1st Duke of Albemarle), 200
Monteverdi, Claudio, 92, 94, 96, 121, 217
More, Alexander, 173, 177
More, Henry, 23, 52, 206
Mosely, Humphrey, 150, 154
Moses, 133

Naples, 86, 88
Naseby, Battle of, 148
Needham, Marchamont, 162

Neoplatonism, *see* Platonism
Newcomen, Matthew, 100
Newman, John Henry, Cardinal, 136, 175

Offspring, Charles, 3, 27
Olivier, Isaac, 62
Origen, 23
Overton, Richard, 139, 180
Ovid, 20, 33
Owen, John, 179
Oxenstierna, Axel, Count, 75
Oxford, 119, 121, 127, 154

Paget, Dr Nathan, 217, 219–20, 254, 259
Palmer, Herbert, 138
Pan-Protestant League, 75
Paris, Matthew, 58
Parker, Samuel, 255–6
Parker, W. R., 116, 218, 231
Patrides, C. A., 195
Paul, St, 11, 251
Pembroke, Mary Herbert, Countess of, 15
Penington, Mrs Mary, 230
Penn, William, 230
Pepys, Samuel, 251
Percy, Thomas, quoted, 157
Peter, Hugh, 159
Petrarch, 80, 169, 184, 190
Philaras, Leonard, 181–2
Phillips, Anne, *see* Agar, Anne
Phillips, Edward: JM cares for, 95, 111–12; as JM's biographer, 95–6, 110; on *Adam Unparadised*, 107; on Mary Powell, 113–17, 148, 150; on grandfather, 128; on JM's academy, 142; on JM and politics, 153; on High Holborn house, 156; on JM and Salmasius, 168; relations with JM, 186; on JM's religious interests, 194; on JM's daughters, 218; on *Paradise Regained*, 229; on *Samson Agonistes*, 231; on JM and Samuel Parker, 256; at JM's funeral, 259
Phillips, John: JM cares for, 95–6, 111–12; 'Life', 141, 196; relations with JM, 186; dislike of Cromwell, 187; satirical writings, 187; at JM's funeral, 259
Picard, Jeremy, 194
Plato, 11, 18, 22–4, 58, 72, 136, 144; *Phaedo*, 47; *Republic*, 42, 57, 207; *Timaeus*, 23, 57
Platonism, 22–4, 52, 195, 228; and *Paradise Lost*, 205–7
Pope, Alexander, 31
Pory, Robert, 18, 30

Powell, Anthony, quoted, 17
Powell family, 113, 116–17, 146–8, 154–6
Powell, Mrs Anne (*née* Moulton; JM's mother-in-law), 114, 116, 156, 171–2, 238
Powell, Mary, *see* Milton, Mary
Powell, Richard, 111–13, 123, 145, 154–5, 178, 258
Powell, Robert, 29–30
Presbyterians, 130, 136–9, 158, 162–3, 200
Press, freedom of the, 138–41
Prynne, William, 73, 98, 126, 135, 142; *Histriomastix*, 45–7
Psalms, 16, 180
Pye, Sir Robert, 155–6, 162
Pym, John, 124

Ranelagh, Lady, Katherine Jones, Viscountess, 36, 129, 141, 218
Ravenscroft, Thomas, 16
Redrish, John, 18
Restoration, *see* Charles II, King of England
Richardson, Jonathan, 186
Richelieu, Cardinal, 74–5
Ridley, Nicholas, Bishop of London, 98
Robins, John, 134–5
Robinson, Henry, 139
Rogers, Dr Lambert, 182
Rogers, Samuel, quoted, 70
Rome, 84–6, 89
Rouse, John, 110, 112, 152–4, 169
Rousseau, Jean-Jacques, 159–60
Royal Declaration of Indulgence to Dissenters (1671), 257
Rupert, Prince, 120, 137, 146–7
Rutherford, Samuel, 125

S., G.: 'Britain's Triumph', 203
St Amant, Marc Antoine Gerard, Sieur de, 167
St Paul's Cathedral, London, 13–14
St Paul's School, London, 9–10, 13–14
Salmasius, Claudius, 167–8, 173–5, 177, 204, 209
Sandys, George, 53
Scipioni, Alberto, 71
Scott, Sir Walter, 252
Scudamore, John, 1st Viscount, 71, 75, 184
Seneca, 136
Sewell, Arthur, 195
Shakespeare, William: in London, 2, 3, 6; influence on JM, 33–4, 50, 72, 221; JM's

lines on, 35; profession, 53; audience, 83; output, 170; sonnets, 190; on eclipses, 241
Shelley, Percy Bysshe, 35, 99; quoted, 252
Sidney, Algernon, 77
Sidney, Sir Philip, 12, 15, 22, 53, 69, 75, 77; *Arcadia*, 77, 166, 232
Siena, 71, 84
Simmons, Mary (Mrs Matthew), 242
Simmons, Samuel, 242
Skelton, John, 14
Skinner, Cyriack, 169, 174, 183, 185, 189, 217, 237, 254
Skipwith (servant), 44
Slater, William, 128
Small, William, 162
'Smectymnuus' and Smectymnuans, 100, 103, 130, 141
Smith, John, 52
Spencer, Sir John (of Althorp), 39–40
Spencer, Stanley, 245
Spenser, Edmund: influence on JM, 11, 32–3, 72, 140–1, 221; reveres Plato, 22; and Countess of Derby, 38, 52, 217; career, 53; and Italian poets, 80; output, 170; *Fairie Queene*, 11–12, 22, 69, 140; *The Shepheardes Calendar*, 63
Springett, Gulielma (*later* Penn), 230
Spurstow, William, 100
Stanton St John (Oxfordshire), 5, 6
Stock, Richard, 3, 6, 11, 52, 76
Stoicism, 249–51
Stow, John, 6
Strafford, Thomas Wentworth, 1st Earl of, 73, 94
Stubbe, Edmund, 32
Svogliati, Accademia degli, 81, 83, 89–90
Swift, Jonathan, 98
Sylvester, Josuah, 11–12, 33, 212
Symmons, Charles, 191

Tasso, Torquato, 72, 80, 86–7
Tawney, R. H., 224
Taylor, George Coffin, 211
Taylor, Jeremy, 28
Tennyson, Alfred, Lord, 93, 214
Theocritus, 63, 66, 72
Thirty Years War, 74–5, 84
Thévenot, François, 181–2
Tillyard, E. M. W., 100
Tolstoy, Leo, Count, quoted, 240
Tovey, Nathaniel, 19
Traske, John, 250

Trinity College, Cambridge: Milton MS, 96
Turnham Green, Battle of, 121–3

Urban VIII, Pope, 84, 90
Ussher, James, Archbishop of Armagh, 102

Vane, Sir Henry, 161
Venice, 92
Victoria, Queen, 198
Vincent, Thomas, 32
Virgil, 32–3, 72
Voltaire, François Arouet de, 242

Walker, Clement, 162
Waller, Edmund, 150, 154, 230
Waller, Sir William, 150
Walton, Izaak, 205
Walwyn, William, 139
Warton, Thomas, 203
Waugh, Evelyn, quoted, 224
Webber, Mrs Isabel, 149
Westminster Abbey, 127
Wheatley (Oxfordshire), 171
Whichcote, Benjamin, 23

Whitelocke, Bulstrode, 161
Wilde, Oscar, 44
Winchester, Jane Paulet, Marchioness of, 36, 61
Wood, Anthony à, 114
Woodcock, 'Captain', 188
Woodcock, Elizabeth, 188
Woodcock, Katherine, see Milton, Katherine
Wordsworth, William, 24, 99, 170
Wotton, Sir Henry, 70–3, 76, 83, 192, 227, 242
Wren, Sir Christopher, 244
Wright, Parson, 256
Wyatt, Sir Thomas, 15

York, James, Duke of, see James II
Young, Thomas: tutors JM, 7–8, 22; in Hamburg, 25, 89; and JM's 'Elegia quarta', 25–6; and JM's 'Letter to a Friend', 55; friendship with JM, 76, 129–30; and Of Reformation, 99–100; and Smectymnuus, 100; disagrees on divorce, 134–5; as Master of Jesus College, Cambridge, 134–5; JM's disillusionment with, 141, 163; Latin letters to, 254

ETA __ 4:20
FH __ 6:00
(BOS)
HOT __ 6:20
RM __ 6:30
CALL __ ↓ ↓
        6:45
Swim __ 7: -8:00
Eat __ 8:00-9:00
Rm (9:15)